ON A WING
AND A PRAYER

Searching for the real Steve Coppell

STUART ROACH

KNOW THE SCORE BOOKS SPORTS PUBLICATIONS

CULT HEROES	Author	ISBN
CARLISLE UNITED	Paul Harrison	978-1-905449-09-7
CELTIC	David Potter	978-1-905449-08-8
CHELSEA	Leo Moynihan	1-905449-00-3
MANCHESTER CITY	David Clayton	978-1-905449-05-7
NEWCASTLE	Dylan Younger	1-905449-03-8
NOTTINGHAM FOREST	David McVay	978-1-905449-06-4
RANGERS	Paul Smith	978-1-905449-07-1
SOUTHAMPTON	Jeremy Wilson	1-905449-01-1
WEST BROM	Simon Wright	1-905449-02-X

MATCH OF MY LIFE	Editor	ISBN
BRIGHTON	Paul Camillin	978-1-84818-000-0
DERBY COUNTY	Nick Johnson	978-1-905449-68-2
ENGLAND WORLD CUP	Massarella & Moynihan	1-905449-52-6
EUROPEAN CUP FINALS	Ben Lyttleton	1-905449-57-7
FA CUP FINALS 1953-1969	David Saffer	978-1-905449-53-8
FULHAM	Michael Heatley	1-905449-51-8
IPSWICH TOWN	Mel Henderson	978-1-84818-001-7
LEEDS	David Saffer	1-905449-54-2
LIVERPOOL	Leo Moynihan	1-905449-50-X
MANCHESTER UNITED	Ivan Ponting	978-1-905449-59-0
SHEFFIELD UNITED	Nick Johnson	1-905449-62-3
STOKE CITY	Simon Lowe	978-1-905449-55-2
SUNDERLAND	Rob Mason	1-905449-60-7
WOLVES	Simon Lowe	1-905449-56-9

PLAYER BY PLAYER	Author	ISBN
LIVERPOOL	Ivan Ponting	978-1-84818-306-3
MANCHESTER UNITED	Ivan Ponting	978-1-84818-500-1
TOTTENHAM HOTSPUR	Ivan Ponting	978-1-84818-501-8

GREATEST GAMES	Author	ISBN
SCOTLAND	David Potter	978-1-84818-200-4
STOKE CITY	Simon Lowe & David Lee	978-1-84818-201-1
WEST BROM	Simon Wright	978-1-84818-206-6

GENERAL FOOTBALL	Author	ISBN
A GREAT FACE FOR RADIO	John Anderson	978-1-84818-403-9
A SMASHING LITTLE FOOTBALL FIRM	Nicky Allt	978-1-84818-402-2

BEHIND THE BACK PAGE	Christopher Davies	978-1-84818-506-7
BOOK OF FOOTBALL OBITUARIES	Ivan Ponting	978-1-905449-82-2
FORGIVE US OUR PRESS PASSES	Football Writers' Association	978-1-84818-507-4
JUST ONE OF SEVEN	Denis Smith	978-1-84818-504-3
MANCHESTER UNITED MAN & BABE	Wilf McGuinness	978-1-84818-503-6
MR JOHN	Mel Henderson	978-1-84818-514-2
NEVER HAD IT SO GOOD	Tim Quelch	978-1-84818-600-2
NO SMOKE, NO FIRE	Dave Jones	978-1-84818-513-5
NORTHERN AND PROUD	Paul Harrison	978-1-84818-505-0
OUTCASTS: The Lands That FIFA Forgot	Steve Menary	978-1-905449-31-6
PALLY	Gary Pallister	978-1-84818-500-5
PARISH TO PLANET	Eric Midwinter	978-1-905449-30-9
PLEASE MAY I HAVE MY FOOTBALL BACK?	Eric Alexander	978-1-84818-508-1
TACKLES LIKE A FERRET	Paul Parker	1-905449-46-1
THE DOOG	Harrison & Gordos	978-1-84818-502-9
THE RIVALS GAME	Douglas Beattie	978-1-905449-79-8
UNITED NATIONS?	Tim Webber	978-1-84818-405-3
WARK ON	John Wark	978-1-84818-511-1

RUGBY LEAGUE	*Author*	*ISBN*
MOML LEEDS RHINOS	Caplan & Saffer	978-1-905449-69-9
MOML WIGAN WARRIORS	David Kuzio	978-1-905449-66-8

CRICKET	*Author*	*ISBN*
ASHES TO DUST	Graham Cookson	978-1-905449-19-4
GROVEL!	David Tossell	978-1-905449-43-9
KP: CRICKET GENIUS?	Wayne Veysey	978-1-84818-701-6
MOML: THE ASHES	Pilger & Wightman	1-905449-63-1
MY TURN TO SPIN	Shaun Udal	978-1-905449-42-2
THE BEST OF ENEMIES	Kidd & McGuinness	978-1-84818-703-1
THE BODYLINE HYPOCRISY	Michael Arnold	978-1-84818-702-3
WASTED?	Paul Smith	978-1-905449-45-3

Know The Score Books Limited
118 Alcester Road
Studley
Warwickshire
B80 7NT
01527 454482
info@knowthescorebooks.com
www.knowthescorebooks.com

A CIP catalogue record is available for this book from the British Library
ISBN: 978-1-84818-517-3

Printed and bound in Great Britain
By Athenaeum Press, Gateshead, Tyne & Wear

Acknowledgements

I am indebted to a vast number of people who joined me on the search for the real Steve Coppell, particularly those who gave up their time to share memories of the man himself.

My thanks, therefore, go first and foremost to: Brian Barwick, Ian Branfoot, Martin Buchan, Tommy Docherty, Nick Hammond, Bob Harris, Paul Hince, Dick Knight, Glen Little, Lou Macari (and Buddy), Eddie McGoldrick, David Meek, Graeme Murty, Phil Neal, Alan Pardew, John Salako, Willie Stevenson, Kit Symons, Gordon Taylor, Geoff Thomas, John Wark and Bobby Zamora.

Bob Harris gets a second thank you for allowing me to use quotes and sections of Steve Coppell's diary from *Touch and Go*, the book he collaborated on with Steve in 1985 and which became my travelling companion on much of the early search for the young Steve. Thanks, too, go to the book's publishers, Collins.

Other books which helped in my research for this story included Jim White's *Biography of Manchester United*; Tommy Docherty's *The Doc, Hallowed Be Thy Game*; Ron Greenwood's *Yours Sincerely*; *Mr Wright* – the biography of Ian Wright; *Determined* – the biography of Norman Whiteside; *Kicking and Screaming, An Oral History of Football* by Rogan Taylor; *Broken Dreams – vanity, greed and the souring of British football*, by Tom Bower; Mihir Bose's *Sports Babylon*; *1966 And All That* by Geoff Hurst; my treasured *Post-War History of the FA Cup* by Ivan Ponting and, as ever, my trusted collection of Rothmans and Sky Sports Football Yearbooks.

Two very impressive websites also proved valuable bookmarks and I am grateful to the MCIVTA (Manchester City online newsletter) and Holmesdale (unofficial Crystal Palace FC fans' site) sites for helping me to understand the background and feelings of fans during those times.

Even with that mountain of research, I required an army of researchers and proofreaders. Above all my tireless father, Brian Roach, who is still trying to teach me proper English, but also Margaret Moore, the acceptable face of mother-in-laws, Simon Schafer (what he doesn't know about Coke cans is not worth knowing), Rachel Roach and Jonathan Stevenson, Andy McKenzie, Chris Bevan, Simon Austin and Paul Fletcher at BBC Sport. Thank you to Humber and Bob for your input and for jostling for top-ten positions.

To those who shared parts of the journey, whether they liked it or not: Nick, Charlie and Tom Barker at Fulham; the Weymouth posse – Schafes, Sue, Paul, Trina, Longy, Sarah, Eileen and the kids – who allowed me a leave of absence to include a day trip to Southampton in a week's holiday.

And to those who helped plan the route by organising meetings and interviews, or simply offering advice and feedback: Mel Austin, Jonathan Pearce and Mark Bright at BBC Sport, Nada Grkinic at the Football Association, Paul Camillin at Brighton and Hove Albion, the media team at Southampton Football Club, Anthony Smith at the *Reading Chronicle* and Johnny Phillips at Sky.

I also need to say a big thank you to Matt Smith at French Jones for his work on the brilliant front cover image and probably the biggest thank you of all to Simon Lowe at Know the Score Books. You showed patience that allowed me to properly carry out this search and valuable advice and feedback when I needed it most, for which I am hugely grateful.

Thanks, of course, to Steve Coppell himself, not only for everything he did for the club I love, the valuable source of post-match interviews and the stream of hysterical one-liners, but also for giving me his approval to talk to those closest to him in researching this story, when a book about himself was the last thing on the radar of such a modest man.

Finally, a thank you dressed up as an apology. To my amazing wife, Rachel, and my beautiful children, Sam and Jessica, who may have forgotten what I look like. Thank you for affording me the time and space to see this through but still being there when I needed you. I love you very much.

Stuart Roach
October 2009

CONTENTS

IN BED WITH STEVE COPPELL

WHEN I HAVE ENTERED those competitions where the prize is to watch any game of my choice, anywhere in the world, I have agonised unnecessarily as to which match I would choose. Boca Juniors v River Plate in La Bombonera; the Milan derby; Real Madrid v Barcelona home and away? It's a harder question than the one set to win the competition, that's for sure.

But why not a game that has already taken place? Where would I go, if someone offered to transport me to a terrace from the past, to witness a game that had already taken place? What if there was a football turnstile in the back of the changing room belonging to Mr Benn, the time-travelling cartoon character I grew up watching in the 70s?

I know some will say that such nostalgia releases already exist and that they are known as ESPN Classics, or involve Jeff Stelling talking to the boys from the good old days about the good old days before Sky apparently invented football. But what if you could *really* go back? What if you were killing time in an episode of *Life on Mars*? Which terrace would your flares be flapping on then?

I am now fairly certain that I would choose Old Trafford on 1 March 1975. Manchester United v Cardiff City. Not because I hold any allegiance to United – and, let's face it, there would be more glamorous a choice of fixture than that one if I did – but because it would allow me to see the moment Steve Coppell first ran out at Old Trafford in a Manchester United shirt.

It is a moment Coppell says he will never forget; a moment only 43,601 people in the world can say they witnessed. I was not one of them, but the events of the past few months leave me feeling that, strangely, I *was* there; and also at Wembley for the FA Cup finals in 1976, 1977 and 1979, or two years later for England's key World Cup qualifier against Hungary, a game memorable only for Paul Mariner sealing qualification for Espana 82 and for Coppell suffering the injury that was to ultimately end his playing career.

I have absorbed these events with an almost rabid appetite, most of them shared with those who knew Coppell best – his managers, his players, his friends. In a bid to discover the man himself my research material has seen Steve Coppell come on holiday with me, come to bed with me and wake me up in the middle of the night just to bounce some ideas around.

I know I am not the only one to have dreams about Coppell. United fans of a certain age still do – right-backs from the Coppell era would call them nightmares – even advertising guru Charles Saatchi confessed to his wife, Nigella Lawson, that he dreamed she was having an affair with the then Reading manager. Such is the impact Steve Coppell has on people.

It was during that Reading era that I got to know Coppell. Not well, but from a relatively short distance. Well enough to develop a respect that led me to turn down the opportunity to write a biography of his life when he was still Reading manager and I was covering his team. But when he quit as Royals boss after six years in which he became the first manager in Reading's history to take them to the Premier League, it was the end of an era; a pause for reflection in his own life and the start of my journey to get to know him better.

I remembered him as a player, wearing the red, white and blue Admiral shirt of England more clearly than the red of United, such are the memories of football fans. And I remembered him as a young manager, for fantastical comic-strip stories of creating heroes from underdogs and working miracles on a shoestring.

I wanted to return to those times, to rewind beyond the Reading era in which I shared big-match experiences with him and to uncover the stories behind the earlier games that charted a course throughout his life. Not one career, but two hugely successful callings. As I talked to those who had been involved with Steve and read more and more about his achievements, trials and tribulations, I realised that I didn't just want to go to one game, I wanted to put myself on every terrace of every game that defined his career. It hasn't been easy and there have been times when I have woken up at four in the morning thinking it's 1975. Like the secret lemonade drinker!

If Mr Benn did have a turnstile in his dressing room, Coppell himself would probably choose the Kop at Anfield in the days when the famous terrace housed the boys' pen. There, the seven-year-old Coppell would stand wide-mouthed in awe of Bill Shankly's pride and joy, allowing his gaze to snap from the hallowed Anfield turf only when it was absolutely necessary to protect himself from the big kids trying to steal his Mars Bar.

Coppell's dreams then were merely to grow up watching this team every week, given that his diminutive frame meant that he was deemed unlikely ever to make it as a player himself. Or so everyone kept telling him. To say that the career which unfolded was beyond his wildest dreams would, therefore, be entirely accurate if simplistic. But it makes for a fantastic sporting and human story of triumph and disaster; highs and lows; tears and laughter. Plenty of laughter.

I am grateful to the players, managers and friends who know Steve Coppell best for sharing their memories and respectful of those who preferred not to, given Coppell's own reluctance to put himself in the spotlight. The subject of my research is a complex and very private person, making my search for the real Steve Coppell a challenging, but hugely rewarding experience.

Choose your terrace and enjoy the journey.

CAREER CROSSROADS

The sky over Dam Square grows brighter as the morning sun draws its strength. And, in the increasing light of an Amsterdam April Sunday, things start to draw into sharp focus as Steve Coppell slowly sips his coffee. It is over, yet at the same time it is only just beginning.

At 28, Coppell should be in his playing prime. He should be part of Ron Atkinson's Manchester United squad and their perennial trips to Wembley; aiming to add to his 42 England caps as Bobby Robson's squad sail through their qualifying campaign for Mexico 86.

Instead, he is learning to walk again – properly and without pain – attempting to rebuild his life, as well as his left knee, after three operations which have failed to rebuild his playing career. Today, though, is his day off. Sunday mornings remain Coppell's great escape, a chance to catch up on the week's events back home and forget about the previous six days of agonising torture as he undergoes the drastic treatment that could yet offer a footballing lifeline.

That third operation, six months ago, has failed to arrest the gradual deterioration of his knee following a crunching tackle from Hungarian full-back Jozsef Toth two years earlier. The routine had represented his final realistic hope of playing again, but now Coppell's recovery is merely about trying to get through life without feeling pain; to be able to play golf or walk up the stairs without wincing. Looking forward to one day playing football in the garden with the kids or grandkids is as ambitious as he now dares to dream.

After the first two operations the feeling had been different. There had been progress, there had been games and, crucially, there had been hope. But after the third operation things felt different. There had been some progress, but no more games and, apparently, no more hope.

Coppell looks up from his papers and pushes away the empty coffee cup. The final throes of winter in Amsterdam have given way to early spring sunshine and, for Coppell, it is also a changing of the seasons. Time to go home and face the music.

KNEE SURGEON JONATHAN Noble unintentionally marked a crossroads in Steve Coppell's life on the morning of Friday 30 September 1983 when he whispered the words: "I am afraid I am going to have to advise you to retire."

Noble had represented Coppell's one last realistic hope of a return to the ranks of professional football, to fulfil a playing career that was only truly a little more than half complete. But the surgeon had removed the final shred of aspiration on that bleak September morning, along with what remained of the damaged cartilage in Coppell's left knee.

"I felt my world had fallen in on top of me," Coppell later recalled. In the days which followed Noble's 13-word verdict there were tears – rivers of seemingly endless tears – and there were beers, a brief anaesthetic to numb Coppell's anger, frustration and pain. But there was no hope. Deep down, there was none.

Coppell's phone barely stopped ringing, the postman became an overworked friend and newspaper columns read like obituaries as they were filled with tributes from players and managers. But still there was no hope.

Even when Ray Wilkins, Coppell's friend and former team-mate for club and country, phoned to insist his wingman had to believe he would one day return, Coppell's response was that he was wrong. By then, it was official. Coppell's mounting depression collapsed into total despair when he watched Ian St John announcing his retirement on television before the injured player had even summoned the courage to break the news to his parents. St John, admired from the Kop by the young Coppell, had once represented dreams and aspirations for Steve – an iconic symbol of hope for the young emerging player. Now that same Anfield icon was announcing the end of the dream. The end of the hope.

For two years Coppell had played through the pain of his injury, with steroid injections and anti-inflammatory drugs becoming a part of his pre-match routine. It seemed a small price to pay for the reward of representing Manchester United and England, week in and week out. In one incredible four-year period between 1977 and 1981, Coppell did not miss a single game for his club. Two hundred and six consecutive appearances during which three managers – Tommy Docherty,

Dave Sexton and Ron Atkinson – came or went at Old Trafford but the little right-winger remained a constant.

"He was as reliable as the number 27 bus," said Docherty, who signed Coppell from Tranmere Rovers for a down payment of £40,000 and immediately made him a star. But the bus had finally broken down, and it was beyond repair. The pain of that third operation disappeared quicker than the black cloud which lingered as its legacy. Yet it took barely more than a week for Coppell, ever the pragmatist, to count his blessings and begin to plan for his future. If he could not play the game, that did not mean he could not stay in the game.

Six months earlier Coppell had begun to keep a diary to help chart the progress of his recovery. It provided a kind of self therapy, but also now represented a basis from which to move forward. Yet the job offers which began to land on his doorstep were not exactly what he'd had in mind. A wine importer and an insurance company offered him roles which would probably have helped their own profile more than assisting the former player move into business; a role with a sports goods firm was as close as he got to remaining in the game.

Third Division Wigan tentatively discussed the opportunity of Coppell becoming their chief executive, but it was a vague approach and Coppell still had the air of a schoolboy daydreaming in class as the offers were made.

It was a conversation with his United team-mate Arnold Mühren that finally snapped Coppell's attention back into focus. The Dutch international, recognising Coppell needed help simply to lead a pain-free existence, recommended Richard Smith, an Amsterdam physiotherapist who had helped several leading Dutch sportsmen. The physio believed he could not only free Coppell from pain, he could get him fit enough to play professional football again. It would mean spending three months in Amsterdam, but Smith offered his services for free and even welcomed Coppell into his home for the full three-month period. If Coppell still was not cured by the end of April, Smith would not charge him a penny for his services; though if the doctor fulfilled his outlandish promise, Coppell agreed to pay him ten per cent of any future earnings from the game as a player.

Still scarred by Dr Noble's verdict of a few months earlier, Coppell refused to allow the hope to return, yet he viewed the Amsterdam opening as an opportunity to clear his head as well as to treat the knee. "There wasn't a moment when I believed that I would play professionally again, but I was doing the sort of exercise which I would never have had the will-power to do on my own at home," Coppell recalled.

Those exercises were part of Smith's cruel-to-be-kind method of treatment known as Cyrriax and involved deep friction massage which was violent but effective. Weekends brought some respite and the undoubted highlight of Coppell's week was Sunday morning, when he would dissect the football reports in the English newspapers. Sipping coffee as he analysed the results and reports, Coppell slowly realised that his heart remained in English football, even if his legs could not. Smith's treatment and his unorthodox techniques were helping but the three-month agreement was close to an end and Coppell knew that it was not going to result in a return to the playing fields of top-flight football.

When he read about his own situation in one of those Sunday papers, Coppell also knew that the doctor had broken a gentlemen's agreement not to talk to the press about their arrangement – and that it was time to leave. His departure for Holland had been that of a fugitive, slipping out of the country with only a few belongings and even fewer people knowing what he was leaving in search of. His cover was that he was studying Dutch football and coaching methods, but now the truth was out.

As Coppell turned his thoughts to London for the PFA awards dinner where, as chairman, he was due to make an address and reveal Liverpool's Ian Rush as the 11th recipient of the players' Footballer of the Year award, he was already making plans for the future. He read about himself in the gossip columns – a top job at the Football Association, the Football League or even back at Old Trafford were all mooted – and he pored over reports detailing United's 4-1 win over Coventry to keep them within two points of Coppell's boyhood idols Liverpool at the top of the First Division. But those stories blurred into the background as he wrote his own agenda, setting a self-imposed July deadline to find a job in football, or think again.

After returning to England, life became a social whirl for the retired footballer as awards dinners, presentations and PFA work filled his time and brought him into contact with all the right people. But the only firm offers to come Coppell's way were the restaurant manager's job at Old Trafford and confirmation of the Wigan opening – until, that is, a chance meeting at the Football Writers' Awards dinner. During a conversation with Charlton chairman John Fryer, Coppell was introduced to Crystal Palace chairman Ron Noades, who was about to appoint Dave Bassett as manager and was on the hunt for a potential assistant. Shortly after that brief encounter Bassett went back on his decision to accept the job, returning to Wimbledon to leave Noades back in the market for a new manager. At last Coppell's phone rang with good news.

The interviews which followed saw Coppell ask Noades more questions than he answered himself. The two had done their homework on each other. Coppell had quizzed several people about Noades and Palace, including outgoing Palace manager Alan Mullery. To a man, they told him not to go near the job. Noades, meanwhile, sought references from the likes of Sir Matt Busby, Ron Greenwood and PFA general secretary Gordon Taylor. They proved glowing, though Taylor admitted he had hoped Coppell might join him at the players union, the PFA chairman having been forced to relinquish his duties when his playing days officially ended. "He tried so hard to get back from the injury and when he realised life would never be the same he thought seriously about becoming a full-time administrator," Taylor told me as I began my search for the real Steve Coppell.

"Steve was a genuinely good lad and we got on well. My predecessor Cliff Lloyd had approached Steve to come onto the committee and I was delighted when he finally agreed to come on board. We had a lot in common, we were both wingers, both graduates with a degree and I knew that he had a good head on his shoulders. It was a tragedy that his tenure was cut short by his injury – but I knew then that he was destined to be top quality in whatever he did."

The football writers present when Coppell had his life-changing encounter with Noades were already speculating on the retired star's next move, but were, unwittingly, witnessing the start of a new life for Steve Coppell; a second football career path that would in many ways plot a similar route to the first when laid out in parallel. *Manchester Evening News* journalist David Meek, who had covered Coppell throughout his eight seasons at Old Trafford, was not surprised by his change of direction and told me: "I always thought that he would go into management because he always had a quiet authority with him. I did wonder whether he was too nice a man to be a successful manager because you have got to be a little bit hard at times and that side of Steve wasn't regularly on show – he didn't open up all that much.

"I would have liked to have worked with him as local reporter and manager because he would have had to come out of the shell that he built around himself as a player. He might well say that I didn't press him enough – I found him quite hard work – but as a manager he would have had to come out with his views a lot more and I think I would then have seen the real Steve Coppell and enjoyed working with him."

The real Steve Coppell? My journey had begun in earnest.

WIN WHEN YOU'RE SINGING

Little Stevie Coppell awaits the verdict. He wants this break and is convinced he is good enough, but the competition is tough and there are too many candidates for too few places. But Stevie is not afraid of a bit of competition.

Trials have been nerve-wracking to say the least, but Stevie is a determined character. Despite being one of the smallest boys in his year at Ranworth Square County Primary School, as well as one of the quietest characters, Stevie makes up for his stature in pure hard work and determination.

The school motto, 'brave and calm', could have been written for him and he has already represented the school at cricket, as a batsman and wicket-keeper, and athletics, running the 100 yards, as well as excelling in his studies sufficiently to be made head boy. But there is one ambition he still holds at the school and Stevie is confident that today's announcement will be a positive one.

The verdict though, when it comes, is damning. Rejection. In a nutshell, he is not good enough; little Stevie Coppell, not good enough for the Ranworth Square County Primary School choir.

Delivered with a tap on the shoulder and a whispered word from the music master, the decision hardly seems fair – in a city dominated by football and pop music, all Stevie Coppell wants is to sing and play football. It is a judgement that provides an early lesson that you don't always get what you wish for and the young schoolboy understands he has to work harder . . . at every level.

WHEN BRIAN BARWICK left a message on my phone to say he would be happy to meet up and talk about his old mate, I was excited to say the least. Not only would this be the ideal insight in my bid to find out more about the young Steve Coppell, it was also likely that our conversation would take place in a celebrated football location. "I'll call later in the week, to confirm a meeting place," Brian had said.

My mind raced. Brian was still well connected with the Football Association – no favour too great for the man who masterminded the delivery of Fabio Capello to the England manager's chair – so perhaps we could meet at Wembley, strolling around the greensward and pointing out the rough locations of where, in the old stadium, Steve would have run out for his England debut, or watched Ian Wright so nearly win Crystal Palace the FA Cup?

We could meet in one of the FA's swanky Soho Square offices, surrounded by pictures of England internationals celebrating goals as we talk through the career paths of two former school and university pals, or failing that one of the nearby bars or restaurants in which I am sure FA deals are sealed or celebrated.

So it was with an air of mild anti-climax that I drove up the M3 to Hampton and Richmond's Beveree Stadium on a wet and windy Tuesday night, not even for a first-team game but to watch the reserves in action against Cove's stiffs. Disappointment soon gave way to the anticipation of catching up with Brian, who had given me my first interview for a job at the BBC when he was Head of Sport and, more importantly, knew Steve Coppell from the age of 11.

At least it provided our conversation with a football backdrop that actually turned out to be highly enjoyable. My £3 entry provided me with five goals, all of them for Hampton and three of them for new signing Michael Lee Charles and, once we had established there was no memorable reason why Brian didn't give me the *Grandstand* job in 1993, I settled in alongside former West Ham and England midfielder Alan Devonshire, now firmly established as Hampton's most successful ever manager. Devonshire played in the same England team as Coppell in the goalless draw with Greece at Wembley in 1983, memorable only in that it meant Bobby Robson's team failed to qualify for the 1984 European Championships; and that it saw Coppell win his 42nd and final England cap. At the Beveree Stadium, Devonshire was busy running the rule over his reserves and I was there to talk to Hampton's recently appointed director, who seemed as happy in the surroundings as he did in the VIP seats at Wembley. "It's real football," said Barwick, "and it's nice being able to watch my local team and enjoy a game without all the officialdom that goes with it," he told me, ignoring the fact that he was the one who opened the bar before kick-off.

It did somehow seem appropriate that we were watching 'real' football given that Barwick saw Coppell cut his teeth on a muddy school field, albeit one once graced by John Lennon, long before the manicured lawns of Old Trafford, Anfield and Wembley.

"He was the year below me, but we played in the same team – I was a pretty ordinary right-back and he was the right-winger who we would give the ball to and watch him go," Barwick told me. "I got to know him better because we both got the same bus to Quarry Bank School. He lived about three miles away and we'd travel in to leafy Allerton on the number 61."

"We'd play tennis against each other too – for two weeks every year. Whenever Wimbledon fortnight came up we would re-enact it on our local public court with two really bad rackets and two tennis balls that had seen too much tennis. But he was happiest playing football. He shot through the team and it wasn't obvious to us that he was as good a player as he obviously was because he wasn't a stand-out centre-forward that scored ten a game or a goalkeeper who tipped everything over the bar. Steve's ability was based on his industry and his touch and technique, and he was a better player than most in the team.

"He had good pace so he was able to get away from people, but he was a tiddler. He grew bigger through university and into his Manchester United days, but he was a small kid. Clubs like Everton and Liverpool would have had a look at him then but they were very size conscious and it's easy to reject the little 'uns."

The football clearly came more naturally than the singing to Coppell. In fact, it all came rather easily to him. Most of the other boys were bigger than Steve, but it didn't make much difference to the youngster who had honed his talents on the unforgiving streets of Sparrow Hall, a tough suburb of Liverpool, from the age of seven. Young Steve would sprint from the front door of his family's ground floor flat in Coronation Court to get involved in the mass street kickabouts typical of most English suburbs in the 60s. When it came to picking teams little Stevie was not exactly the first name on the team sheet. He had two positions; in goal, when no-one else wanted to play there; or up front, where he could goal-hang and not get in the way. He quickly developed a knack for poaching goals – the two-yard tap-in became a trademark – and as the tiny striker started to have more of an impact in the street games, or the occasional trip to 'Wembley' – the title bestowed on West Derby Cemetery in Norris Green due to the simple fact it had grass – he found himself moving up the pecking order when it came to picking sides.

Even so, he wasn't sure of the answer when Miss Lydiate, the primary school teacher who organised the Ranworth Square County Primary School team, asked which his best position was. Showing some astute instincts for a primary school teacher who probably had better things to do with her after-school hours than run the football team, Miss Lydiate suggested he tried the left wing.

In headmaster David McKay and games master Owen Griffiths, Coppell had found two early role models. McKay took a keen interest in the football team and was especially proud of Joe Royle, a Ranworth prodigy who had gone on to Quarry Bank and had already been picked up by Everton. McKay was keen for Coppell to follow the same path, especially when Coppell was named in the first ever representative side for Liverpool Primary Schools alongside Billy Rodaway and Joe Gallagher, who both went on to play professional football, and future Liverpool apprentice John Highams. The team photo betrays Coppell as easily the smallest player in the squad and, though his pride was doubled as he followed his sporting achievement by winning a place at Quarry Bank – the first in his family to pass the 11-plus – his size gradually became an issue when it came to football. If it was obvious in that team photo, it became glaringly so over the next few years as Coppell's peers grew more quickly. Bigger and stronger players all too easily knocked the skilful youngster off the ball and when it came to attempting to emulate Royle by securing trials for Liverpool, Coppell was not even given the chance to mix it with the big boys.

Barwick explained: "Joe had been an iconic player at Quarry Bank. The most famous man to come out of the school was John Lennon, by some distance, but in terms of sport Joe was the most famous to come through. The headmaster at the time, Mr Pobjoy, was a really brilliant headmaster, but he just felt the amount of time asked of Joe when he was playing for Liverpool schoolboys affected his education and promised himself that if ever he had a player as good as Joe he would deny him the opportunity. So Steve made the Liverpool primary school team, but never got the chance to try for the senior schoolboy teams."

I could not help pondering what role fate plays in football and a player's progress. Even at Hampton on a night of foul conditions; what if a scout from any of the London clubs from Chelsea to Dagenham had decided to wander down and stumbled upon Charles bagging a well-taken hat-trick? What if they had come the previous week before he arrived at the club? Yet Coppell's lack of progress through the youth team ranks owed more to policy than fate and so may have been even harder to stomach.

"He has always been a very level headed feller, Steve. I don't know whether he was kicking the proverbial dog and cat at the time, but he was a very talented lad and even though he probably stood out to astute football watchers more than his team-mates, his manner was quiet and his stature was small. He wasn't one of these rock 'n' roll centre-forwards," Barwick insisted.

Coppell, like Barwick, was already a passionate supporter of Liverpool and would go to Anfield with his Dad, Jim, and elder brother, Kevin, who would drop him off in the boys' pen while they stood on the Kop to which he aspired to graduate. The pen was an eye-opener to a young lad in Liverpool and boasted its own micro-community, where overaged kids would sneak in and rule the roost, taking possession of the younger kids' sweets and drinks if they were not well hidden.

The young Coppell kept as far out of sight as he could, preferring to concentrate on events on the pitch where a Liverpool side captained by Ron Yeats were dazzling crowds of more than 40,000 fervent fans on a regular basis. 'I recall only too well that first great Bill Shankly side and especially Peter Thompson. I had a soft spot for him because he was a winger, but I also admired Ian St John and Rowdy Yeats while Shanks was my idol,' Coppell wrote in his 1985 biography, *Touch and Go*. He added: 'Ronnie Moran, such a key backroom figure with Liverpool during their great years, also stands out because whenever we hung around waiting for autographs he would not only sign them but also make the effort to stay and chat for five or ten minutes, asking what school we went to and what positions we played in.'

Coppell yearned to be a part of that scene and in a sense the pen toughened him up more than any series of games ever could. The combination of protecting himself within his surroundings and educating himself on a diet of pure Anfield gold was a powerful cocktail and instilled in Coppell a determination to succeed. So, when the terrace-hardened youngster was invited to play for Norris Green in the Boys Clubs League, it was the perfect stage on which to step. Coppell quickly formed a tidy partnership with Colin Shennan, a 6ft 3in rangy striker who scored his fair share of goals and, crucially, took the knocks which allowed his diminutive strike partner to flourish. So successful was the combination that Norris Green progressed to the final of the Liverpool Boys' Clubs Association Cup, a showcase game played at Anfield. Despite losing 2-0 to Tuebrook Boys' Club, Coppell had at least achieved his dream of playing on the hallowed Anfield turf – no matter what future lay ahead.

That box ticked, Coppell started to think about his career path. Where would he head if football did not give him his chance? One theory was that he would become a teacher, but the obvious choice was to follow his father into the Royal Navy and Coppell made the decision that he would take to sea if he failed to pass enough O-Levels to allow him to study A-Levels at sixth form.

Coppell seemed to surprise himself, but few others around him, when he managed six O-Level passes, allowing him to further his education by returning to Quarry Bank to study English, History and Economics A-Levels and still continue playing regular parks football. Yet, invisibly, his professional career was already taking its first tentative steps.

Tranmere Rovers scout Eddie Edwards had watched Coppell playing in a parks match at Aintree and saw enough to ensure he became a regular spectator of the young Norris Green side. "Although he was small I was impressed by his ability," Edwards later revealed. "You are always on the look-out for players who have a certain edge to their game; you don't find many of them but Steve impressed me because he made up for his lack of height with his great tenacity. He showed he was a terrier for hard work and was dangerous coming forward from midfield. I watched him in several other parks games to check his progress, but he never knew I was there, who I was or what I was doing. This is part and parcel of scouting. You keep yourself to yourself and your cards close to your chest."

When Edwards had convinced himself he had discovered a genuine talent, he recommended the diminutive midfielder to Tranmere boss Ron Yeats, the very centre-back who had led the Liverpool team Coppell had loved to watch from the Anfield pen. Yeats and Coppell could hardly have been more different. The Tranmere boss had worked in a slaughterhouse before becoming a footballer and was such a man mountain that when Liverpool signed him, manager Bill Shankly invited journalists to "come in and walk around him". Coppell, even though he had grown half a foot in his final school year and was no longer dwarfed by his team-mates, was hardly a player in that mould, but Edwards was told to offer him a trial and the young winger's big break was about to be realised.

Incredibly, after years of yearning to make the ranks of professional football, Coppell turned down Edwards' approach. With his A-Level exams just a couple of weeks away and a place at university within reach, Coppell decided he could not afford to gamble his place on the outside chance of impressing a Third Division football club. In many ways his stubbornly sensible reaction endeared him even more to Tranmere and certainly set the standard for his early years in the game. A fortnight later Edwards came calling again and this time encountered the frustrated student, bored with revision and ready to take the opportunity of a football-related distraction.

Shennan was also offered a chance, so it was with a familiar foil that Coppell headed to Tranmere for a trial match. The pair combined perfectly, Shennan setting up two of the goals as Coppell scored a hat-trick, yet after the game only Coppell was asked back for a second trial. One had secured a foothold on football's conveyor belt, the other was on his way to a career as a draughtsman in Liverpool. It was another valuable lesson to Coppell that he needed to continue his studies to ensure he had something to fall back on if he did not make the grade as a footballer.

Then, having worked so hard to ensure he secured at least one line of progress, two came along at once. Just as the Coppell family – mum and dad Ena and Jim, with Steve and younger sister Christine – were getting ready to head off for their family holiday in Tenby, Coppell was offered a place at Liverpool University to study Economics to Bsc level and amateur terms with Tranmere

Rovers. He later admitted that the biggest decision he had to make was whether or not to go on the holiday as planned, as he had already decided that the university life was more important than a fledgling football career.

Coppell had also applied to Leeds University, but his interview there was a tough one and the A-Level grade requirements were high, so Coppell settled on Liverpool. He believed he could use the experience of joining Tranmere as a springboard to finding a non-league club that would allow him to play football to a relatively high standard whilst continuing his studies. But Tranmere were already setting their own precedents as young Birkenhead-born midfielder Mark Palios was being allowed to combine professional football at Prenton Park with a degree in psychology at Manchester University. It was a model the club were keen for Coppell to follow and he was treated as a professional, despite remaining very much the amateur. That meant training with the first team and playing for the reserves in the Northern Floodlit League during the week, then the A-team in the Lancashire League at weekends. As an amateur, Coppell could even duck out of cleaning the senior professionals' boots, as was required of his professional peers, and he also managed to squeeze in an occasional third game every week by turning out for his university side.

"I got to know Steve really well when he got to university because, like him, I didn't leave my home town," Barwick told me. "Steve was a year behind me and the Liverpool clique within Liverpool University stuck together. Football was a big part of that and we had a department team called Comecon, which is commerce and economics thrown together. I played centre-half and centre-forward and most of the time Steve watched from the touchline and coached us.

"He was very committed to remaining as much of a student as he could and I really respected that. We were conscious of him making his progress in football because when he went to Tranmere that was big news for us. I went to see his debut, playing against Aldershot, and whenever I could I got over to Tranmere to watch him and was really proud to see him play."

But if the students were proud to have a real footballer amongst their ranks, how did the footballers feel about having a student amongst theirs? In a bid to capture the moment when the young Steve Coppell first walked into Prenton Park I tracked down former Liverpool favourite Willie Stevenson. The 33-year-old Stevenson had played more than 300 games in 14 years as a professional at Rangers, Liverpool and Stoke when Yeats signed him for Tranmere just a month before Coppell's arrival.

The former Scottish international talks in a growl that descends into a purr when he recalls Coppell's shy yet sudden impact at Tranmere, where seasoned and hardened professionals were humbled by a raw teenage talent. "Stevie was more laid back than most of us," Stevenson recalled of the youngster's arrival. "He was not one of those guys who was in awe of his surroundings, though the training ground then was not as elaborate as the grounds now. It was almost like a park. He'd speak his mind and was always asking questions, he was a very keen lad, but even then he was too good for Tranmere. He would make mistakes, like teenagers do, but there was immediately something different about him – he was a cut above the rest."

That natural ability and obvious talent earned Coppell a debut at the age of 18 as he pulled on the Tranmere number seven shirt against Aldershot at Prenton Park on 20 January 1974. Terry Bell's goal secured a 1-0 win for Aldershot that Sunday afternoon in a game that few (possibly with the exception only of Bell and Coppell) will remember.

Coppell's studies never impacted his commitment to football and he was able to cope in the same way that most of his peers held down part-time jobs to supplement their studies. Even so, the wide-eyed teenager started only five more games that season and it was the following campaign in which he started to truly make an impact. Despite featuring in the pre-season trip to Scotland and a 2-0 League Cup win over Southport, Coppell was left out of the opening game of the 1974/75 season at home to Bournemouth, but started the next 29 games in succession as he began to display the goalscoring instinct first honed in Coronation Court.

Having started life at Tranmere as a striker, Coppell was now being used in a wider position and Yeats was quick to explain in the local paper: 'You can play him anywhere. We know he's an upfield player, but he is so strong we play him in midfield. He will finish up as an attacking player because he has got what a lot of full-backs hate – speed and control.'

His first goal in professional football gained some measure of revenge over Aldershot as Tranmere recorded their first win of the season at the third attempt and Coppell went on to score nine more goals, making him the club's leading goalscorer and attracting more attention as the Prenton Park crowds were soon swelled by increasing numbers of scouts coming to watch the young winger in action. "We knew the scouts weren't looking at us because we were all knackered," Stevenson recalled with a smile.

"Steve had pace and knew what he was doing with it. He hugged the line and did his job, getting past the full-back and getting crosses in for the forwards to get on and score. It worked. The thing about Steve is that he didn't beat people from four or five yards, he would come to you and then go past but leave you no time to turn and do anything about it. We only played against him in five-a-sides thankfully. Not only did he play well, he was very articulate. He was bright, sharp and a good listener, but above all he had a wee bit more talent than anyone else there."

Yeats was trying to recreate the Liverpool model in lower league form at Prenton Park; an Anfield model village. Training was highly professional and Yeats always insisted on the best facilities the club could manage. He also strengthened the Liverpool connections by signing former Anfield stalwarts such as Stevenson, Ian St John, Bobby Graham and Tommy Lawrence, then, with Rovers struggling to stay out of the bottom four, brought in recently-retired Bill Shankly in an advisory capacity.

"What a thrill it was when the great man turned up at training one day. Just his being there helped – he possessed great presence and charisma," said Coppell, adding: "the important thing to me was that I was learning about the game. Although we were a small club with few resources and precious little money, big Ron Yeats insisted that everything should be done properly and I would not be exaggerating if I suggested that I owed a great deal of the successes that were to follow to him. He was intent on giving youth an opportunity and under another manager I may never have been given my chance in what was a struggling team. When I was, I had people like Willie on hand to offer practical advice."

Stevenson clearly recalled the first time he became aware of Coppell's sponge-like ability to absorb everything he experienced. "I can remember sitting on the bus chatting – just chatting, rambling on about Liverpool – and he wasn't just listening, he was analysing it all. You knew immediately that he was sharp. He was bright, intellectual and articulate and he seemed to be in control of himself. I was a joker and it was a laugh to me at that time, at the end of my playing career, but he was serious."

Perhaps that is why Coppell thought he was the victim of a practical joke when his studies were interrupted by a phone call from Tranmere's general manager, Dave Russell. Coppell had stayed behind to study while his team-mates headed to the Aldershot army base for a five-day training camp ahead of their Friday night game in Hampshire. When Russell told him that Manchester United wanted to talk to him, Coppell's first reaction was that he was being wound up.

Thankfully he didn't hang up, because he had an appointment with the Doc – first thing in the morning.

A VISIT TO THE PALACE

The scene is just like any other nine-year-old boy's bedroom; clothes, books and toys twisted together in a tangled covering of floorspace so tight it is hard to tell whether the bedroom was carpeted or not.

A Rothmans Football Yearbook sits on a shelf, spared the killing fields of the bedroom floor partly to protect its pristine condition and partly because it spotlights Norman Whiteside skinning Alan Hansen in the Milk Cup final.

Posters fight for space on the walls, team-mates seemingly jostling for elbow room as Ray Wilkins, Bryan Robson and, of course, super Stevie Coppell smile down on the boy like guardian angels. All heroes, all legends and all looking down on the youngster, inspiring him to work harder, to keep practising, to be like them. One day.

Now the boy is going to get the chance to meet one of them in the flesh – to smile at his hero and see him smile back just as he has done a million times from the wall; only this time for real. First, he has to find those pictures. They are here somewhere; not on the floor – they are too precious to have been left on the floor – but in an envelope in a box in a drawer in a cupboard in that bedroom. Somewhere.

There is the box. The boy, hurrying almost frantically now, flips off the lid and digs out the envelope, then smiles as he looks down at the two photos he treasures so much. Steve Coppell smiles back. A voice behind him snaps him out of his daydream. "Come on Glen, it's time to go."

The drive to the Crystal Palace training ground is only a short one, but it feels like a lifetime as Glen Little and his father twist through the streets of south-east London towards Godstone. Glen is the stand-out player of his generation in the area and the Palace scouts are well aware of his talents. Keen not to lose him to the lure of other London clubs, they know when to play their trump card the moment they see him wearing a Manchester United shirt.

"STEVE COPPELL WAS my favourite player from the age of about six," Glen Little told me from the Sheffield hotel that he had made his temporary home during an early-season trial with Kevin Blackwell's Sheffield United.

It seemed poignant that we were discussing Little's recollections of his days under Coppell during an extended hotel stay, typical of the nomadic existence footballers share with travelling salesmen and Alan Partridge. Poignant because it was a brief encounter with Coppell in a hotel dining room – when the Burnley player was introduced to the Reading manager – that finally gave Little his chance to play for his hero, years after having those pictures signed at Palace.

"He was the reason I went to Palace. I was at primary school and the people at Palace said 'do you want to come and train with us and meet Steve?'" Little admitted. "I was a right-winger as soon as I started playing at five years old; I grew up having the red number seven on my back and he was my idol. It's only when I look back that I realise how young he was when I met him. You know how you react when you encounter your heroes, but he was only 29 years old. At the time, I thought he was an old man.

"I always remember him running down the wing; he was a fantastic crosser of the ball. I knew all about him and I once had a quiz question: 'how many England caps did Steve Coppell win?' I knew the answer straight away – he won 42 caps by the time he was 27 years old and it's frightening what a great player he was. The game just wasn't as big then without Sky and all the media attention it now gets."

Coppell had been a manager only a matter of weeks, but Palace were clearly keen to use his influence wherever they could, even if it was simply to ensure they attracted the best kids in the area. Even more encouragingly, the new manager looked an absolute natural from the day he walked in.

"It was the trick question – who is the best player at Palace? People would answer 'Ian Wright', 'Geoff Thomas', and you just kept saying no as they rattled through 20 names before giving up. Then you'd say 'Steve Coppell'. He used to train with real enthusiasm and that's when he was happiest, when he was on the pitch," Little told me.

Of all his memories of Steve Coppell, though, that first meeting rates as the best. "I took my Steve Coppell pictures for him to sign and we had a chat," remembered Little, reflecting on the fulfilment of an ambition that inadvertently started a relationship that would be landmarked throughout his career. "I was nervous, but so happy. I went with my dad, Dave, and he was a United fan, so it was as great for him as it was for me. Steve was my dad's favourite too, so he was happy to be there."

Coppell was happy to be there too. Despite all advice to the contrary, despite Ron Noades having parted company with five managers in his three years at the club and despite Palace struggling to find £150,000 every year to pay bank interest alone, Coppell had accepted the job at Selhurst Park with a real sense of anticipation. Though, in all honesty, it had been the only firm offer.

'The task of management did not daunt me,' he wrote in *Touch and Go*. 'I said all along that all I wanted was a chance and this was it. I was prepared to ignore my misgivings and the question marks. I was not frightened of failing and, inwardly, I hoped that my arrival would act as a catalyst to the future growth of the club. I am sure every new manager feels like that.'

Noades took over as Palace chairman in 1981, attempting to arrest a slide of mounting debts caused by dwindling support. Terry Venables had taken the Eagles from the Third Division to the First but, following his move across London to take over the reins at Queen's Park Rangers, Palace's fortunes took a nosedive. Malcolm Allison, Dario Gradi, Steve Kember and Alan Mullery all came and went before Coppell was given a chance to make a name for himself as a manager. There was no master plan, but there were aspects of the Anfield and Old Trafford models in which Coppell had been schooled that he was keen to adopt.

The barrier was that Coppell knew it would take patience and time; yet time was a commodity Palace could ill afford and patience a virtue the chairman was not renowned for. Coppell, though, used his wealth of knowledge to persuade Noades that his vision needed building brick-by-brick, and not overnight. "The first thing to strike me at Palace was that everyone was living in the past," he recalled. "The word 'potential' still dominated everyone's thinking. The reality was a £1.3 million deficit which could only be reduced to sensible proportions by shrewd financial and football management. If I had gone in heavy-handed, generally throwing my weight around, there would have been civil war in the dressing room – and that was the last thing we wanted when we were beginning a season trying to stop the rot and avoid relegation.

"I have to confess that I was extremely nervous, as I suddenly found myself at the helm of a very large business with absolutely no experience at all. A lot of people were relying on me to pay their wages and I did not want to let anyone down, least of all myself. I certainly did not need a degree in economics to tell me that Palace's overdraft and the bank's refusal to raise the limit meant I would have to develop a youth policy to replace Alan Mullery's emphasis on experience. The club had not been taking in youngsters of 13 and 14 and so there were no young players ready to challenge the seniors for their places.

"I stood back and took stock of the situation and I was not particularly pleased. Some players on the staff commanded no respect at all and were happy picking up inflated wages while playing for the reserves with no ambition to move on or to try and make first-team football. Quite clearly we were not going to become a good side overnight with players who had struggled at the bottom of the Second Division since being relegated from the First."

Two of those decisions had already been made for Coppell; Billy Gilbert was on his way to Portsmouth by the time the new man was in place and Vince Hilaire insisted he was determined to leave for Luton. Coppell's first piece of business as a manager was to persuade Luton striker Trevor Aylott to swap places with Hilaire and winger Alan Irvine, now manager of Preston North End, also joined from Everton.

Other transactions proved more complicated. Coppell's experience of mediation during his time as PFA chairman came in handy as his early weeks were spent trying to negotiate settlement payments with several players who were in no hurry to move on and ease the club's financial plight. It was a fast learning curve for the young manager, who admits now that he might have struggled without the support network he was able to fall back on from former managers Tommy Docherty, Dave Sexton and Ron Atkinson and his former international managers, Ron Greenwood and Bobby Robson.

A Selhurst Park crowd of 6,764 saw Steve Coppell's managerial debut result in a 1-1 draw with Blackburn Rovers, but a run of three straight defeats – to Shrewsbury, Birmingham and Brighton – followed, before the rookie manager was able to celebrate a first victory, a 2-1 win at Sheffield United after Palace had trailed 1-0 at half-time.

Palace eventually finished a steady, if not spectacular, 15th that season, but Coppell admitted: "I was very young and inexperienced and it was a case of the blind leading the blind. On many occasions I wondered what on earth I was doing and, when we'd lost, I readily admit that I would have been happier going to prison than driving into the training ground. At the time I was totally lost. I did not have a clue."

Crucially, help was also on hand in the form of assistant manager Ian Evans, a former Palace player whose career had also been cut short by injury and who had been recommended to Coppell by his new chairman. Evans was happiest on the training ground, a weight off Coppell's mind as he learned to grapple with the intricacies of football management. It was the following summer when Coppell's natural leadership started to show through and the shoots of new growth at Palace began to appear as the manager shopped locally to make his most significant signing in the type of deal that was to become his trademark.

Ian Wright was 22 years old and working as a labourer, hardly the ideal grounding for a potential Second Division footballer. But, with Palace having long flirted with administration, Coppell was on the lookout for raw materials with which to work – and they did not come much rawer than Wright. Southend and Brighton had both rejected the striker as a teenager and so Wright had resigned himself to a career as a plasterer, satisfying his football needs by playing non-league for Greenwich Borough, before Palace scout Pete Prentice invited him for the trial in which he caught Coppell's eye.

"You just need a chance in life, and I was still working on a building site a week before I went to Palace," Wright said. "Steve gave me the faith, he gave me the chance and he coached me through. The thing about Steve is that when he looks you in the eye, he tells you how it is. It is something I discovered when he signed me for Palace."

Wright was quick to lay down his own marker too, as Coppell remembers well. "On his first day at Palace he told me he wanted to play for England, a bold statement for someone who had just walked in off a building site."

Wright signed professional forms two weeks before the start of the 1985/86 season, but had to wait for his chance as Palace won their opening two games while the new recruit found his feet during training. He made only four substitute appearances in the opening 11 games of the season, but when he came off the bench to secure a 3-2 win over Oldham at Selhurst Park on 12 October 1985, a glorious career had begun in earnest. Eight more goals, half of them as a substitute, followed that season as a strong finish to the campaign lifted Palace to fifth place and offered huge hope for the future. People were using that word 'potential' again, but by now it was in respect of Coppell's burgeoning side, especially when six wins in their first nine games, culminating in a 2-1 home win over local rivals Millwall, sent Palace top of Division Two early in 1986/87.

Wright had started every one of those games but, with Trevor Aylott having departed for Bournemouth, Coppell was keen to continue his rebuilding programme by finding a new foil for his burgeoning star and in November he paid Leicester £75,000 for 24-year-old former Port Vale striker Mark Bright. Coppell fielded his assonant strike force for the first time against Ipswich on 15 November, just 48 hours after Bright's arrival, and the effect was immediate, Bright opening the scoring on his debut and Wright also on target in a 3-3 draw.

Palace's hard-working commercial department funded the £12,500 signing of Anton Otulakowski from Millwall – though injury limited his Palace career to just 12 games – while Coppell also moved to sign central defender

Gary O'Reilly from Brighton for £40,000, paving the way for veteran defender Mickey Droy to depart. Two more players key to the restructure were Alan Pardew, signed from Yeovil in March, and teenage winger John Salako, who was handed his debut just two weeks short of his 18th birthday. Mindful of his own route into the big time, and with his own fatherly responsibilities to the fore following the arrival of his son Mark on 14 March 1986, Coppell was keen to mentor Salako, though the youngster's opportunities were limited to four substitute appearances in his first campaign.

"As a winger he was very much one of the players I admired and I felt I was one of the lucky ones to be playing under him," Salako told me. "I think he had frustrations, but part of management is understanding players and their strengths and, having so recently been a player, he had a lot of things in his head. He was fresh and focused.

"The way he man-managed players was subtle and we didn't see him much – he doesn't do much coaching but he talks and puts things in your head. He would tell me, 'if you put ten crosses in we will get one goal' and would set targets to make sure you were focused on what you are doing and try to win the game. He had a very natural way of getting his point across; a lot of managers have a side to them and get angry if they don't understand players, but Steve understood how it worked."

Despite an erratic run of form towards the end of the campaign, Palace remained within sight of the play-off places and when Wright secured victory over second-placed Portsmouth in the penultimate game it left Coppell's side tantalisingly close to the end-of-season knockout. Victory at Hull on the final day of the season would have been enough to secure their place if Ipswich failed to beat Reading but, with Bobby Ferguson's side only managing a draw, Palace crashed to a 3-0 defeat which left them agonisingly short. It did, however, mark further progress which continued the next season, boosted by the strengthening of the midfield with the arrival of Neil Redfearn from Doncaster and, in particular, Geoff Thomas for a bargain £55,000 from Crewe.

"I had grown up watching Steve Coppell play but he was always on the other side as I was on the blue side of Manchester," Thomas told me. "He was a great player and you tend to forget how young he was when he had to stop playing. He started so young as a manager and when you look back you realise what he had already achieved at such a young age, but at the time it wasn't obvious."

Thomas did not need much persuading to join the Coppell revolution and was quick to sense the air of renaissance at Selhurst Park. "Some of the players he was bringing together had come to the game late or been rejected by clubs. There was hunger in a lot of lads in that squad. He had so much respect from the players – probably because of the way he played the game. He was a 100 per cent guy with crossing ability and goals and when we were playing five-a-sides in training he was still one of the best in the squad.

"He also had this air about him that he was always in control; there were some personalities in the dressing room at that time, but he kept it together. He would sometimes let it go and there would be bickering going on, then he would step in and say a few words.

"He was quick to learn his management skills, but my feeling has always been that ex-players, no matter how old they are, are either a manager or they are not. Steve is. There are some players in the game you expect to go on and become great managers but they don't have that ability to hold back their frustrations when players don't match up to the standards they played to themselves. Steve had that potential to work with players of all sorts of abilities – not all managers have that ability and they are the ones who come to lose the dressing room."

Thomas was named the club's player of the year in his first season, while Salako was young player of the year as he began to emerge along with another teenager, central defender Richard Shaw. But, for the third successive season, Palace fell just short of the play-offs. So when promotion finally came 12 months later it was perhaps poetic that it came via the play-offs.

That was some reward for Coppell's refusal to panic, despite the increasing number of near misses and the frustrations of some fans unhappy at his decision not to re-sign club legend and captain Jim Cannon after 16 years at the club, instead replacing him with Jeff Hopkins, a £240,000 buy from Fulham. Though the fans were upset, Cannon was the last of the old guard to leave and saw Coppell complete his clear-out of the ageing and struggling squad he had originally inherited.

There was no room for sentiment in Coppell's rebuilding of the squad and, along the way, there had been training ground clashes between some of the elder statesmen and several of the young outspoken crop of emerging talent who did not readily offer the respect the senior pros felt they deserved. Coppell organised training games of old boys v youngsters or even black v white that often saw those tensions explode, but the young manager remained in control and ready to step in when necessary.

Wright added in his autobiography, *Mr Wright*: 'I joined Palace when the dressing room was divided virtually down the middle between the seasoned old pros on one side and the young kids who were the future of the club on the other. It didn't help that a lot of the youngsters were black, people like Andy Gray, Tony Finnigan and myself, and I will never be able to swear, hand on heart, whether some of the older lads were prejudiced or jealous of the fact that our careers were just starting and theirs were ending. What I do know is that the likes of Cannon and George Wood seemed to single the young lads out and give them a really hard time.

'Looking back, it was probably a case of the old pros trying to teach the kids a thing or two about life, but at the time I couldn't handle it. Things got so bad with players having a go at each other that Steve had to call a meeting to sort it out. That didn't really help because he couldn't hide the fact that he liked Andy, Tony and the rest of the youngsters, so in training it was a case of the senior players saying, "oh, we mustn't touch Stevie's little boys or they'll go crying to the gaffer."'

A focused Coppell simply continued with his rebuilding programme, gradually moving on those older men, and Thomas told me: "He was always calm and was made for management – he has that demeanour about him. He didn't do too much visually or bang his fist on the table, but he knew when to react and did it in a way where the morning after it is all forgotten."

Salako described his former manager as: "very gentle and very subtle," adding: "I have never seen him lose his temper, but you know when he is happy and he is strong enough to make sure you pull your weight. The words get in. He was never a ranter and raver but he had you pumped and ready and enjoying what you do, which was such a rare thing."

Coppell's reconstructive surgery at Selhurst ensured an air of liberation about the Palace squad that season that was self-perpetuating: the momentum built as the self-assurance grew and, as confidence bred results, Palace became harder and harder to stop. It was like an all-night party that none of the neighbours seemed able to pull the plug on and is a mood captured by the official team photograph at the start of that season. There are 40 faces in that photocall on the Selhurst Park pitch and just about every one of them is smiling. It is as if the photographer has told a joke, or revealed that this would be a top-flight roll-call next time around. Glad all over? It certainly appeared so.

A run of eight wins in nine league games propelled them towards a late promotion push and included a remarkable 2-1 win over Brighton which saw referee Kelvin Morton award a Football League record five penalties – four of them to Palace and three of those missed. Wright opened the scoring and Bright scored the first penalty to put Palace 2-0 up, but Bright then missed a second spot-kick before his strike partner took over the duties and also missed. Alan Curbishley showed them how it was done as he pulled a goal back for Brighton from their one and only penalty of the game before John Pemberton became the third Palace player to miss from the spot as he blazed high over the bar from the game's fifth award.

Those missed opportunities could so easily have come back to haunt Palace as they went into the final day of the season needing a major mathematical twist in order to secure automatic promotion. "We needed to beat Birmingham by five goals and for Manchester City to lose at Bradford," remembered winger Eddie

McGoldrick, signed by Coppell from Northampton Town earlier that season despite interest from Leicester and Norwich. "We were 4-0 up after about 25 minutes but it was murder because Birmingham had brought about 7,000 fans and they wrecked the place and got on the pitch. The game was abandoned for a while and I remember some of the directors coming down and saying if we could just get one or two more we might go up as City were losing to Bradford. Then Trevor Morley scored City's equaliser in the 88th minute and they were up."

It was a surreal end to the campaign for Palace, not least because the Birmingham pitch invasion had an air of pantomime about it. With most of the away fans in fancy dress to mark the end of the campaign, the police attempts to restore order became pure *Keystone Cops*, as Wright remembers: "It will stay with me forever," he said, "Adolf Hitler chasing a nun, with a policeman on horseback chasing the pair of them!"

Palace had to compose themselves for the play-offs where, in a delicious twist of fate, the semi-finals saw Coppell come up against his former Old Trafford ally Lou Macari, who had taken Swindon Town from the depths of the Fourth Division to within touching distance of the top flight. Macari recalled: "We battered them in the first leg and should have won four or five, but we had to settle for a 1-0 win [courtesy of a Hopkins own goal], then Wright and Bright scored in the second leg at Palace and they won 2-1."

Coppell's ambition of managing in the top flight was within reach, but in the first leg of the play-off final Palace slipped to a 3-1 defeat away to a Blackburn Rovers side that had already beaten them 5-4 in the league that season. Howard Gayle was the hero of the first leg for Rovers as he scored twice, but, crucially, also missed a penalty and Palace were given hope by a goal from winger McGoldrick.

McGoldrick told me: "The first leg at Blackburn was a disaster for us. It was howling with wind and the rain was lashing down from the heavens; we were awful that night and didn't do ourselves justice. It was a case of after the Lord Mayor's show and we played so poorly as Gayle absolutely tore us to shreds."

The atmosphere in the Palace dressing room at half-time had been tense, but tempers boiled over after the final whistle as Coppell's players blamed each other for a result they clearly believed had wrecked their chances of reaching the top flight. Several players almost came to blows, presenting Coppell with the biggest test of his managerial skills so far. "We all wanted to kill each other," Wright remembered. "We called each other every name under the sun and how Steve stopped a massive brawl breaking out I'll never know. I was totally depressed because I could see my chance of the big time slipping away, and there was nothing I could do about it."

Coppell, though, kept the lid on the situation at Ewood Park and used his players' frustrations to his own advantage for the second leg, insisting that

McGoldrick's goal had handed them a lifeline and that, in fact, there was plenty they could do about it.

Roared on by a crowd of 30,000 at Selhurst Park, Palace battled back to take the game into extra-time with goals from Wright and a penalty won by McGoldrick and converted by David Madden, the midfielder signed from Reading at the start of the season, who took over spot-kick duties after the farcical scenes at Brighton.

With 24 league goals and two play-off strikes already under his belt, the stage was set for Wright to step into the spotlight and when McGoldrick skipped to the bye-line and crossed to the near post, the striker got across the first defender and headed down into the bottom corner for one of the easiest goals he had scored all season.

"Selhurst Park erupted and what a feeling that was," said McGoldrick as he recalled demented scenes of celebration that saw Selhurst Park invaded by the crowd once again. This time there were no attempts to contain the surge of emotion as Wright, the hero of the hour, found himself carried shoulder high as fans ripped every shred of clothing from him in a bizarre search for a souvenir of the night Palace were promoted. Wright was left wearing nothing but his jockstrap, cheering wildly as he was paraded through the crowd. Forget after the Lord Mayor's Show; this was the Emperor's new clothes and Coppell was king of the Palace at last.

The Eagles, after an eight-year absence, were back in the top flight and the word 'potential' was finally banished to the Selhurst Park history books.

AN APPOINTMENT WITH THE DOC

Steve Coppell is nervous. He has told a fib and he might soon be found out. What's more, Dave Russell has told him to tell another one; a big fat porky that surely no-one will believe. Russell wants Coppell to tell Tommy Docherty that he is earning £30 a week, three times the wage he is currently pulling in, to help drive up the value of the youngster's potential move to Manchester United.

Coppell is convinced that Docherty will never believe him, surely not swallow that a struggling Third Division side are paying their teenage winger 30 quid every single week? And what if the Manchester United manager asks Coppell about his own book, Tommy Docherty's Teach Yourself Soccer? *That was one of the two titles Coppell told journalists he had used to work out his own training routine when Tranmere had signed him as an amateur. It sounded better than 'kicking the ball against a wall' when they asked him how he preferred to train on his own.*

Coppell did at least own Docherty's book, that much was true, and he knew enough about it to remember extracts if the Manchester United manager asked him. But he didn't ask; the Doc didn't want to know about training routines, about bedtime reading, or about anything other than whether or not Steve Coppell wanted to sign for Manchester United.

"What sort of money do you want?" said Docherty. The reply was quick, rehearsed and avoided the use of downright lies.

"Make me an offer," said the teenager.

"I was thinking about 50 or 60 quid?"

"Done."

WHEN I BEGAN my search for the young Steve Coppell, the first person I wanted to talk to was Tommy Docherty. Few, if any, in football knew the teenage Coppell better than the Doc – and it was clear from the many interviews and post-match press conferences I had been part of at Coppell's Reading that much of the Doc's influence had rubbed off on him. Although, at least at first, Docherty allowed the raw young winger to simply go out and do his thing, he clearly had a massive influence on the way Coppell approached a game. More than that, he affected Steve Coppell the manager – and the man.

It was less than ten years after Docherty signed the teenager from Tranmere when Coppell was taking his first steps into management. Those post-match conferences would be laced with regular traces of Docherty adages or anecdotal evidence from Coppell's years under the Doc. "I remember at United, the Doc would always say . . ." was a regular prelude to a Coppell maxim. Docherty anecdotes were ten to the penny.

The mutual appreciation is clear. When I first called Docherty to tell him of my project his wife, Mary, answered and listened patiently to my explanation for calling. "Oh yes, Steve Coppell," she said, as if recalling a childhood sweetheart. "One of Tommy's absolute favourites."

When I spoke at length with Docherty, he was preparing for a ten-day cruise; a couple of bouts of after dinner speaking payment in kind for a summer holiday. I wondered if he had planned to include any stories about Coppell and wished I was going with him; not so much for the holiday, but so that I could hear him wax lyrical about the good old days.

Predictably, he was happy to oblige with the limited time he had, leaving Mary to do the packing while he talked to me – probably citing the need to try out some new material as an excuse not to help her. He was soon off and running: "Steve has a very sharp wit – well, he's a Scouser, isn't he? I did a dinner with Tommy Smith recently and first prize in the raffle was an alibi for two weeks."

Thank you, God bless, I'm here all week.

Our conversation lurched between the now and the then; like a fast-paced episode of *Life on Mars* in which Coppell plays the leading role. Out of the corner of my eye, I watched Sky Sports News fill hours of rolling news with just one story – Cristiano Ronaldo's £80 million move from Manchester to Madrid – and at the same time Docherty was also talking Old Trafford superstars, only of a different age – and one in particular who would regularly wear the number 7 shirt bequeathed to the likes of Robson, Cantona, Beckham and Ronaldo.

"The game as we know it has gone to the dogs now," Docherty said, shaking his head in disbelief. "The way the money is now, the Stevie Coppell I knew would probably be worth about £50 million. And he'd be worth every penny. Finding Steve Coppell," he added, "was like winning the lottery."

Docherty was not looking for a bargain when he went to meet Coppell at Prenton Park that morning in 1975. He was looking to make sure he got his man. Or boy. As Mary packed the tuxedo for their cruise, it became apparent Docherty was never told the full truth about the money, but it was also clear he doesn't care now, and didn't care then. "I think he was on about 25 quid at Tranmere and he would probably have settled for half what I offered," he told me, "but I wasn't taking any chances."

Docherty was building an exciting young team as he looked to steer United back to the First Division at the first attempt following a humbling and disastrous relegation and in Coppell he had discovered an absolute gem. With United's push towards a top-flight return faltering slightly, Docherty was growing concerned over the form of Jim McCalliog, while his experimental replacement, Eric Young, had also failed to provide the drive and penetration Docherty was craving.

Docherty told scout Norman Scholes that he wanted a young player who could play on the wing or as an attacking right-sided midfielder and, in February 1975, a seemingly perfect scouting report from Scholes landed on Docherty's desk. The player in question was Coppell, Tranmere's teenage winger who had started life as a striker, and Docherty travelled to Prenton Park with chief scout Jimmy Murphy to run the rule over the player for himself.

Coppell was blissfully unaware that the paltry crowd of 2,914 that saw the 1-1 draw with Gillingham included two key figures from one of the most famous clubs in world football. "He was brilliant, a real joy of a talent," Docherty told me. "After ten minutes I was thinking: *good God, why is he still here?*"

"I have always fallen in love with wingers – right and left, going down the line and getting past their full-backs. It was enough to convince me; though in truth I'd already made my mind up when I read the scouting report. At half-time I'd seen enough and we headed for home, and the next day I went straight to Tranmere and made an offer."

With gates having fallen below 3,000, Rovers needed to cash in their prized asset. The clubs agreed a fee of £40,000, rising to £60,000 if Coppell made more than 20 appearances, an add-on clause which seems laughable now given that Coppell went on to play more than 400 games for United. The fee was less than Tranmere chairman Bill Bothwell thought Coppell was worth and his initial judgement was ultimately proved to be correct. "He would have been a bargain at £150,000," admitted Docherty.

The fee agreed, Docherty arrived at Prenton Park for those brief talks with Coppell and the pair departed agreeing to meet again at Old Trafford 24 hours later, where the contract would be ready and waiting to be signed. "Go home and think about it," he told the youngster.

As far as Coppell was concerned, there were only two things to think about: what should he do about his studies, and where on earth was Old Trafford? The latter problem was easily solved, as Russell offered to drive him to Manchester, and Coppell also made the gut-wrenching decision to give up his studies in order to fulfill the opportunity of playing for United. "As I drove down the East Lancs Road to the stadium I knew I'd made the right decision," he later recalled.

Yet Docherty surprised Coppell when he insisted the youngster completed his studies. "You never know what might happen, son, and an education is a great thing to fall back on," he said, somewhat prophetically given Coppell's ultimately premature retirement from the game. The agreement was that Coppell would remain at university during the week and join up with United on matchdays, keeping fit by training in Liverpool and playing whenever he got the chance. In effect, the world's biggest club were signing a part-timer.

"He was absolutely a part-time player for us at that stage," Docherty confirmed. "In fact, there were times when we never saw him and he didn't even seem part-time! We really only saw Steve on matchdays; Saturdays if we were at home and Fridays if it was an away game and we were travelling. He'd take his tracksuit and boots to college and would join up with us on the Friday to head off to wherever we were headed. He was the type of pro you could trust with your life. He would never dodge training – there was never any doubt that he might say: 'I can't make it today because of my college commitments' and not mean it."

University pal Brian Barwick corroborated that theory, telling me: "People respected the fact that he was still turning up. It would have been very easy for him to pack it in, but to Tommy Docherty's credit he was keen for Steve to finish his studies and that still involved him doing another 15 months.

"We all helped him in those 15 months and, because I was a year ahead, I was able to give him notes. It has become apocryphal that we all took exams for him but I can assure you I never did that – do I look like Steve Coppell? I would never have got away with it, but people did help him if he couldn't get to a lecture by taking notes for him. He was genuinely a really hardworking character and he got the same degree as all of us which was a great achievement.

"When he signed for United, the footballer/student thing became a bit of a story because lads like Brian Hall and Steve Heighway had played for Liverpool while studying and Mark Palios, who was with Steve at Tranmere and in years to come with me at the FA, had done the same. Steve was featured on *Football Focus*, who did a story at the university. They used some footage from a great programme in the north called *Granada Kick-Off*, a Friday night review which had filmed us playing. I scored in that game, so my goal was actually on *Football Focus* 30 years before I was working on the programme."

The player-student arrangement at that time seemed largely unimportant given that Docherty had only meant to sign the youngster as cover, his fears over the health of the last of the Busby favourites to remain at Old Trafford increasing. "Willie Morgan had damaged a retina in the close season playing tennis and I needed cover in the event that his operation wasn't successful," Docherty recalled, but he still intended to fast-track Coppell into the first-team set-up as quickly as possible.

So quickly, in fact, that the ink was barely dry on Coppell's United contract by the time he was pulling on a red shirt in anger for the first time. With Docherty considering including his new signing on the substitute's bench for the league game against Cardiff three days later, he casually told Coppell that it would be a good idea to have a run-out in the scheduled practice match later that day. Coppell panicked. He hadn't slept properly, he didn't have any boots with him and he had not even met his new team-mates. But Docherty insisted and, just a couple of hours after being signed, Coppell was wearing a pair of boots borrowed from Stuart Pearson and playing for the reserves against the first team in a Manchester United practice match.

"God knows what my new team-mates must have thought of this player from the depths of the Third Division because I didn't get a kick for the full match," Coppell recalled. "I could have been crucified." Either Coppell was playing his performance down, or he did better than expected, as the manager had already made his mind up.

Docherty took out his pen and amended his notes for the Cardiff game. From wind-up phone call to fantasy land, Coppell's world had changed in the space of 48 hours. Instead of travelling to Aldershot to catch up with his Tranmere Rovers team-mates and prepare for their crucial Friday night relegation battle, he was getting ready for a curtain call at the Theatre of Dreams.

NO PAIN, NO GAIN

The bath scalds as if handing out some form of punishment, but Crystal Palace's players sink deeper into the water; as though indulging in a cleansing process, or even self harm, to take away the pain of a shocking defeat.

There is virtual silence in the Anfield dressing room, but noise from beyond the door. Constant noise; shouting; laughter even. Palace are being laughed at. The football world is starting to mock the First Division newcomers and it is embarrassing. It hurts. It hurts like hell.

Alan Pardew sinks further into the bath. Red faces all round are caused mainly by the punishing temperatures but symbolise Palace's feelings. "Fucking hell," Pardew says, piercing the silence at last. "Seven-nil. Unbelievable." He looks at John Pemberton and repeats the phrase in the hope it will sink in. "Seven-nil!"

Pemberton, Palace's right-back who has been run ragged all night by Liverpool's mercurial John Barnes, shakes his head. "It was nine," he says, then waits for the impact to take effect. Pardew doesn't look back as he slides still further below the water's surface. "Fucking hell."

AS ADVENTUROUS AS Palace's return to the top flight was, there are basically four games which sum up their season and which, between them, arguably define Steve Coppell the manager. One of them was a win, one a draw and the other two were defeats, including the now infamous 9-0 thrashing at Liverpool; the very pitch that had held Coppell's wide-eyed gaze as a youngster now the horrific subject of his jaw-tightening stare as a manager.

Alan Pardew played in all four games, a hero in the FA Cup semi-final against Liverpool which afforded Palace revenge and redemption in equal measures, and a vital part of the Palace team which came so close to beating Manchester United in the final before losing the replay a few days later.

Coppell became Pardew's mentor as a player and a manager, the Mr Miyagi to Pardew's Karate Kid, so it made sense that he should be one of the first names on my interview list when it came to asking the Palace class of 1990/91 what made Coppell tick.

I worked with Pardew for several years during his Reading days, carrying out pitch-side interviews and reporting on post-match conferences, and I interviewed him for the BBC during his spells at West Ham and Charlton, so there was an aura of déjà vu when we met again in the late summer sunshine of Southampton's training ground at Marchwood. "Why are you writing a book on Steve Coppell?" he asked me. "He hasn't got any stories to tell." But he then spent the best part of an hour undermining his own quip with countless tales which spotlight an obvious admiration for the man who helped shape Pardew's footballing life.

"When I signed for Palace, my game was really uneducated," Pardew told me. "There was a lack of discipline – although I really worked hard, I did it in a weird way. Steve helped me understand what the game was about with his coaches, Ian 'Taff' Evans and Alan Smith. I got to understand how the game was played and he played a very simple game, so that helped me. I wasn't asked to do too many pretty things, just hit it in the corners to start with and get in the box and win my war. That is basically what I did for Crystal Palace in all my time there, so he never complicated it.

"Steve expected discipline and the biggest discipline he had was what he took from his own game – his work rate. When I used to watch him play for Manchester United he was probably as diligent a wide player defensively as there was and he installed that in all his players; his strikers, everybody. We had a work rate that few could match."

Coppell had little input into Pardew's move from non-league Yeovil, other than a late scouting trip to rubber-stamp a player who had been earmarked as an ideal candidate for the Coppell school of football education. When the hungry midfielder first swaggered into the Palace training ground the manager was slightly taken aback by his confidence.

"Ron Noades and the Palace scouting team more or less decided to have a punt on me, because I was so cheap," Pardew told me. "Steve inherited a raw non-league player with strong opinions – I had been the main man at my previous club, so I wasn't a wallflower from the moment I walked in. I kept calling him Steve because I wasn't used to using the word gaffer or boss, so after I'd been there three or four weeks he said to me, 'I think it's about time you started calling me gaffer. You have to understand this is how it works here.'

"Because I was a London boy, the terminology I would use would be perhaps a bit over friendly and I would say 'mate' to him until he reminded me that I wasn't his mate. Someone said to him that somewhere down the line that either I was going to sack him or he was going to sack me – there is a closeness between player and manager but you have to keep a distance when you are the boss. I understand that now."

Pardew's bluster matched that of his fellow non-league graduate Ian Wright, whose presence at Selhurst Park assured Pardew he was in the perfect place to further his football education.

"The budget decided that they had to take some chances, but they were educated ones that came off, Wrighty being the typical example," Pardew continued. "He came to us and had a work rate that was installed in him from day one and he grew as a player very quickly. When I was at Dulwich Hamlet [Pardew was on Hamlet's books as a youngster before joining Yeovil in 1986] he came for a trial and he was so outstanding that there was no way he could play for us. I had visions of becoming a professional player myself and this boy came in and was a different class to me – and he wasn't a professional. That really knocked me back.

"Once Palace had signed him, it really was about educating him in the right way because he was as raw as I was. It was a case of making sure you recruited good players and Steve, at that time, recruited very good players."

Defeat against QPR on the opening day of the 1989/90 season marked an inauspicious return to the First Division for Palace, but it was appropriate that Coppell's first point as a top-flight manager came against Manchester United, Wright's first Division One goal securing a 1-1 draw. A home defeat to Coventry was followed by a first win of the season over Wimbledon and it was with a degree of confidence – and no end of pride – that Coppell took his young Eagles to his home city for that showdown with Liverpool at Anfield.

"It was the first time Steve had taken his team up to Merseyside in the top league. He was having a bit of banter on the bus going up there and I could tell he was really excited about taking his team to his own town," said Pardew, shaking his head as he added: "To get that result, blimey, it must have killed him. I couldn't imagine as a manager after having that result how you would sleep, but he picked himself up."

Palace were 3-0 down at half-time and Pardew believes a collective naïvety led to the scoreline reaching embarrassing levels. "It was a lesson from a footballing side against a direct team that just forgot what they were doing. That night we started thinking that we could play, but we were never that good. Only Ian Wright would have got in that Liverpool team, the rest of us probably could not have got in their reserve team," Pardew recounted.

"We were naïve. At half-time we were all thinking – and that included Steve – how we were going to get something out of it rather than thinking, *let's put the lid on this and save our dignity for another day.* You have to do that in football occasionally, rather than go into the next game with confidence even lower, but we had an ego because we'd only had success up until that point. I won a penalty, only for Geoff Thomas to blaze over the bar at 4-0. We would probably have won from that point if he'd scored!"

While Palace learned the hard way that sometimes you need to down your football medicine, no matter how foul the taste, Liverpool rubbed salt into their gaping wounds when they plotted to give John Aldridge a farewell present of a final goal for the club before his imminent move to Real Sociedad. Liverpool were already 5-0 up when they were awarded a penalty and Peter Beardsley volunteered to be substituted to allow Aldridge to come off the bench and take the spot-kick. Aldridge obliged with his 63rd goal in 104 matches for Liverpool and the rampant Reds went on to score three more.

"I think that was an error on the part of their management team," insisted Pardew, wincing at the memory as he adopts the face of a man trying to get a piece of bitter lemon out of his teeth. "They quickly rushed Aldridge off the bench and it was all a big joke. We had to wait while they substituted Beardsley and that didn't get forgotten. I'll be honest, I lost count of the score afterwards. I thought we'd lost 7-0, but that incident really was the icing on the cake for us in terms of wanting some sort of revenge if we could ever get it."

Coppell did not use that as any kind of excuse in his post-mortem of the match, but did launch an uncharacteristic attack on his own players after their dismal display. It was an early lesson in management for Coppell, who had rarely criticised his own players up to that point and has hardly made a habit of it since.

"I think like a lot of things in football the 9-0 defeat was a lesson," adds Geoff Thomas, the captain of that humiliated side. When you look at the stats of that game, which I have many times, Liverpool didn't actually have that many shots. Teams can have 25 shots and score two. Liverpool had 14 shots, 13 on target and nine went in. We had to hold our hands up and say they were far better on the day – but for large amounts of the game we felt we held our own in certain parts. We were just naïve, but rather than sinking and fighting relegation we learned from that. We didn't set the league alight, but we learned and we knew we had got enough to compete."

The result was particularly cruel on goalkeeper Perry Suckling, who never really recovered from the mauling. Coppell, who had already talked to Noades about needing to invest to ensure survival, was quick to make Bristol Rovers's Nigel Martyn football's first £1 million goalkeeper and he also snapped up Andy Thorne from Newcastle for a fee of £650,000.

"It was a terrible game for Perry," remembered Pardew. "The football world laughed at us, but at him in particular and it hurt him. Steve's reaction was quick and he signed two or three players, including Martyn, that made us immediately stronger. And, of course, we used that defeat amongst us all, learning never to have that happen again."

A 2-0 win for Liverpool at Selhurst Park in January meant that Palace appeared to have missed their chance of revenge, especially as Coppell lost Ian Wright to a broken leg and winger Eddie McGoldrick to a serious knee injury in that game, but an even sweeter opportunity to make amends was presented to Coppell's young and hungry side when three home wins and a 1-0 victory at Cambridge took Palace to the semi-finals of the FA Cup. With Manchester United and Oldham also having progressed, the team to fear most in the final four was league champions-elect Liverpool, yet it was with poetic inevitability that Palace were drawn to face the team that had humiliated them earlier that season.

"My gut feeling was that it was Liverpool's time and the overriding emotion I had was that we were going to give it a go and make sure we came out with dignity, but ultimately probably lose," Pardew confessed. "We were certainly going to give it a real go and to let them know that thrashing would never happen to us again. It wasn't like we were going into that game on the back of the 9-0 defeat – we had come pretty close to beating them at Selhurst but in the last 10 or 15 minutes they were by far the better side. We tried to get a bit of revenge in that game, there were a few tackles flying about and some verbals going on, which was part of our make-up then and, in truth, the make-up of the First Division then. It was a tough, proper man's league.

"We were going into the semi-final without Wright, but Steve sets his team up to win the game. He might set the team up in a defensive formation, but ultimately it will be with a tactic to win. That day we genuinely believed we could get something out of the game."

Much of that was down to the fact that Coppell and his coaches, Ian Branfoot and Alan Smith, had spent the week re-educating the players to play a completely alien system. First, though, the coaches had to convince themselves that Coppell's plan to play five at the back, with John Salako man-marking Ray Houghton, could work. "We'd played strictly 4-4-2 and had done for two years," recalled Branfoot.

"There were talented and hard-working players in the team – they were Steve's players and they reflected his own character.

"On the Monday morning before we played Liverpool he called us in and told us he wanted to play with three centre-backs and two wing-backs. We both looked at Steve and said, 'what? No chance!' But Steve insisted, so we said, 'ok, you're the gaffer' and spent a week coaching a system that was new to me and to the players. It was totally out of context, we had never done it before and Steve never explained why, he just said, 'this is what I want to do.' We were puzzled, but had total respect for him and did what he said. If he had been a plonker we might have told him to piss off, but it worked."

Even now, if you ask the 11 Palace players who started that match to tell you the tactics employed that day the chances are that you will get close to 11 different responses. Yet the fact that everyone accepted their individual roles without question and carried them out virtually to the letter underlines how committed to the Coppell cause his players were.

"Obviously the semi-final was special," remembered Thomas. "For me, if you are going to get to a Cup final you really want to play the big sides. We'd had an easy run to get to the semi-final and I wanted a test for us – and there was no bigger test to prove we deserved our place at Wembley. Steve had a big say in that famous win, not least because he got us all fit for the end of the season. A lot of clubs would be winding down towards the end, but his mentality was to work harder. We were fitter than anyone and were mentally stronger with the confidence we were gaining.

"We had a game plan to keep the first half even and Steve said beforehand that even if we were 1-0 down we could go on and win it. Steve was clever, putting that in our minds, and the first plan was to kill the game in the first half. If you are a Palace fan that was a fantasy 90 minutes and extra-time, but the truth is that first half was one of the worst games of football you will ever see!

"Liverpool had a couple of chances and Ian Rush scored just before half-time, but hardly celebrated. We traipsed off at half-time feeling we had a fantastic chance to reach the final; at that stage at Anfield we had already been three down and getting our backsides kicked, so we were very positive for that second half."

Pardew recalled the atmosphere in the Villa Park dressing room at half-time: "It was similar at 1-0 down to how Steve had been at 3-0 down at Anfield. I had given the goal away having made a sloppy pass in midfield, so I was feeling particularly angry with myself and feeling I'd let the lads down. We had kept a good shape and although they had opened us up a couple of times they had not really run riot with us, so I was a little bit more determined in the second half that we were going to do well."

Seconds after the restart, Palace turned the game on its head as John Pemberton raced forward and crossed for John Salako, whose shot was saved by Bruce Grobbelaar, but thumped home on the volley by Mark Bright. The goal completely changed the atmosphere inside Villa Park and the belief amongst Palace's hungry fans exploded.

Thomas revealed: "TV replays make things easier to remember, but my first memory of that second half was Pemberton tearing down the right wing. Kenny Dalglish was not even sat down and we were level. It was sunny and warm and suddenly the atmosphere was electric – there was a real wave of optimism amongst our fans."

Coppell's master plan had included trying to exploit Liverpool's one big weakness – aerial deficiencies at the back. Twenty minutes from time, the tactic was showcased when Bright flicked on an Andy Gray free-kick and Gary O'Reilly stole into a crowded area to put Palace in front. The delirium amongst the Eagles supporters was punctured when McMahon quickly equalised and a John Barnes penalty after Pemberton had fouled Steve Staunton appeared to have ended Palace's brave challenge. Then, in the dying seconds of normal time, Liverpool failed to clear another corner and Gray stole in to send the game to extra-time.

Thomas continued: "We used to work a lot on free-kicks defensively and in attack, so we had run that routine many times before. Right before full-time Thorne skimmed the bar with a header and I was behind him waiting to hopefully knock it in. Liverpool were creaking every time we had a set-piece; they didn't like it and Alan Hansen didn't like playing against us as he had the physical presence of Brighty to contend with. In extra-time we had another corner; Thorne flicked on and Pardew did what he did . . . Super Al."

Pardew still remembers the drill and added: "Set-pieces were the strength of us. We had a set-play that we had practised, floated to the near post and flicked on – something that Nottingham Forest had done many times in that great team they had. My job was just to finish in the middle of the goal and to take everything that was in the way into the goal with me. For the winner, I got a free run at it, so it was a simple goal for me, but the emotion and everything that went with it was incredible.

"At the final whistle I remember Steve running off the pitch and down the sidelines and that was typical of him. He wanted the players to get the credit and I don't even remember seeing him in the dressing room. Ron Noades was pushed in the bath, but Steve was kind of detached from the celebrations and, when I think about it, he always was."

Coppell looked as though he was running for a train in rush hour, dodging in and out of a crowd scene along the touchline as he made for the tunnel and the sanctuary of the Villa Park dressing room while his players celebrated on the pitch.

His explanation at the time was simple as he insisted: "There is too much emphasis put on managers and coaches in football." But he was clearly bursting with pride, as he added: "We have gone through the full range of emotions this season – it is humiliating to get into the record books for all the wrong reasons, so to come through at all and to win a semi-final is the finest feeling ever."

He could not resist a joke as he added: "I thought in extra-time both teams had settled for a replay. I was panicking then, because I hadn't re-booked our hotel for midweek." But his demure departure was in stark contrast to the acrobatics on crutches performed by Ian Wright, thrilled that his team-mates had given him a footballing lifeline. The hungry striker had rushed back from a broken leg in a bid to be fit for the semi-final, only to suffer an even worse double fracture. There seemed little chance of him coming back again, though Wright clearly believed in miracles.

Coppell was keen to give his striker every chance of returning for the final, but also wary of protecting the players who had got Palace there and ensuring they were fit to take their Wembley bow. So, when their penultimate game of the season was a fixture at Wimbledon, it is fair to say Coppell would not have seen it as the ideal preparation.

"There was a great rivalry between us and Wimbledon – the Crazy Gang were at their real height then, but they couldn't beat us," Pardew told me, his eyes growing wider at the memory. "We used to love it that they couldn't beat us and we had some real battles with them, but we always won them and the main reason was that we had the same war ethic as them, but we had better strikers.

"I was sub for that game at the end of the season. I think Steve was aware of a whisper that went round that Wimbledon were going to sort us out and I think he was trying to protect certain members, me being one of them, knowing that I had a bit of a hot head. It was a real war – a proper war. Dennis Wise elbowed me off the ball in the face and things like that were going on all over. It was a nastier game then than it is now – and thank God those days are over."

After the bruising encounter with the Dons and a Wembley send-off in a 2-2 draw with Manchester City on the final day of the season, Coppell took his team for some rest and recuperation in Tenerife, ensuring they got some sun on their backs and recharged their batteries ready for their big day out.

"We worked, trained, bonded, had a few drinks and relaxed, then we came back Thursday, trained Friday and went to the game on Saturday," explained Salako, sounding a little like he was reeling off a Craig David classic.

"That's how Steve was before the final. He was totally relaxed, but he never had to scream. He let the lads have a little freedom and treated us like adults. He'd just say, 'if you go out, just make sure you don't drink too much and get fluids in before you have a drink; sit down if you are injured – and don't dance.' He was not a preacher. The game has changed with sports science, but we worked hard and played hard and that was all part of the bonding."

There were pre-final duties to perform too, though Thomas was slightly disappointed that the FA Cup final build-ups he remembered as a youngster appeared to have been phased out. "The final was always a showpiece. When all of us were kids growing up the FA Cup was really special and being part of the build-up was all part of it," he told me. "When we got to Wembley, the cup was just starting to lose a bit of its gloss and football was at a bit of a low ebb, so there was no *It's a Knockout* this time, like I used to watch. We still went to Abbey Studios to record a Cup final song, some of the lads were on *Blue Peter* and I met the Duke of Edinburgh with Ron Noades. It was a surreal time, but despite all the build-up training was so focused on the job at hand."

The distractions of Tenerife and the media commitments helped take the pressure off Coppell and his players and when they emerged from their country house base near Luton on the sunny May morning of the final against United, they could hardly have been more relaxed. "It was a special dressing room," remembered Salako. "I remember we went for a walk on the morning of the final and a reporter came up to do an interview with Ian. He asked, 'are you ready for today?' and Wrighty looked at him and said, 'I was born for today'. That was our attitude."

After the drama of their semi-final win, coupled with United and Oldham sharing a 3-3 draw on the same weekend before United edged a replay to deny a Steve Coppell v Joe Royle final, few could have predicted as much theatre in the Wembley final. It was the perfect stage for the young manager, leading his side out against the club that had made him a household name, and in the returning Wright on the substitutes' bench, Coppell had an ace up his sleeve.

"Wrighty was training hard and showing how fit he was – and it was so nearly the Ian Wright day," recalled Thomas, almost fantasising in reliving the moments before he was robbed of the chance to climb the Wembley steps and get his hands on football's most famous trophy.

The captain added: "I don't think Ian was ever close enough to start, it was a case of whether he would be fit enough to be on the bench. The squad had put in a lot of work to get us to the First Division and then the Cup final and people like David Madden deserved their place in the team or on the bench. Steve respected everyone and knew that he would have the pace of Wright coming off the bench and he was proved right. When Ian came on he gave us a spark as if we had just started the game."

Salako agreed, adding: "We should have won. The night before the final I went to bed and had butterflies, but not because I was nervous. I just wanted it. We weren't intimated by playing United or playing at Wembley; Steve just said, 'do your stuff' and he let us do what we wanted. He would let you express yourself, but would tell you to play in the right areas and just do what you were told. Getting players to understand their individual jobs was half the battle and he would forever be telling us, 'a team is only as strong as its weakest link'. We knew it was easy to mess the whole thing up.

"Steve would often let the dressing room look after itself; the senior players like the Wrights, Brights and Thomases. You've got to have a blend and that's an important part of the preparation. In that sense, it was no different for the final."

Coppell later insisted the thrill of leading a team out at Wembley was as special as playing in a Cup final, saying: "Being there as a manager was just as good as being there as a player – probably because Palace hadn't been fancied by anyone to get anywhere near the final. Walking out at Wembley as a manager was a really heart-stopping moment."

Alongside Coppell that day, Alex Ferguson was under huge pressure to deliver for United. His side had finished in 13th place in the First Division, ahead of promoted Palace only on goal difference and, nearly four years after Ron Atkinson was sacked having won two FA Cups on the back of some free-flowing football, Fergie was facing up to the fact that his £13 million spending spree had produced no silverware – and precious little style by way of compensation.

The tabloids had long since speculated that failure in the cup would have spelled the end of Ferguson's reign and, though chairman Martin Edwards has always denied that, an early cup exit – or even defeat in the final against Palace – would have been hard to justify.

So when Gary O'Reilly headed Palace in front on 18 minutes those United fans amongst the first all-seated FA Cup final crowd would have been on the edge of theirs. Inevitably, the opening goal was straight off the Palace training ground; Danny Wallace fouled Andy Gray wide on the Palace right and Phil Barber's bent free-kick saw O'Reilly beat his marker Gary Pallister in the air and flick the ball beyond a stranded Jim Leighton.

Thomas wasted a glorious chance to make it 2-0 when he shot straight at Leighton and that miss was punished ten minutes before half-time when Bryan Robson's header deflected in off Pemberton. Just past the hour mark United went in front as Mark Hughes produced a trademark clinical finish and when McClair and then Robson had chances to put the game beyond Palace, Coppell knew it was time to throw on Wright.

The substitute sprinted into the action and was on the scoresheet within three minutes, skipping past Mike Phelan and cutting inside Pallister before firing a low shot across Leighton and into the far corner. Pandemonium washed over Palace like a tidal wave and Wright remembered the release of months of pent-up frustration as his shot hit the United net: "Whenever you see people score in a final, they don't actually say anything, they just make a noise of pure, unadulterated joy, a kind of roar that you can't put down on paper and make it sound like it does. I made that noise. From somewhere deep inside me it came into my mouth and I just screamed. The tears were coming down my face because I had made a difference on the greatest day of my life. I ran past John Salako, but he caught me and I went down on the pitch and all of a sudden there were four or five people on top of me making the same noise."

The game lurched unpredictably either way, Robson heading against a post before the additional 30 minutes of extra-time. Then Wright struck again. Thomas fed a long pass out wide to Salako and his deep cross was judged to perfection, eluding the woefully ill-positioned Leighton and dropping invitingly for Wright to slide home despite the challenge of Steve Bruce.

Gray wasted a chance to put the game beyond United, who responded by launching wave after wave of attacks. Martyn pushed a long-range Paul Ince effort over the bar and Phelan chipped just over. Just as it seemed Palace would hold on, Hughes broke their hearts again, turning the ball beyond the outrushing Martyn after Wallace's pass had evaded O'Reilly.

The looks on the faces of Martyn and Richard Shaw, frozen in eternity by the cameras behind the goal, tell the story of how close Coppell came to Palace's first trophy that day. Martyn is almost willing the ball to spin wide, though the agony etched across Shaw's face makes it painfully clear that it is a forlorn hope.

"We all had defensive roles to do which were well thought out and ultimately should have made us win the game," remembered Pardew, the heartbreak of having victory snatched away still painfully evident. "We are all part of a team, but we should not have conceded the last goal – Gary O'Reilly in my opinion made a major error and cost me a winners' medal, but that's how it is with Cup finals."

Wright has since questioned whether Martyn should have resisted the temptation to rush out, while Thomas is more simplistic, adding: "I look back and think that if we could have just held on for another seven minutes we could have changed the history of Crystal Palace."

Whatever the reasons, Coppell had to dust his players down and rebuild their hopes for a replay at Wembley five days later, but few expected them to be given a second chance. "It felt weird," Salako said. "It should have been all over on the Saturday and coming back was strange and surreal. That always plays into the hands of the bigger teams."

It might be unfair to argue that Palace were still picking over the bones of the 3-3 draw, though the fact that the players' memories of that first game are patently more vivid today might tell its own story. And while Coppell appeared to change his approach to the replay, there was still no place for Wright.

'For all the wisdom that Steve Coppell has and all the respect that I have for him, there's still a small part of me that cannot forgive him for not having me on from the start in the replay,' Wright wrote in his autobiography. 'I know he'll understand that, because he knows how badly I took it when he told the players that he was going with the same team that started the final. Brighty took him aside and said that I should play but Steve told him he was looking at the wider picture and that he couldn't afford for me to do my leg again and miss the start of the next season.

'Steve was wrong. I knew that the sort of buzz that I was on, the sort euphoria I was feeling could – and would – have made a difference. I knew that Gary Pallister and Steve Bruce were wary of me, that they knew I was a danger. Paul Ince told me that when United found out I wasn't in, they were truly relieved. All I needed was an hour, 60 minutes to run at them and score or set something up, not for selfish reasons but for the good of the team, because I think the rest of the boys wanted me out there.'

Coppell did adopt more of a traditional Palace formation, despite the unchanged personnel, and he underpinned the speed and power of his side with the physical edge they had shown themselves capable of in those battles with Wimbledon. It was an approach that was announced within two minutes when Bright was booked for clattering replacement goalkeeper Les Sealey, preferred to the hapless Leighton despite having played only twice all season on loan from Luton.

"One thing I've never worked out is why Steve changed his tactics for the replay," mused BBC TV commentator Jonathan Pearce. "They captured the nation's hearts with the first game on the Saturday but on the Thursday they went out and were so physical – you don't expect that from a Steve Coppell side."

Rival manager Ferguson, looking back at that final, was diplomatic, claiming: "He had a really feisty team, all warriors. It was an example of how he's able to bond together good pros with a good, winning attitude."

Palace had their chances again in the replay, but it was United who won the trophy courtesy of an unlikely source, young full-back Lee Martin choosing the perfect stage on which to score just his second senior goal as he chested down Neil Webb's pass and lashed a shot beyond Martyn on the hour.

"We didn't change the plan," argues Thomas. "What happened was that we thought we had a chance of winning. In the first game we just enjoyed the occasion and you had two sides giving 100 per cent to win the game, but in the replay you had two teams not wanting to lose. I don't think it was an over physical game, but it was a bit stop-start. The final was decided by a player who had only scored once before and that kind of summed it up. Wembley is a horrible place to lose. It is sickening looking up and seeing the lights flashing as the other captain lifts the cup."

As Bryan Robson became the first captain to savour that moment for a third time, it signalled the start of a new era for United. On fine margins are such dramatic twists of history carved and Coppell displayed little doubt that Ferguson's ruthless casting aside of Leighton – stark in contrast to Coppell's loyalty towards his own starting 11 – not only turned a Cup final, but also helped define a manager.

Coppell said, "For what he knew was going to be a massive occasion, to change a player he had previously shown a real allegiance to showed that cold, cutting edge that all top managers need. Inadvertently, we were the catalyst for an empire."

PLAYING IT BY THE BOOK

"This used to be a hell of a town, officer," the doctor says to Lew Slade, as the pair try to come to terms with what has just happened. "Yeah," says Slade, but speaks not another word as his eyes flicker from left to right then back again, his mouth taut in pensive resignation and every twitch of the face clear to see in perfect Panavision as Slade takes in the scene of devastation around them. Buildings, what remains of them, burn as far as the eye can see and smoke drifts across the sky in black clouds that increase the room's descent into darkness.

Most of the people still in their seats are almost scared to move; fearful their legs might buckle after what they have just experienced. Slowly, they shuffle out; some smiling – laughing, even – others puffing their cheeks or shaking their heads; the clatter of tilting seats and the increasing babble gradually drowning out the Oscar-winning surround sound which had earlier, literally and deliberately, shaken their chairs, as people start to talk about what they have just seen.

Big-money blockbuster, all-star epic or disastrous disaster movie? Whatever it was, Steve Coppell is hardly in the mind for reviewing Earthquake as he leads girlfriend Jane out of the cinema and back into the street where photographers from the national papers had earlier taken snaps of the young couple going in. Coppell's life has suddenly become as surreal as the big-budget movie he has just sat through.

The latest Hollywood epic, with oscillating seats an added bonus, was meant to take Coppell's mind off the teenage footballer's own Hollywood script, but that distraction failed from the opening scene as Charlton Heston's lead character, construction engineer Stewart Graf, announces he has got an autographed football for a young fan.

It would probably take an earthquake to distract Manchester United's latest signing from his own outrageously scripted blockbuster which lies ahead; his next outing is a trip to Old Trafford, where he has a date with Cardiff City.

IT IS FAIR to say that Steve Coppell was ill-prepared for his Manchester United debut. In fact, his preparations for the day bordered on the shambolic. His boots had been packed up in the Tranmere kit bag and taken to Aldershot ahead of their Friday night game, leaving Coppell still reliant on Stuart Pearson's spare hand-me-downs. Then, as Coppell pointed his Austin 1100 in the direction of Manchester, he realised he still did not know the way to the team's rendezvous point at the Lancashire County Cricket Ground. Quite what the helpful passer-by in Eccles made of the teenage driver asking for directions to Manchester United's meeting place is a mystery, but the chances are the anonymity of the driver would have remained, given the reaction of United's own team captain.

"My first impressions, in all honesty, were 'who is this guy?'" Martin Buchan told me, after I followed my meeting with Tommy Docherty with a wonderful tea-time chat with another Old Trafford legend. "I hadn't heard of him – he wasn't high-profile, even at Tranmere. These days, there is wall-to-wall coverage of football across all the divisions, but back then it was just papers – and a lot of players preferred not to read papers. So I think everybody thought 'who is this?' to a certain extent."

Clearly United's matchday programme editors were amongst that group. As Coppell finally arrived at Old Trafford to prepare for his debut, he grabbed himself a copy of the programme and turned to the team page, probably in a bid to confirm to himself that it was all real. He read through the names, repeating them in his head like a Panini sticker album playground swaps roll-call: Stepney; Forsyth; Houston; Greenhoff; James; Buchan; Morgan; McIlroy; Pearson; Macari; Daly. Then, a sure sign that even the club were unprepared for the youngster's debut, substitute: Kopel.

Apparently confusing him with former United favourite Frank Kopel, the editors had not done their homework, though Coppell insisted it did not lessen the thrill of seeing his name on the team sheet. He soon got the chance to make a name for himself, whatever the spelling, when Willie Morgan made way for him in the second half of that game against Cardiff.

He needed to be quick to prove himself to the 43,601 fans who witnessed his debut, many of whom were angry at Docherty's decision to substitute Morgan, a crowd favourite and one of the last remaining links with Busby. With the scores still goalless half an hour from time and United looking to improve on a run of just one win in seven games – hardly promotion form – there was increasing frustration in the ranks as United won a corner and Coppell was told to go on.

"Running on to the pitch for the first appearance will stay with me for the rest of my life," Coppell said in *Touch and Go*. "I could vaguely hear a section of the crowd booing the decision to bring off Willie Morgan, but all that concerned me was the fact that I was going to play. It was one of those moments when your stomach is in your mouth and you feel so elated that you could jump the stand."

It was also the moment when his own fairytale of Old Trafford really began. As Coppell ran on, the corner was taken and Stewart Houston broke the deadlock before the substitute had even reached the penalty area. Minutes later, Coppell's first touch as a United player led to the score being doubled, one pair of Stuart Pearson's boots crossing for another, worn by their rightful owner, to apply the finishing touch. Sammy McIlroy made it three before Coppell got another touch in the game, a complete mis-kick which fortuitously rolled straight to Lou Macari to make it 4-0. Manchester United's new signing, it seemed, was blessed.

"It was beyond a fairytale," he said. "My heart was jumping out of my chest and I've never had another experience like it. I wasn't running; I was floating across the grass. Words do not do the experience justice; it was a drug-like euphoric trance. I've had a few operations and it was like that little pleasant stage after the anaesthetic. Only multiplied by a hundred."

The promotion drive was back on and the atmosphere in United's dressing room was electric after the game. Coppell talks of being brought back down to earth by Buchan when he asked if he could borrow the captain's shampoo; Buchan refused, but the team leader and his Red Devils squadron had clearly accepted the new boy as one of their own. "When a new player comes into your dressing room, you don't care whether they are black, white, green or whatever; the only thing players care about is 'can he play?' and he could," Buchan told me.

I pointed out that it was not merely Coppell the footballer that the team were accepting, it was Coppell the part-time footballer. It was an alien format for top-of-the-range players and Buchan and his team-mates would not see Coppell's face again before the team bus headed for Bolton the following Friday.

"It was a different experience for most of us," he admitted. "When I first joined Aberdeen at the age of 12, they had part-time players, but by the time I signed professional in 1966 they had fazed the part-timers out. So it was surprising for a big club for United to have that at that time."

Buchan, more than most of Coppell's team-mates over the years, is well qualified to commentate on Coppell's career. He also faced the dilemma of staying in education or pursuing his football dream, before representing Manchester United with distinction and, later, following Coppell into the offices of the Professional Footballers' Association, where he now works as an executive advising the clubs' delegate liaison officers.

Buchan, who turned 60 in early 2009, is still very much at home in Manchester. His PFA office is tucked into the corner of a courtyard area at the heart of Bishopsgate, in a building which at first sight could easily be mistaken for a private house. One of the meeting rooms boasts a wall full of football memorabilia and, as Buchan leaned back into his chair to reflect on Coppell's career path, his own memories stretched back to his graduation from Robert Gordon's College, the top school in the north-east of Scotland whose motto translates to: 'Now you should use all your masterly skills'.

"In my sixth year at school I had gone back three days a week to secure my university entrance. I passed my exams, but Aberdeen invited me to go full-time, so that is the route I took. I talked to my parents about it and we decided I would give this football thing a go until I was 21 then go back to university if it didn't work out. So I could relate to Steve in that respect.

"I didn't study on the coach, but I did prefer to sit and read a book than play cards. It meant I soon got a reputation as a loner – I wasn't, but people are quick to pigeonhole you. So I was the loner and Steve was the student. He did so well to combine both aspects of his life and I have got nothing but admiration for him. It would have been a big enough move for anyone at that age – I'd played six seasons and international football by the time I moved to United."

Yet the distractions of his university studies might actually have helped the teenage Coppell cope with the demands of helping United to regain their top-flight status. While others trained throughout the week and prepared for every game under the weight of expectation that was building around their promotion campaign, Coppell was absorbed in his books and making sure he secured the education Docherty had insisted he complete.

"It might be true to say it helped him because his mind was focused on two things at different times. He was not pressured by the build-up to games in the way he might have been," Buchan told me.

The lack of training was never a problem, it seemed, particularly as Coppell's immediate success on his debut secured him enough games to keep him ticking over. It meant he continued to train alone at university to relieve the stresses of studying, while regular first-team action meant his match fitness was increasing;

hardly an unfamiliar concept to his United team-mates under the watchful eye of trainer Tom Cavanagh.

"Steve had a natural fitness about him and we all looked at a good pre-season as money in the bank anyway," recalled Buchan. "When we were playing twice a week, training just needed to tick us over and Tommy Cav knew how to judge how much we needed and when. I remember a European coach coming over and watching a United session where Tommy was working us really hard. The coach turned to Tommy and said, 'how long do you train them like this? For 80 minutes, for two hours?' Tommy snapped him a look back and said, 'my eyes are my judge'.

"One morning, Tommy sent us back in to get changed after only 40 minutes or so. He just said, 'well done lads, I'm pleased with what I've seen, off you go'. No-one took it for granted though and if anyone was messing about Tommy would let you know. We worked hard and played a short, sharp style of football with a very quick midfield."

Coppell's dramatic introduction to the United first-team earned him a starting place for the trip to Bolton and he remained a permanent fixture for the remainder of the season. Morgan was in and out of the side, his seven-year spell at United slowly drawing to an inevitable close. Docherty, though, insists he had not bought Coppell with a view to squeezing Morgan out, merely to cover him for any absences.

"Willie was always an awkward customer, but he took it wrongly. The truth is that Steve was just cover, yet when he got into the team it was just impossible to leave him out. He couldn't be shifted." Morgan, it seemed, could, with Docherty selling him back to Burnley at the end of the campaign, though Coppell himself later insisted he felt no bitterness from the last of the Busby favourites.

The win over Cardiff kick-started an unbeaten run of 11 games, eight of them victories, as United strolled back to the First Division as champions of Division Two. With five matches remaining, Coppell's first goal for the club clinched a 3-2 home win over Oldham Athletic that all but sealed promotion. It was still mathematically possible for Aston Villa and Norwich to overhaul United, so Docherty kept on ice a bottle of champagne given to him by Sir Matt Busby when United had been relegated until a 1-0 win at Southampton made their return certain.

Two games later, a point in the 2-2 draw at Notts County clinched the title, ensuring the home game against Blackpool on the final day of the season was, as Docherty put it, "a victory parade". A 4-0 win with two goals from Pearson and one each for Macari and Brian Greenhoff delighted an Old Trafford crowd of 58,769 and sent United back to football's top table in some style. The trophy presented to Docherty and his burgeoning young side, Coppell marvelled in the euphoria of a lap of honour to a terrace soundtrack of "United are back".

Amidst the champagne and singing, though, Coppell could not help but spare a thought for his former Tranmere team-mates, relegated to the Fourth Division and with Ron Yeats, the manager he respected so much, sacked when their fate had become clear. In any case, there was little time for extended celebrations as Coppell faced a scheduled operation to have his grumbling appendix removed. He took his books into hospital with him, desperate to revise for his summer exams and not waste the opportunity Docherty had given him.

"I scraped through my exams that year as, typically, I had left everything until the last moment," Coppell recalled, harsh on himself given the remarkable circumstances of his double life. His football revision for the new campaign revolved around a pre-season tour to Hong Kong, Coppell's first-ever flight on an aeroplane, involving a near 20-hour journey. The rest of the United squad had already travelled as Coppell stayed behind to complete his exams, but he was joined on the flight by Sir Matt Busby, who sat at the back and calmly puffed on his pipe as the nervous Coppell rode white-knuckled for almost the entire journey.

The youngster remained wide-eyed at all the different experiences coming his way, though he admits to being totally overawed by most of them. The tour took United from Hong Kong to Australia and New Zealand and, finally, a brief stop in Los Angeles, but the inexperienced traveller stuck to a diet of steaks and hamburgers and preferred to sleep off his jet-lag rather than enjoy a spot of sightseeing.

There were other problems off the pitch too, as Coppell found himself in the middle of a row between the players and the manager over the payment of laundry bills. The players, who had been away on tour for several weeks, wanted their washing done at the hotel at the club's expense, but Docherty refused. Then, when the United manager was asked to select three United players to take part in a head-tennis tournament in Australia, he chose Coppell, along with Brian Greenhoff and Sammy McIlroy. The promoters paid the players 150 Australian dollars each and the rest of the squad insisted the money be added to a players' pool and used to cover the laundry bill.

Young, naïve and eager to please, Coppell was quick to agree, but Docherty was furious and turned on his young protégée, threatening to throw him out of the club. The laundry row was a prelude to the following season, when a fine FA Cup run took Docherty's United to Wembley to face underdogs Southampton. It was a game United were expected to win at a canter, especially having seen off main rivals and league champions Derby County in the semi-final, but the build-up to the Wembley final was peppered with public appearances and endorsement opportunities which threatened to cause factions in the squad. It was a worry for the captain, who grew increasingly concerned that some of his team-mates were taking their eye off the ball, or becoming over confident as they prepared to face Second Division Southampton.

"I wasn't getting as carried away as some of my colleagues. Some seemed more worried about what they could make on the side rather than concentrating on the game, so I had misgivings about that," Buchan recalled.

Coppell was involved in one of the more high-profile fund-raisers when Gillette turned to United to promote their new twin-blade razors. Their slogan was 'give your beard the old one-two' and Coppell and Hill were the ideal players to accompany Docherty in marketing the product.

"They were two great players who liked to play push and run and give and go, two great wingers, and they were thrilled to do it, so we all went along and filmed it," Docherty told me. He added, "It created a bit of animosity because some of the players said they should be entitled to a share of the spoils, but they *weren't* entitled to it. What Stevie and Gordon did with the money was up to them, but there was a bit of friction there for a couple of weeks."

The atmosphere was not helped when the press were asked to make a donation to the players' fund in exchange for pre-Cup final interviews, adding to the pot swelled by advertising endorsements and public appearances, an approach that did not amuse Buchan as many members of the fourth estate were not happy bunnies. "The press were the lifeblood of the game and that alienated people," he said, "but Steve wasn't distracted by what was really a storm in a teacup, he was too level headed for that."

Whether it was the distraction of the build-up or simply United thinking they only needed to turn up to win, the final itself went horribly wrong. Coppell and Hill, the wingers around which Docherty had built his tactics, let alone his advertising campaigns, were identified by the media as key to the outcome and Saints boss Lawrie McMenemy had clearly formed the same opinion, as he had United's wide boys closely policed by full-backs Peter Rodrigues and David Peach.

Coppell had the first effort on goal, shooting straight at goalkeeper Ian Turner from distance, and McIlroy hit the bar, but McMenemy's side was bursting with experience, veteran skipper Rodrigues joined by the likes of Peter Osgood, Mick Channon and Jim McCalliog, who Docherty had sold to Southampton following Coppell's arrival to immediately recoup the £40,000 he had spent on his new winger.

Southampton's key to winning was to stop United from gaining any momentum and McMenemy's side remained alert and tackled fiercely from the first whistle, ensuring United struggled to get out of first gear. Southampton played on the counter-attack, quickly regrouping when their forays broke down, and while Rodrigues defiantly shackled Hill, United's attempts to find their key men were constantly defied by Southampton's tactic of cutting off the supply lines of passes.

Many purists suggested Southampton's tactics were a crime against football, strangling United's free-flowing creative play at birth in order to win the match with a display of counter-punching, but to Southampton's players, under the auspices of manager Lawrie McMenemy, it was simply a job which needed doing and one which was done clinically well.

"Myself and David Peach had to contain Hill and Coppell," recalled Rodrigues, who was told by Docherty that the FA Cup was 'only on loan' as he prepared to receive the trophy. It hardly dampened the moment, as Rodrigues revealed: "The greatest feeling I had was taking the cup from the Queen, turning half a metre and raising 33,000 Southampton voices. To turn and show the cup to our supporters was the greatest moment of my life."

It was a salutary lesson for Docherty and his team, who had been frustrated before falling to a breakaway goal from Bobby Stokes, sent clear by former United man McCalliog. "Every time I have seen it since, Bobby Stokes gets further and further offside just before he scores," lamented Buchan.

Docherty remains philosophical to this day, and he told me: "We should have beaten Southampton, but I have always said that if your name is on the cup you will win it. Bill Shankly said that the FA Cup is a sprint and the championship is a marathon and he was right – 99 times out of 100 we would have beaten Southampton, but that day their name was on the cup."

Coppell didn't know whether to laugh or cry, recalling: "I didn't feel too bad, as I appreciated being in the FA Cup final at all. It was only afterwards I realised it might have been the only chance I'd ever get, but just to have taken part in an occasion which I'd grown up watching was very special and I had a medal – even if it was a losers' medal – to prove it."

Defeat at Wembley was, however, harder to take given that United had also seen the First Division title slip from their grasp in the final weeks of the season, a legacy of their Wembley distractions. Having carried the momentum of their promotion year into the start of the 1975/76 season, United got off to a flying start. Docherty's team were largely unknown to most sides in the division and Coppell, who had been nervous over whether he would be technically capable of making the step up, was an unexpected force. Five wins and a draw in their opening six games of the season sent Docherty's side racing to the top of the table. The only defeat – and Coppell's first experience of losing in a United shirt – was a 1-0 reverse at Loftus Road where David Webb struck the winner after only 45 seconds and before any United player had touched the ball.

Coppell also began to rediscover his goalscoring touch. He netted twice in a 3-1 win against Arsenal in October, denied a hat-trick only by a brilliant Pat

Jennings save, and also fulfilled a boyhood dream of scoring in front of the Kop, albeit a late consolation goal in a 3-1 defeat at Liverpool.

In the same week, Docherty bolstered his squad by signing Gordon Hill from Millwall for £70,000. "He is the last piece of the jigsaw in my team building," said Docherty, who four days earlier had allowed errant former wonderboy George Best to leave Old Trafford and sign for Stockport County.

The sense of timing was never lost on Hill, who recalled in Jim White's excellent *Biography of Manchester United*: 'Before every game I used to get in my kit and sit on the toilet. I'd look at the shirt – it was a lovely shirt then, a different red from now, a deeper more pure red. I'd almost have to pinch myself it was true, and I'd say to myself, this is real, this is you. You are playing in George Best's shirt, now go out and play like George.'

The anxieties Coppell had faced before the start of the new season returned as new signing Hill watched rivals Manchester City thrash United 4-0 on their way to winning the League Cup. "It was my own inferiority complex rather than any newspaper speculation and I was worried simply because I was still very much a part-timer," Coppell said.

He need not have worried though, as Docherty's intention had always been to play the two young wingers on opposite flanks. Docherty said: "My priority at the start of the season was to find a left-winger to complement the work of Steve on the right. I believed if United had direct wingers on either flank who could take full-backs on and beat them, we would stretch defences and provide more opportunities for goals from Pearson and Macari."

"Steve and Hilly were special," Docherty told me. "Stevie would get 10 or 12 goals a season, but he would cause havoc in the box. If he took his man on 20 times he would beat him 20 times. If he finally got stopped on the 21st, Steve would go back again and beat him the next time. He wore defenders down – he was quick and strong and his crosses were lethal, they were like cannonballs and Pearson and Macari would stick them away. Hilly was a goalscorer, the 20-a-season man, but they complemented each other on the wings."

The wing pair's first outing together came against Aston Villa at Old Trafford, Coppell opening the scoring in a 2-0 win. It was a result which left them in third place behind Liverpool and QPR in the race for the title and, though United returned to the top in January, the distractions of the FA Cup arguably caused them to fall just short as Liverpool sealed the title ahead of Rangers, with United trailing in third.

It was in January that their FA Cup adventure began, though there were few signs of what was to come as they edged past Oxford United 2-1 courtesy of two second-half penalties and then saw off Third Division Peterborough 3-1 in round four. When Macari inspired Docherty's side to a 2-1 win over Leicester in the fifth round most Manchester United fans begun to see Wembley in their sights, among them former World snooker champion Alex Higgins. United fan Higgins had tried to celebrate the win over Leicester by visiting the team's dressing room and congratulating the players, but hadn't banked on the security guard-like presence of Cavanagh, who was highly protective of his players and manager. Higgins was graceful in the face of rejection and when United reached Wembley he adopted a different approach, sending every single player an individual telegram to wish them luck.

It could have been so different though, as Wolves had provided a tougher than expected barrier in the quarter-finals, forcing a 1-1 draw at Old Trafford and racing into a 2-0 lead in the replay before United roared back to win in extra-time. By then United knew their semi-final opponents would be reigning league champions Derby, while the other semi-final had paired Second Division Southampton with Third Division giant-killers Crystal Palace. Docherty, despite telling his players not to be drawn in by any journalistic probing, could not help himself. Describing the other semi-final as "a bit of a joke" he said: "this is the real Cup final – we should have been meeting at Wembley, not Hillsborough in the semi-final".

Determined to keep his players out of the media spotlight he so readily garnered for himself, Docherty took his squad to the familiar surroundings of Mottram Hall, the Cheshire hotel which United used as a meeting place ahead of many home games. The club had originally been booked to stay in a hotel in Buxton, closer to the semi-final venue, but when Docherty decided the accommodation was not up to the standards he had expected he ordered the players back on to the coach and headed back for Mottram Hall. Docherty was keen to take out his frustrations and to relax ahead of the semi-final with Derby and so organised a personal shooting trip with Mottram Hall's head waiter and some friends. His wingmen, Coppell and Hill, were invited along as his gun-bearers, but it turned into a marathon outing as Docherty tried in vain to bag himself a kill. "It could have proved disastrous with a semi-final to play the next day – we had walked so far that Gordon and I were very stiff," Coppell recalled. "We traipsed over the countryside for hours trying to find our manager something to kill, finally giving up and heading back to our hotel where Tom, after a furtive glance around, let fly at the tame ducks on the ornamental pond. He even missed those!"

Fortunately, Hill was more deadly the following day when, despite his aches, he scored two fine goals to seal a deserved 2-0 win for United and secure their place at Wembley. Even more notable was the fluent style with which United had played and it seemed clear to most who witnessed that semi-final that Southampton could not have lived with a similar approach in the final. Yet United suffered a hangover from that performance when they were beaten 3-0 by Bobby Robson's Ipswich at Portman Road just a few days later, a result which put a massive dent in their title chances. It was a full month before the FA Cup final, but the football writers were quick to suggest that United's players were already making sure they did not get injured and miss their big day out. "They had a point," conceded Docherty, sparing only Coppell, Buchan and goalkeeper Alex Stepney from blame.

The FA Cup run had left United playing catch-up and facing five League games in a fortnight. Docherty's side responded to his criticism with victory over Everton, though ironically the wholehearted Coppell suffered an ankle injury which was to keep him out of the next three games, all of them crucial.

"The only downside that afternoon was Steve's injury in a 50-50 with Mick Lyons – proof if ever it were needed that minds were not simply on Wembley," remembered Docherty. Without Coppell, and with Pearson also forced off through injury, Macari's goal sealed victory over Burnley to keep their hopes alive, but a first home defeat of the season at the hands of Stoke rocked United once more, this time terminally. Peter Shilton was the hero for Stoke, performing miracles to keep out wave after wave of United attacks before defender Alan Bloor headed an injury time winner to sound the death knell for United's title hopes.

Another defeat at Leicester three days later followed and, though Coppell returned in time for a 2-0 derby win over rivals Manchester City on the final day of the season, the damage had been done. "Losing Steve for those three games was some blow and it was no coincidence that we tailed off when Stevie was injured," Docherty told me. "I can't know for sure that things would have been different with him in, but if United lost Best or Ronaldo for six games the results wouldn't be good either, would they?"

Coppell had exceeded his own expectations and his disappointment at missing out on the title was tempered by his excitement of playing at Wembley. He even had another final to look forward to a few days later, having helped his university department side through to their own showpiece game; and his student fan club was ready to give him a lift – metaphorically and literally!

"He tried very hard to hard to maintain his student links and a group of four or five of us tried to get to as many games as possible to see him and support him," university pal and future FA chief executive Brian Barwick told me. "I went with a feller called Sammy Sinclair and a lad named Keith White, who owned a Volkswagen and was basically the mug who drove us everywhere. It was quite a thing for me because I was a dyed-in-the-wool Liverpudlian and had to watch Manchester United. At the time I weighed up in my mind that I was supporting Steve and not Manchester United and it was terrific to see him get on so well and become an established player in the team.

"When we got to the university cup final he played for us in goal. We went to see him play at Wembley on Saturday and on Wednesday he played for us. He was very committed to remaining as much of a student as he could and I really respected that because he had signed for Manchester United, but still wanted to enjoy as much as possible of the student life.

"That summer we celebrated his 21st birthday with two days in Southport. There were four of us and we created all sorts of forfeits for the weekend. I will never forget it, because I absolutely hated roller coasters and they conned me onto one and made me stand up at the very top. We played a lot of pitch and putt and there were forfeits there too – I won't go into what they were, but suffice to say they were typical of being 21 years old." I pondered aloud whether those forfeits included the ceremonial dropping of trousers and Brian did not pause for a second before saying: "That's easy for you to say."

That jolly boys' outing was the perfect way for Coppell to let off steam after the frustrations of such a promising season, but Docherty had been adamant that the end of the campaign should be marked by celebrations and not a wake, having bounced back so admirably from relegation just two years earlier. Half a million United fans responded to that rallying cry as they crammed into Albert Square the day after the shock Cup final defeat to Southampton to welcome their team back at a civic reception. Buchan's PFA office is a mere 500 metres from Albert Square, his venues of now and then separated only by the Central Library and St Peter's Square, and when we met he could picture the scene all too easily as he glanced out of the window in the direction of the Town Hall, transporting himself back 33 years to when those 500,000 fans had come to pay their respects.

"We should have won the cup, but we could have won the league too," Buchan said with a mixture of pride and deflation. "We would have done better in the league if we weren't distracted by the cup run and I'm always disappointed when I look back because our form at the end of the season was average to say the least. Yet, in truth, no-one expected United to be in the top half-dozen having only just come back up.

"We all stood over there on the first-floor balcony of the town hall overlooking the square and Tommy Doc said to the fans: 'never mind, we'll go back next year and win it'. He was just trying to console people – himself too, probably – but it was a fairytale statement."

Docherty didn't believe in fairytales, but he did genuinely believe that United's name was on the FA Cup. Next year.

THE EAGLES HAVE LANDED

This is what paradise must have looked like. Golden sands, sweeping like a soft carpet towards an inviting sea that shimmers in the afternoon sunshine. Water warm like a bath and so shallow and clear it seems there must be a filter hidden behind the rocks, artificially cleaning the bay in which bodies and boats bob to the rhythm of the tide.

Speedboats fizz along the horizon, towing happy water-skiers who have graduated from the shallow learning pools closer to the beach, where amateur skiers don virtual L-plates as they aspire to the deeper waters of experience. John Salako, Crystal Palace's young winger, is learning the ropes, literally, while his mates look on and laugh every time he fails to maintain his composure on the crystal waters of the Caribbean.

Others try their hand too, but most of the group on the beach are happy to be still, resting aching limbs in a bid to repair their bodies for a new season of challenges. As Salako wades back to the shore after an hour of learning his new hobby he still cannot submit to the calm, instead joining in an impromptu kickabout on the beach. His skills draw admiring glances from the men on the beach, his physique equally approving stares from the ladies and Salako looks as though he has been schooled on the beaches of Copacabana.

"Brazilian, yes?" asks a local, after several minutes of waiting for a pass. "Yeah baby, that's what I want to hear,' Salako replies, then adds, to bemused responses: 'I should have been Brazilian."

Crystal Palace were living the dream. Once dubbed the 'team of the seventies' they were very much the side of the 70s and the Caribbean break that Ron Noades had treated them to was a reward for their FA Cup run and an opportunity to unwind and reflect on how far they had come in such a short space of time. And, crucially, to focus on where they were going.

The FA Cup semi-final win over Liverpool and the way they had taken the game to Manchester United in the final had underlined what Coppell's burgeoning side were capable of, even though a 15th-place finish in the top flight barely hinted as much. Their televised heroics had also secured them a big following in faraway corners of the world as Jamaica, Trinidad and Grand Cayman; a good excuse to combine the three destinations on a summer holiday.

None of the players have ever seen Steve Coppell look so relaxed. With a beer in his hand and a smile on his face, Coppell could be forgiven for never wanting to leave this beach. There is not a cloud to spoil the view . . . or so it seems.

IAN BRANFOOT FELT as though he had lost a pound and found a fiver as he lay on that Caribbean beach.

A former Sheffield Wednesday, Doncaster and Lincoln defender, Branfoot had developed a reputation as a coach when youth team manager at Southampton, before Reading gave him his big break as a replacement for Maurice Evans. Alan Brown insisted Branfoot take his coaching badges as a young player at Hillsborough and, having played under Graham Taylor at Lincoln and worked under Lawrie McMenemy at Southampton, Branfoot had enjoyed a sound coaching education that became evident as he steered Reading to the Third Division title, breaking records along the way.

When the Elm Park magic wore off and his own Royals reign came to an end, Branfoot had wondered where his next move might be. He only had to wait 48 hours for the answer, as Steve Coppell had a proposition for him.

"It was a shock when Steve approached me. A lovely shock. He phoned me only a couple of days after I had been sacked by Reading and offered me the job as first-team coach," said Branfoot, who was an easy target on my journey to discover what makes Steve Coppell tick, having been a family friend of the Roaches for the past 25 years.

He told me: "I agreed verbally straight away. I jumped right in. I had no hesitation, but I had to wait 14 days for my settlement to be completed at Reading before I could actually start at Palace. I never asked Steve why he offered me the job, I just assumed he had seen what I had done at Reading and watched my teams. I didn't know a lot about him other than that he had a good track record and was an intelligent guy who had a degree.

"I turned up on the first morning and Steve left that first training session to me. We had players like Wrighty and Brighty in the side and for the first couple of weeks I just got on with it, doing all the normal things like working on set-plays. Palace had bloody good players, hard-working players; people like Wrighty and Brighty worked their nuts off, chasing everything down a bit like Tevez does these days.

"They had fit players too. We used to go to the park and do cross-country runs and they hated it but loved it at the same time. From being a manager, I became a coach who came in in the morning, did my coaching and maybe watched a game in the evening if Steve asked me. I had none of the pressures of being a manager, Steve did all that. He told me, 'that's your job, get on with it.' We could only work like that because of the relationship we had and I always acknowledged that he was the boss; I would suggest things but always did it his way."

Coppell's lieutenants were as important to him as his players – all part of the machinery that made up his Palace engine room. To the untrained eye it was a complicated formula, but Coppell based his theories on simplicity. Branfoot runs the qualities off as if he is compiling an ad for an online dating agency: "He is one of the best people I have ever met in football. He is straight, honest, not pretentious, not a big-time Charlie. He is totally trustworthy and has never been a shouter. He is an intelligent guy and says what he thinks."

All that, and no mention of a good sense of humour! But that was a given, if those pre- and post-season tours were anything to go by. "The most enjoyable parts of my time at Crystal Palace were the end-of-season trips and the pre-season tours," Branfoot told me. "We used to go to Sweden pre-season and it was perfect; we played four games in ten days. And there was that post-season tour to Jamaica, Trinidad and Grand Cayman. Steve was just the same off duty as on duty – quiet and reserved – he would have a drink but nothing stupid. He was good fun and would have a few beers and a good laugh round a table. They were my most enjoyable two and a half years in football."

That much showed as Palace took their momentum into a new season. Coppell's side were unbeaten in League and Cup until a 2-0 defeat at Old Trafford on 3 November 1990 and defeats at Southampton and Chelsea were the only further setbacks as they ended the year with a 1-0 win over Liverpool, further redemption and proof that the wounds of 14 months earlier were all but healed.

Coppell, though, had not brought the carefree attitude of the Caribbean back into the day-to-day rigours of English football and remained wholly focussed; feet planted firmly on the ground, no matter how much Noades tried to persuade him to live *la Dolce Vita*.

"We were doing great and Ron turned up and gave Steve this really garish Porsche that even I wouldn't drive, and that is saying something," said Pardew. "Ron had just bought it for Steve to say 'you are doing great, just take this' but Steve just could not drive it; he wouldn't be seen in it and he wasn't going to have it. That tells you a little bit about his personality: he is not out there, his clothes are awful, his hair has always been the same, but he loves the banter, the dressing room Mickey-taking. He loves all that."

The atmosphere was good as the Eagles continued to fly. Wright and Bright formed one of the most feared goalscoring partnerships in football, Salako and Eddie McGoldrick supplying the vital ammunition, Thomas and Andy Gray marauding through the heart of midfield and Nigel Martyn outstanding behind a rock-solid defensive unit.

"Wright and Bright would sometimes give me and John a raw deal because they were at the top of their game – they were scoring a lot of goals at that time and if they didn't get the balls where they wanted they could give us a really hard time," McGoldrick told me, but added: "When you did get the ball where they wanted it, everything was fine and dandy. John and I were both quite young, but Steve let us deal with that because he knew it would make us stronger. The criticism from Wright and Bright would either send us one way or the other and he saw it as a test of character. It was part of his management style and it worked well."

Salako's recollection of the Coppell mantra 'a side is only as good as its weak link' rang as true as ever, for Palace simply didn't seem to have one that season. Incredibly, they kept the pace they had set before Christmas and finished the campaign third, behind champions Arsenal and runners-up Liverpool and five points clear of fourth-placed Leeds.

"It was such a short time in which we had moved from a mediocre Second Division side to a top-flight team, but it was the way we did it, playing decent football and scoring for fun," recalled captain Geoff Thomas. "I just remember everything coming together – we only lost a couple before Christmas and whether we were home or away we went out knowing we had a chance of winning. The only side we were ever battered by was Arsenal; they were a step in class above us and seemed to have some kind of spell over us, but for the likes of Manchester United and Liverpool we had no fear factor and were performing pretty well."

Palace also exorcised some Wembley demons by claiming the club's first ever piece of silverware thanks to a 4-1 thrashing of Everton in the Zenith Data Systems Cup final, a competition created to give those clubs who would have been involved in Europe some consolation for the ban which kept English clubs out of UEFA competitions for five years. It was only minor consolation for their defeat at the same venue the previous year, but a trophy all the same. Even so, there were still those who sought to tarnish Palace's first silverware with criticism over their style of play, claiming Coppell's side had bullied their way past Everton.

Even the remarkable achievement of steering a club on limited resources to third place in the top flight was belittled by many who felt Palace's style of play did not merit such lofty reward. But while Coppell's methods were undoubtedly direct and simple, they were built on solid footballing foundations and carved out of the same work ethic he had boasted as a player. Perhaps the critics were just sore that so-called glamour clubs like Chelsea, Tottenham and Manchester United were left trailing in Palace's wake.

Yet, just as Coppell seemed to have perfected his system and completed his Palace jigsaw, it all started to fray at the edges. While fourth-placed Leeds added Eric Cantona and Rod Wallace to their squad in the summer of 1991 and went on to win the First Division championship the following season, Palace failed to add significantly to their squad and their captain feels to this day there was an underlying credibility issue; and is adamant that the legacy of their FA Cup near-miss played its part.

Thomas told me: "We did ever so well to finish third in the top flight in 1991, but if we had won the FA Cup the previous year and then done that, then people would have looked differently and realised what a decent side we were. In truth, we were not big enough to keep hold of the likes of Wright and Bright, so it was frustrating – but no more so than for Steve.

"As quickly as it all came together, it broke up just as swiftly. The realism is that not having been a top-flight team for decades makes it hard to sustain that position. Millions of pounds coming in to a club was massive back then and the money on offer for our best players was just too much to turn down. It was not the first time a club had gone so close to trophies and then been broken up, and with Sky making more of a showpiece of football there was an opportunity to start to create better characters off it. Football was just about to take off after years of crowd trouble and seats being ripped up. Sky played a big part and revved things up."

Wright was undoubtedly one of the characters already and, after a season of speculation in the press and on the terraces, not to mention within his own dressing room, Wright joined champions Arsenal in a £2.5million deal. Winning at Wembley, albeit a minor trophy in the shape of the ZDS Trophy, had given Wright the taste for silverware and he was hungry for more.

'We didn't just win, we battered Everton both in a footballing way and a physical way. They went away whingeing that we'd been like bullies in the playground, but we went away with winners' medals and for me that cancelled out all the criticism that anybody threw at us,' Wright recalls in *Mr Wright*. 'I finally had a medal and I'd been a winner at Wembley and suddenly it dawned on me that I liked the feeling, that I wanted it all the time. I needed to be winning things, to see my trophy room full up with silverware and mementos and everything else that went with being a winner, but I also realised that it wasn't going to be with Palace.

'I knew there had been interest from Arsenal, and Spurs were also in the background, and I began to get impatient and made it known to Steve and Ron that I wanted to get away. They both knew what the score was; £2million is a hell of a lot of dough to a club like Palace and they had also made plans for my replacement. Stan Collymore had come down from Stafford Rangers and I think that they were grooming him to play alongside Brighty when I left.'

Perhaps with that in mind, it was with typical understatedness that Coppell broke the news to Wright that a deal was in place for him to join Arsenal. Wright revealed: 'I went into training really fired up. I was going to storm in to see Steve and tell him that if he or Noades tried to stop me leaving I'd play up. I'd make a nuisance of myself and make it so unbearable for everybody that they'd have to let me go. Instead, Steve pulled me over before training started and said, "You've got to go and speak to Arsenal, the club have accepted a bid." I went from having all the front in the world, ready to give it the big time, to a scared little kid terrified that a club like Arsenal wanted to speak to me.'

It was the end of an era for Palace, whose manager, in keeping with the yawning silence from the big-club obsessed press even then, failed to receive the praise he deserved for such a remarkable rise through the football ranks. Yet while many critics claimed Coppell had taken Palace to the top by playing the wrong kind of football, Wright was well aware of the difference his manager had made to his own game.

He said: "I'll be eternally grateful that Steve always allowed me to play the way I wanted to. He told me to play with my instincts and never let anyone take that away from me. Steve Coppell has played an integral part in my life, not just my career. He means the world to me – he is like a father to me and I certainly love him like a father – I speak to him all the time with everything that's concerning me, personal and professionally. Between him and Ron Noades they had a major influence on my life, not just on my career.

"Ron and Steve were the two main reasons I became such a success at Palace. Steve put me on the stage, he gave me the chance and I will never be able to thank him enough for what he did for me. He saw something in the cocky little kid who came along for a trial and gave me the opportunity to fulfill my dream. I've had a few managers in my time, but nobody has ever been so honest with me. If he thought I'd played well he'd always tell me, and if he thought I'd been useless then he would let me know. There are no grey areas with him: what you see is what you get and if you don't like it, then tough. I owe him virtually everything."

Coppell neatly summarised his Mark One era at Selhurst Park when he added: "I wanted to win football games and I felt, given the kind of players I had and the financial resources I had available, the style of play that I was adopting was the best way for me. If I'd been at another club where there had been greater financial resources then I certainly would have adopted a different style of play. I used to go and watch other teams and I obviously used to watch Wimbledon, who were just down the road, and had great spirit for each other. They played a style of football which perhaps wasn't pleasing on the eye but which was exciting; I used to see fabulous goalmouth action every game and Wimbledon won more games than they lost and they were up at the top of the table. Having seen that I felt, looking at my problems, the solution was to adopt a more direct style and please my chairman, who was employing me to win games."

Those financial restraints meant Palace sold more than they spent over the next two seasons, though Coppell was quick to invest much of the Wright cash on Sunderland's Marco Gabbiadini for a club-record £1.8million. It proved an expensive mistake though, as Gabbiadini failed to make an impact at Selhurst Park, scoring seven goals in 25 games before making Derby County his third club in a single season as he moved on within three months for barely half the fee Palace had paid out.

Pardew also left to join Charlton and the likes of Paul Bodin and Jeff Hopkins departed, yet Palace still managed a creditable top-ten finish, with Collymore establishing himself where Gabbiadini had failed to fill Wright's boots. But Collymore and Bright had a falling-out before both strikers followed Wright out of the door early the following season, Bright joining Sheffield Wednesday for £1.375 million in September and Collymore heading to Southend in November.

With midfielder Andy Gray, now an England international, also departing to join Spurs, the haemorrhage of players over two seasons wounded Palace and Coppell, despite replacing Bright with Millwall's Chris Armstrong, was unable to stop the bleeding. Palace struggled throughout the 1992/93 season, but appeared to have survived with a couple of games to spare when they beat Ipswich 3-1, only for a single away point from their final two games, coupled with Oldham's 4-3 win over Southampton on the final day of the season, to send them down on goal difference.

The collapse taught Coppell a vital lesson and, to this day, he has refused to publicly predict the footballing future beyond the very next game. "When I try to predict it doesn't work – I found that to my cost," he told me. "Palace got relegated on 49 points and we celebrated the week before because we had reached 48. I have stopped crystal ball gazing now. I don't bother. One of my abilities is to compartmentalise and, although 'one game at a time' is a cliché, it works for me."

The biggest irony on that day of relegation was that it was Wright who hammered in one of the final nails, scoring the opening goal in a 3-0 win for Arsenal at Highbury to leave his former club licking their wounds and contemplating life back in Division One. Coppell immediately fell on his sword, feeling the cycle had been completed, and it was clearly with huge frustration that he left largely unheralded for the footballing near-miracle he had achieved.

'It always amazes me that the long-ball theory is looked upon as being simple – "you just welly it and you win games" – whereas the passing style of football is harder because "there's more coaching involved",' Coppell declared in Rogan Taylor's *Kicking and Screaming*. He continued: 'My experience is that long ball teams are coached, they are told what to do, they are allowed to express themselves but only in certain areas of the field, whereas passing sides are just told to go out and play.

'The Liverpool sides are famous for their training in five-a-sides, whereas the more direct teams spend a long time in dead-ball situations. Reality states that the passing game is expression without the coaching whereas long-ball football is more about coaching. A lot of people say that bad players can't play that style of football. They can, but they can't play it successfully, you need good players to play that style successfully.

'I was fortunate. Over five or six years we got together a side which was excellent: Ian Wright, Mark Bright, Eddie McGoldrick, John Salako, Andy Gray, Geoff Thomas, Eric Young, the goalkeeper Nigel Martyn. We had some good players and with time we gave a little bit more expression to the very rigid framework we started with.'

Thomas left that summer too, the captain following his manager out of the door a year after Coppell had blocked his departure to Blackburn, desperate to maintain some of the existing foundations on which to base his next phase of rebuilding.

"I should have gone the year before I did, to be honest," Thomas recalled with a heavy heart. "I was frustrated because the fee Blackburn were willing to pay Palace was huge. Palace were rebuilding but Steve dug his heels in and Ron Noades says the manager persuaded him to keep me as a player. I respected that, but when I look back I feel everyone would have prospered had I gone then.

"There is no bitterness. Steve had a job to do and I was delighted to be part of that, so when I knew I was not going to Blackburn I just got my head down. But once you lose that five per cent in your game with your mind not fully on it, you suffer a performance dip, so when Steve went it was time for me to go. He was a big part of me being there and [his replacement] Alan Smith was bringing the young players through, so I felt I would be standing in the way of the next stream of talent.

"They were the best footballing days of my career, but it ended on a frustrating note. Wolves signed me for £1 million, but it was officially recorded as £800,000. Blackburn had offered £2.8 million a year earlier, having just paid £3 million for Alan Shearer. That's football; things change and that was proved when I was injured ten games in at Wolves. You can't look back and work out how it would have been if everything was perfect, but I just felt the years came off me after that. It was hard and when the side was relegated I knew I needed a new challenge."

So too Coppell, though that challenge would not be with England, despite the now 37-year-old manager being linked with the job following Graham Taylor's resignation after the dismal failure to qualify for the World Cup in the USA in 1994. 'I wouldn't take the England job for a big gold clock,' Coppell wrote, adding in his *Daily Telegraph* column at that time: 'I have often likened a football manager's life to that of a pimp. You depend on other people for your success and are not in control. The main area in which a manager has control is the selection of players. Although I have never been in the fortunate position of choosing an England squad, I would presume that you choose your best 11 and then add names accordingly. I wonder how many times Graham Taylor has been able to choose his first-choice 11? I would think that, because of injuries, the team that eventually plays for him has more often than not been a mixture of his second and third 11s. This means he has not been in control as much as he would have liked – and certainly not enough for him to be so personally vilified.'

Coppell may also have been wary of the criticism Palace had received for their brand of football after Taylor had been derided and ridiculed in the press, not only on the back of bad results but also a perceived lack of style from his team. Where the England manager had suffered as 'Turnip Taylor', Coppell had no intention of becoming a 'cauliflower', 'carrot' or even 'cabbage'.

'I think Graham Taylor was given the international job more because of his success at Aston Villa when he didn't play long-ball football,' Coppell claimed. 'He played with a very innovative five-man defence with three centre-halves. They were the only team in the country who did it and they finished second in the league and you could argue that with a little bit more luck with injuries they could have won the league. But the "long-ball type", the direct style of play, is a tag you just do not shake off. There's always somebody in the press who will ram it down the readers' throats. Or, people don't remember Graham Taylor for his passing Aston Villa side, they remember the Watford side.'

Relegation hurt Coppell, but he did not leap back into another job as a kneejerk reaction. Not with England; not with anyone. He remained a student of the game, learning from other coaches and absorbing as much knowledge as he could as he recharged his batteries in a break from the day-to-day business of running a club. It was the first of his sabbaticals, with only the occasional newspaper column keeping him in the public eye.

There was another important appointment for him though, his reputation for integrity and his experience of mediation with the PFA making him an ideal choice to form part of the three-man FA panel investigating an increasing number of claims of illegal payments in football. The FA ordered the inquiry on 13 June 1993 following allegations made in the High Court during the case in which Terry Venables attempted to overturn Alan Sugar's decision to terminate his role as chief executive at Tottenham. The allegations centred on the transfer of Teddy Sheringham from Nottingham Forest to Spurs and resulted in the first use of the term 'bung' in football.

During the case details emerged of a cash withdrawal of £58,750 that had then been paid to Frank McLintock's First Wave Management company for 'distribution, network, travel and merchandising' for Tottenham in the United States. Sugar insisted McLintock and Venables had both said the payment was for First Wave's role in the Sheringham transfer and it was those claims that led to football's cash culture being questioned in parliament and the FA ordering a full inquiry into the Sheringham transfer and other similar accusations of illegal payments.

Coppell, Premier League chief executive Rick Parry and Robert Reid QC formed the three-man panel put together by the FA to investigate all allegations, including claims in the national press that George Graham had received illegal payments, and the inquiry took more than three years to complete as an increasing number of cases were referred to it. In the end, more than 60 witnesses were interviewed and tens of thousands of pages of evidence considered in compiling a report that covered the Football League, the FA and 12 other football associations around the world at a cost of more than £1 million. But few answers were revealed.

Ultimately the report, described as "a damp squib" by FA chief executive Graham Kelly, read like an Agatha Christie novel, except without the final explanation of what really happened. The conclusion was an unsatisfactory one for Coppell too, as the report revealed a difference of opinion within the panel relating to the Sheringham transfer. That deal formed the bulk of the 1,000-page report written by Parry and Reid, in which they affirmed that in their opinion Forest assistant manager Ronnie Fenton had accepted an illegal payment as part of the Sheringham transfer. At the last moment Coppell, who like Kelly had been sceptical that a bungs culture existed in football, insisted there was inconclusive evidence to prove wrongdoing.

Coppell's refusal to put his name to the conclusions made for a slightly farcical rewriting of part of the report which stated: 'Two members of the inquiry (Mr Parry and Mr Reid) are satisfied that at the meeting Mr McLintock handed over to Mr Fenton at least a substantial part, if not all, of the £50,000 which he had received earlier that day from Tottenham and that Mr Fenton returned to Nottingham with the money from Mr McLintock. Mr Coppell is not satisfied of this and by extension the conclusions set out in paragraphs 21.15 and 21.16 are those of Mr Parry and Mr Reid and not Mr Coppell.'

Author Tom Bowyer, in his book *Broken Dreams: Vanity, greed and the souring of British football*, claimed: 'Inevitably the cynics would suggest that Coppell's rebuff was "a closing of ranks in the football fraternity." Others were more blunt: "He's been got at by football."'

By the time the report was finally published, Coppell had returned to the football community. Two years after ending his nine-year managerial debut following Palace's relegation from the Premiership, Coppell returned to Selhurst Park as Technical Director, Ron Noades keen to bounce back after Alan Smith's Eagles had won promotion but then been immediately relegated.

Coppell was installed as an overseer, with coaches Ray Lewington and Peter Nicholas as his first lieutenants, but struggled to steady the ship as he inherited a team barely recognisable from the previous season. Salako, Armstrong, Chris Coleman, Gareth Southgate, Iain Dowie, Richard Shaw and Eric Young had all departed and a second successive relegation was a distinct possibility before Noades shuffled his managerial pack once more.

While Coppell remained 'upstairs', Dave Bassett was installed as manager for the second time and nine wins in the final 14 matches took Palace to the play-offs where they were beaten in the final against Leicester by a dramatic last-gasp winner from Steve Claridge at Wembley.

When Palace's promotion push the following season was interrupted by Bassett being heavily linked with the vacant Manchester City job, Coppell looked set to return to the manager's seat for a third time. Instead, there was a huge twist in the tale as Bassett turned down the City job and remained at Palace, leaving the club's Technical Director and one of Manchester's favourite football sons to be tempted by the Maine Road move instead.

Steve Coppell was about to make the biggest managerial mistake of his life.

EVERY CROWD HAS A SILVER LINING

The early morning sun cracks the horizon like a glowing ember and causes the hotel porter to squint as he focuses on the three men in the park, suddenly illuminated by the growing spotlight on a new Sunday. The trio come towards him slowly and something between them catches the light of the morning sun's first rays; flashing, blinking, as though they are signalling to him in Morse code.

Under a new sky as red as the porter's coat, the flashlight flickers between two of the men, then dances back across between the middle man and the third man. Confused, the porter strains his eyes harder in concentration as the men come closer to him, across Hyde Park, but suddenly the flashlight is extinguished as one of the men crouches to the ground.

Then they are on the move again and he can hear them now, voices growing louder. There's laughter; hysterical, uncontrollable laughter, terminated only by a sigh of satisfaction. It is the undoubted sound of blissful, unbridled happiness.

The three men are squinting too, like rabbits in the headlights as they finally come into focus, shuffling out of the park and across the road as they head for the sanctuary of the hotel. The porter does not recognise them at first, but he recognises the object of their play, the conductor that has passed between them and created the flashlight effect in the breaking dawn light. It is the FA Cup, the most iconic trophy in English football, and as it passes within touching distance of the excited porter and into the revolving doors, he is sure he spots a dent in it.

THIRTY-TWO YEARS AFTER Tommy Docherty, flanked by Steve Coppell and his close pal Brian Greenhoff, had carried the slightly scuffed FA Cup across Hyde Park and back through the doors of the Royal Garden Hotel, the memories of Manchester United's 1977 FA Cup win over Liverpool were still fresh in Lou Macari's mind as he reminisced with me while walking his dog.

Buddy, a black Labrador named after Buddy Holly and belonging to Macari's grandson, seemed almost as excited during his walk as United had been on that glorious Wembley day in 1977 when Docherty's team dented Liverpool's treble bid – and then dented the FA Cup trophy itself.

Macari was more relaxed than his dog, but keen to get across to me the mixture of pride and relief that he, Coppell and everyone connected with United felt at unseating the FA Cup favourites just 12 months after being so unceremoniously unseated from that pre-final tag themselves.

Like Coppell, Macari is not particularly one for reminiscing, preferring to look ahead rather than back, but walking Buddy for two hours every day through the park near his home in Stoke-on-Trent means he can't help but let his mind wander from time to time. Especially when I give him a nudge.

"When we left Wembley 12 months earlier we were more than disappointed, but things could not have been more different in 1977," he told me. "Coming a cropper against Southampton was a bit unfortunate in the way it came, but there had been enormous pressure on us. Every pundit in the land had predicted we would beat them; people thought we just had to turn up and win, but it is never that easy.

"When we went back, the exact opposite applied. This time we were the underdogs and all the pundits were saying the treble was on for Liverpool, who were heading straight off to Rome to play Borussia Mönchengladbach in the European Cup final, having already won the League. We were more relaxed and weren't sitting in the dressing room an hour before kick-off thinking 'bloomin' hell, if we don't win this it will be a terrible shock'. I felt it, and I'm sure Steve and everyone felt the same.

"Our preparations were exactly the same as the previous year, but this time there was no pressure on us and all the journalists who had come in to the hotel the previous year and said it was just a case of us turning up to win at Wembley were now saying Liverpool were going to win. Were we going to stop them winning the treble? Probably not."

Talk of underdogs was timely, as it coincided with Buddy being suddenly jumped by a friendly companion. "They are two males!" shouted Macari, and could not stop giggling as he prized the new friends apart. I could not help but be reminded of Macari, the little black-haired terrier, being lifted high by Gordon Hill after United's winner at Wembley that day.

Macari was still smiling, probably more to do with the memory than the analogy Buddy had inspired, when he told me: "All I remember really is chasing for a ball out of defence and I went up and flicked it towards Jimmy Greenhoff and Stuart Pearson, then made my way to try and follow up for any opportunity. The ball fell and I shot – I didn't really know where I was aiming or where it had gone and I had no idea it hit Jimmy, who was trying to get out of the way. When you are on the Wembley pitch you have no idea of half of what is going on. All I knew was that the ball was in the back of the net and no-one was bothered who had scored it, whether it was me or Jimmy. Even after the game, no-one cared, we just cared that we had won."

Macari's wayward snapshot had cannoned off his team-mate and looped beyond the reach of Ray Clemence and into the far corner of the net. Stuart Pearson had earlier beaten Ray Clemence at his near post – "instead of the treble, could it possibly be trouble?" asked commentator Brian Moore – before Jimmy Case levelled with a shot on the turn after Joey Jones had too easily beaten Coppell wide on Liverpool's left. When Macari's shot deflected in for a winner eventually credited to Greenhoff, the sense of relief was as massive as the slice of luck which had produced the goal and United's celebrations – on and off the pitch – were wild.

"Climbing those steps to get a winners' medal, having climbed them to get a losers' medal 12 months previously, was undoubtedly one of my highlights," Coppell said. "It was as though we were avenging what had happened 12 months previously. The key for me was that Kevin Keegan was kept in close check by Martin Buchan – he marked him out of the game." It was a performance put into perspective by Keegan's display in the European Cup final a few days later, where he gave world-class man-marker Bertie Vogts the runaround as Liverpool won 3-1.

"It was not just any old Liverpool team. It was a fantastic Liverpool team," Macari was keen to reinforce, "and the difference in emotions from the previous year was huge. In 1976, after the final I was in bed by 9.30; I was gutted and there were not many United players who wanted to be at that banquet. The year after at the Royal Garden Hotel was different. It was bedlam. All your friends know where you are and head back to see you at the hotel, and the fans normally knew where we were staying, so what starts with four or five hundred ends up with 2,000 and it is pandemonium."

Docherty still insists that party owed its electric atmosphere to fate and told me: "I would have mortgaged my house and bet the proceeds that we would have beaten Southampton, but we lost. I wouldn't have mortgaged my house on us beating Liverpool the next year, but we did because our name was on the cup. Something always happens on the way to the final. That shot which hits the post and goes in during an early round . . . it was our turn."

The route to the final, in which United were pushed to their limits on several occasions, backs up the otherwise unscientific theory. Unconvincing 1-0 victories over Walsall and QPR at Old Trafford offered mixed emotions for Coppell, who was substituted after a poor third round performance but created Macari's winner on an icy pitch in round four against Rangers. Those victories set up the chance for revenge over Southampton, who once again offered stern resistance before relinquishing their grip on the trophy as Jimmy Greenhoff's double forced a 2-1 replay win after a tense 2-2 draw at The Dell.

The quarter-final victory over Aston Villa was more comfortable than the 2-1 scoreline suggests and that set up a mouthwatering semi-final with Leeds United at Hillsborough. Mindful of the previous season's exhausting pre-match shooting trip, Coppell ensured he stayed relaxed and healthy this time around and was not even put off by the giant Leeds defender Gordon McQueen's mind games in the tunnel.

Coppell recalled: "With people like me, Gordon Hill and Lou Macari in the team we were quite a small side. Before the game Gordon, all 6ft 4in of him, was growling in the tunnel, looking at us and saying: 'Look at all these midgets. If we can't beat this lot we need locking up.' Gordon joined us the following year and we didn't let him forget what he'd said."

Nor the result. Coppell had a fine game and scored the crucial second goal, hooking home a Hill shot that had cannoned off Paul Madeley, having earlier forced the corner from which Greenhoff opened the scoring. Allan Clarke pulled one back from the penalty spot but Docherty's side were at Wembley again and Coppell's influence was underlined when he was named man of the match by TV pundit Bobby Charlton. So proud was Coppell at being recognised by the United legend that he never opened the bottle of champagne that marked the achievement.

The champagne was flowing four weeks later, yet amongst the chaos of those Cup final celebrations, Docherty was strangely subdued. "It was the day after I left my wife," he told me, revealing he had kept the news of his split from Agnes, his wife of 27 years, quiet at the time to ensure the focus on United was for all the right reasons. Docherty knew his affair with Mary Brown, the wife of Old Trafford physio Lawrie Brown, would steal the headlines and was desperate not to suffer media intrusions having been distracted so easily the year before.

Drained and emotional, Docherty was nevertheless one of the last to bed as his celebrations culminated alongside Coppell and Greenhoff just as the sun was rising over Hyde Park. "We were playing rugby with the trophy, just lobbing it backwards and forwards with each other," Docherty told me. "When that trophy finally got back to the Football Association, they ordered the club to have it repaired and cleaned up. It wasn't properly damaged, just wear and tear, and it wouldn't be right for me to say who the main culprit was. Put it this way, Steve was a fine winger, but he was no goalkeeper!"

The following day the FA Cup was placed in the safe custody of United's captain, but even Martin Buchan admitted: "One minute I was showing it off on the balcony at Albert Square, the next I had it at a mate's pub in Altrincham. You wouldn't get away with that now. You'd have six security guards with the trophy all the time."

Docherty led the celebrations as United returned to Albert Square, fulfilling the promise he had made to the fans 12 months earlier as he appeared to be marking the dawn of something special with United. Yet, less than six weeks later, he was sacked after revelations of his affair became public. "I am the only manager ever to be sacked for falling in love," he said.

Buchan could not help wondering what might have been as he told me: "We will never know if we could have built on that cup final win, but I'm confident if Tommy had stayed we would have done. Who knows what would have happened, but we beat a team who then went and won the European Cup; we stopped them doing the treble. We could raise our game for Liverpool, but I always said it was at Coventry on a wet Wednesday night where we needed to grind out a win.

"There were not any crunchers in that United team, but if you look across the midfield we had Steve, Gordon Hill, Lou Macari, Sammy McIlroy, Gerry Daly; none of them were going to knock people over, but they were quick. We were the best in the country at getting the ball back. Steve was a very important player for us; he always had a very natural fitness and he can't be much over his playing weight now, unlike me!

"It wasn't all sweetness and light, but those two seasons from 1975 to 1977 were the two happiest of my playing career in terms of football. I always said we could have given teams a two-goal head start at Old Trafford and still won. The atmosphere on Fridays was electric too; we would train on the pitch on Friday morning then have a cup of tea and a briefing in the directors' room before heading off to get ready for the game the next day."

Macari added: "It was different then. You can't compare the game then to football now. Life was less complicated than it is now and, for footballers, there was no shielding from the public, you were part of the public. You were walking through the streets of Manchester during the week, just one of them, not like now where you are not allowed to touch the players. We all came from similar backgrounds and we were delighted and grateful to be at Old Trafford."

The uncomplicated atmosphere suited Coppell, the down-to-earth student who had only just turned full-time professional. He had taken his revision books to the team hotel before the FA Cup final with Southampton, as he was to sit his final exams just a few weeks later, but in 1977 he was not burdened by books as United's players all went into that second successive final with a more carefree attitude.

Amongst the invited guests at Coppell's graduation ceremony to receive his Economics degree at the start of that trophy-winning 1976/77 season had been Docherty, the manager who had so vehemently encouraged his young winger to complete his education and who was keen to see the moment when he officially achieved that. "I was at the UEFA Cup draw in Switzerland with Bill Shankly and Matt Busby, but I had to leave two days early to go to Steve's graduation at Liverpool. It was surreal, going to see one of your players in his passing out parade," Docherty told me.

United's league form was fairly surreal too; another bright start had seen them as early leaders, but an injury which kept Buchan out until Christmas proved crucial as Docherty's United slumped as low as 17th before settling for a 6th-place finish. Their mercurial form was at least derived from some fine flowing football, the cavalier approach highlighted by the form of the two wingers in tandem on opposite flanks.

"Steve was a bright lad and he knew what was required. He adjusted from his background quickly and he did it quite easily," remembered Macari. "Back then, there was pressure around cup finals and big games, but in terms of the build-up to games there was no real pressure on any of us. Any Steve faced in those early months, he could lose in his studies.

"In all honesty, there was not really a lot to learn in those days. It was not as complicated as it seems to be now. He was uncomplicated on the pitch too; if you needed someone to get at defenders and get balls in the box, he was your man, and if you needed someone to track back and help your defenders, he was your man. He was a great success story when you look at his background, but he made it because he was honest and genuine.

"He was a clever lad and it was a breath of fresh air to United fans that we had a flying winger. Then, when Gordon Hill arrived, we had two flying wingers who people loved to watch. Steve's work rate gave him the edge over Gordon – Gordon was a spectacular player and scored spectacular goals; Steve didn't get as many, but he was classier and his work rate was higher."

United eventually finished sixth, but had the consolation of silverware and had enjoyed some European adventures along the way having qualified for the UEFA Cup the previous season. After overturning a first-leg deficit to beat Ajax in round one, United were then hugely unfortunate to be paired with a strong Juventus side. Though Hill's goal sealed an outstanding first-leg win at Old Trafford, the 1-0 lead was not enough as the Italian giants roared back in style in the second leg on their way to winning the trophy.

That 3-0 defeat did, however, leave Coppell with one of his most memorable moments in European football. He laughed as he told me: "The old Juventus stadium [Stadio Comunale Vittorio Pozzo] was a real eye-opener and had a chapel just before you went on to the pitch from the tunnel. We were well beaten on the night to eliminate us from the competition and after one of the goals Marco Tardelli was running past our dug-out, celebrating wildly. It was hard to take, but Tommy Docherty jumped up from the bench and shouted at Tardelli: 'Yeah, but who won the war, then?'"

A CITY SICKENER

If gardening and the great outdoors are therapeutic, then the best job to have at Manchester City at this moment in time is probably that of head groundsman. There's a lot of therapy needed around Maine Road right now.

The only concern for the groundstaff on this fine autumnal morning at the Platt Lane training complex is leaves, but groundsman Paul appears happy enough as he sweeps; a shower of red, yellow, green and brown shimmering in the November morning sunshine as they are tossed to one side in preparation for the reserve team match against Stoke City later that morning.

Stoke's former Manchester City striker Mike Sheron is already there, smiling pleasant recognition in the direction of a few old faces and taking the opportunity to chat to the modest gathering of fans hanging around the entrance to the complex as he waits for the rest of his team-mates to arrive.

Until they do, Platt Lane is a quiet place; more so given the absence of those squad members away on international duty. Those first-team players who remain look relaxed as they head over for the morning training session, joined by coaches Tony Book and Asa Hartford.

The peace and quiet of a crisp, sunny morning is a welcome guest; a breath of fresh November air blowing away the stale wind of turmoil which has engulfed City in the past year. To say 1996 has not been a good year for the Blues would be an understatement – relegation from the Premier League and £26 million of debt still weigh heavily on the club's shoulders – but now there appears to be hope. In the six weeks since Steve Coppell arrived to replace Alan Ball as manager, results have not exactly been renascent, but the general feeling is one of optimism.

The scene is so simple that it might be described as dull had it not been the backdrop for a club who have forgotten the meaning of the word 'normal'. Yet, something is not quite right. As the last of the players jogs across to the training pitch to a soundtrack of car tyres on gravel, of doors opening and closing, the whispers begin. Assistant manager Phil Neal looks ashen-faced as he strolls towards the gathered players, but the manager remains conspicuous by his absence. A notorious early bird, Coppell would normally have been here hours ago.

One of the apprentices reveals he has heard the club has called a press conference at Maine Road for 12 noon. "What's it for?" he asks. The leading expectation is of new money from a wealthy benefactor, perhaps even a takeover to relieve chairman Francis Lee of his responsibilities and to breathe new financial life into the ailing club. Wishful thinking? Perhaps.

The majority of alternatives are negative ones. The end of Umbro's sponsorship of the club is mooted, while one of the groundstaff even suggests Blackburn have tempted Coppell to come and spend Jack Walker's money. The joke falls flat: "he's not that kind of guy – to do that to us after only a month." Although, increasingly, in football, anything is possible.

Another member of the Platt Lane staff cycles into the complex with a worried look on his face. He has been told the news is "bad and sad". The speculation is now frantic, racing out of control on various levels. Has someone at the club died? Is the club facing liquidation? Has Kinkladze joined Liverpool?

In the distance, Neal stands over his players as most of the groundstaff crowd around a few vehicles in the car park, leaning through windows to hear radios tuned in to the mystery press conference. The eldest member of the groundstaff looks on from a short distance and as the news on the radio causes the collective faces to freeze in a mixture of disbelief and sadness, all he can think of was the day in 1939 when he watched his family stunned into silence as they huddled around their radio to hear Neville Chamberlain declare that Britain was at war.

Here, there is no war and no-one has died, but the snippets of information he gains from the gasped repeats of radio information – "Coppell resigned" . . . "overwhelming pressure" . . . "medical advice" – are enough to tell him that City are once again a club in crisis.

EDDIE McGOLDRICK'S FOOTBALLING world has come full circle since he was given the chance to learn the art of wing play from one of the masters of the craft. Twenty years after leaving Northampton to join Steve Coppell's Crystal Palace revolution, McGoldrick is back, making use of his recently-earned Uefa A Coaching Licence.

"It's ironic really," he told me, after putting Northampton's current crop of burgeoning young stars through their paces at Town's neat little training ground that doubles up as an athletics stadium. "It's totally different here now from when I was first at the club. When I first came to Northampton we either trained at the ground or the local park, battling with every bit of dog poo it could hit us with."

I resisted the temptation to suggest to Eddie that he has had to put up with his fair share of shit ever since, partly because his good times outweigh his bad; but it was hard to escape talking about setbacks including two serious knee injuries, missing out on an FA Cup final with Palace and ensuring he would turn out to be an eternal orange question in *Trivial Pursuit* by becoming Coppell's one and only premanent signing in his brief Manchester City tenure.

"It's the old quiz question," Eddie laughed. "I was his only permanent signing and although I'm proud of that and privileged to have been signed twice by Steve Coppell, I was devastated when he quit City."

Devastation had already become an overused noun amongst City fans, but never more so than that November morning in 1996 when Coppell quit after just 33 days in the job, citing stress as the reason for his departure. Chairman Francis Lee had taken 42 days to appoint City's 9th manager in as many years, but had lost him after little more than a month, the briefest managerial spell in City's history. Few would have predicted such a u-turn on the day Lee finally got his man, least of all it seemed Coppell, who suggested the City fans might need "a little patience" before things were right again.

A full transcript of his inauguration to the City ranks that day makes for fascinating reading in hindsight. Coppell said:

> "I'm delighted to come here; Manchester City is a massive club with huge potential. I still consider myself a northern boy, even though I've been away from the area for 12 years, and I'm pleased to be able to come back. Francis and I have been talking about the position for the last ten days, and I came to the conclusion that I'd be a fool not to take it.
>
> It's a golden opportunity and I'm just glad that it's fallen into my lap, and I certainly don't view the job as the poisoned chalice that it's been described as of late. As soon as I saw the set-up here I knew I'd made the right decision to come here. I've been wanting to get back into management for the last six months or so, and I did tell Ron

Noades at Palace that this was my intention. As Technical Director at Selhurst Park I missed the day-to-day involvement of a club, and the job wasn't as satisfactory as I thought it may be. Therefore, I'm delighted to be able to grasp the nettle again at Maine Road.

I will be judged on how many games I win. You've got to be pragmatic about it and I'm under no illusions. If I don't win matches I'll just be another statistic, but if I do, I could be a hero! That's the way football is. Basically, I see myself as a cog in a big machine, and as long as the other "cogs" work properly, we shouldn't have too many problems.

My first priority is to start winning games and to get this team out of this division and into their rightful place in the Premiership. But this league is a very difficult league to get out of. Teams in the Nationwide are more concerned about stopping you playing than playing themselves, and it's a case of all hands on deck. Relegation can knock the stuffing out of a team, and in my experience with Palace it took at least three or four months for us to acclimatise ourselves into a lower division. The same thing has probably happened here, and hopefully I'll be able to steady the ship.

I've been given a blank page to work on, and the players should now take this opportunity to impress me. I have no pre-conceived ideas about their ability, so it's up to them to prove to me that they want to play for Manchester City. If they can play with confidence, can start to express themselves and can get winning some games the crowd will be happy, and so will I. The players are well capable of getting on a roll, and we're in need of a string of good results.

I don't know if I'll be dipping into the transfer market yet – I want to see what talent I've got here before I start spending money; and Ron Noades will tell you that I treated the club's money like my own – it's not for me to say that I'm tight-fisted, but I'm very careful when it comes to signing players. If it's necessary to bolster your squad, well fine. If it's not, I'm quite happy to work with the players I already have here.

The amount of managers that have passed through here has been slightly worrying, but in my case, I'm an animal who tends to roost wherever he stays. I was with United and Palace for nine years apiece, and I hope that City is a long term rather than a short term move.

Although I've still got a huge affection for Manchester United, my links with them now are pretty tenuous. I played my last game for them 13 years ago, and I've actually spent more time at Crystal Palace than at Old Trafford. I'm totally focused on what's happening at City now – to me, United are in a different league in more ways than one, and there won't be any rivalry on my part until we actually play them again face to face. I can't quite see them coming down to Division One, so it's up to us to get back into the Premiership to do that. However, if we can emulate any of the success that United have had I'll be delighted.

The support here is renowned, and to see 200 fans welcome me at the ground when I first arrived was great – there were only about three when I became manager of Palace! The fact that 25,000 fans regularly come to Maine Road, despite recent circumstances, speaks for itself. Their loyalty is amazing, and all I ask is that they're patient.

Fans demand a lot, whatever team they support. Their club is very special to them and is a massive part of their life, and I understand that City fans in particular are in need of a few good times. Improvement can't happen overnight, but I want them to know that I'll be putting everything into this job."

Lee seemed prepared for patience and announced: "With the appointment of Steve Coppell, I really feel we've turned the corner. I like everything I have heard about him, particularly his record with young players and the way he has brought them on. It has taken a bit of time to bring someone in, but we were determined not to rush into a wrong appointment. Believe me, things are looking up."

Within those statements there were hints of the troubles ahead; Coppell anticipating the right to request reinforcements after a period of stocktaking, while Lee appeared heartened by the manager's ability to develop young talent, perhaps largely because it hinted at a potential to be prudent. Yet perhaps the warning signs were already there for both parties. City was Coppell's second-chance saloon, the door opening after his route back in to the Palace job was blocked by Dave Bassett's sudden decision to stay at Selhurst Park as he turned down the Maine Road job Lee had offered him.

Should Coppell not have been wary when the wily Bassett suddenly decided to stay? Should Lee, who had considered taking over as manager himself as his search for Alan Ball's replacement dragged on, have been guarded after Coppell had walked out on Palace following the club's relegation from the Premiership in 1993, or the rumours that he favoured a job near his new home in London rather than a return to the north west? For his part, Coppell may have thought that fate was trying to tell him something. After all, Bassett's u-turn was similar to that which had given Coppell his first break in football management. In 1984, Bassett turned his back on Noades and returned to Wimbledon just four days after accepting the Palace job that was to become Coppell's first managerial role.

Some Manchester City fans were guarded over the appointment of Coppell, partly because of the new man's Old Trafford connections and partly as a result of his resignation following Palace's top-flight demise. Did he have the stickability necessary to make it work at Maine Road? The majority were at least cautiously optimistic, given that City had become a laughing stock following their 5-1 aggregate League Cup exit at the hands of Lincoln a fortnight earlier. After Ball's disastrous reign and the long wait for his replacement, City's fans at last felt they were not going to be a comedy club any longer.

So it was to a backdrop of genuine shock that Lee and Coppell sat side by side again on the morning of 8 November to announce that the manager had quit "on medical advice". Coppell, looking pale and haunted, read a prepared statement which revealed that the pressure of the job had "completely overwhelmed" him and made him ill. As Coppell was reading out his statement, the players were hearing the news from his assistant Neal, who himself was still in a state of disbelief. "It was a shock to all of us. It certainly wasn't something we had discussed," Neal told me. "Stevie didn't even let me know his thoughts – he just came in to training and said, 'you take the first-team, I'm going'. I just looked at him and said: 'WHAT?' It was a bolt out of the blue and he didn't explain his decision at all. He was quite an inward person like that and quite a secretive type. He said he couldn't tell me the full reason and he got my goat because I had to go and take training and there he was at the press conference saying cheerio. He left me in an awkward position, obviously."

McGoldrick added: "There was no indication whatsoever that he was going to walk away from the club. Everything seemed fine, so it was a total shock, especially for me. I did not believe what had just taken place and I thought, *bloody hell, what's going to happen now?* As far as I was concerned, Steve was just beginning to turn things round and get his way, gradually stamping his authority on the football club."

McGoldrick could have been forgiven for thinking his own career was set for a renaissance in parallel with his new club's upturn in fortunes. Having come to Maine Road on loan from Arsenal to gain vital match fitness after a five-month injury absence, he had been quick to agree to a permanent deal following the appointment of his former Palace manager.

"I sometimes hear people say I had a nightmare at Arsenal, but to play 60 games in two seasons for a massive club like Arsenal, for me that was terrific. George Graham was well known for rotating his teams, but I played so many games in succession that Paul Merson started calling me 'Son of George'. Then I picked up a knee injury, the same knee I had injured at Palace, but a completely different injury. When I came back after five months out I needed to play, so I ended up going on loan to City. I was told to come in and steady the ship.

"Soon after I arrived there, I was hearing rumours to say Steve was coming in and one day as I was getting out my car at the training ground I saw him getting out of a taxi. As I walked over to say hello he said: 'I bet you are surprised to see me again!' I told him I was delighted to see him again.

"Steve had an immediate effect with his calmness and his composure. He brought that in straight away to the players and, because I knew him, people were asking me what he was like. I was telling them all he was top drawer and had no hesitation in saying that if the players stuck with him and the supporters stuck with him then he would turn the place around and it would be a great place to play – if you are there when things are going well then there isn't a better place to play."

Kit Symons, for one, did not need any persuading. The central defender was spared Neal's training ground revelation as he was away on international duty, though Wales's 7-1 capitulation in Holland made it a surreal and painful weekend for him. "To be honest, all the lads were really impressed with him when he first came in," Symons told me, adding: "He was very methodical, he did his homework on the opposition and we were all really excited. We thought things were finally going to start going in the right direction for us.

"The early signs were good. He was an affable guy and he didn't come in and make big sweeping gestures. He's more a man of words, Steve, he just goes about his job quietly, but he gave this sense of confidence in his manner. He wouldn't go and make big bold forecasts about us going out and winning our next ten games – he's a bright feller and just gets on with doing his job in what he thinks is the right way of doing it. That gave all the players confidence at that time."

That returning confidence was hardly in evidence during the first 30 minutes of Coppell's first match in charge, away to Queen's Park Rangers. City had reinvented McGoldrick as a sweeper and the new manager kept him in his new role, playing behind Symons, Darren Wassall and Ian Brightwell, with a midfield four of Nicky Summerbee, Nigel Clough, Steve Lomas and Georgi Kinkladze and a front two of Paul Dickov and Uwe Rosler. Dickov wasted a glorious chance to open the scoring early on before McGoldrick, a previously calming influence at the back, put his keeper Andy Dibble in trouble with a weak back header. Dibble rushed out of his goal to head clear, but Trevor Sinclair showed quick wits to fizz the ball back over Dibble and in from the best part of 50 yards.

Worse was to come for City and the last line of Coppell's defence as McGoldrick and Dibble suffered two more defensive misunderstandings which led to the two team-mates squaring up and being separated by Symons. Tempers were still frayed when McGoldrick slipped on a greasy surface and left Paul Murray in the clear to fire the home side 2-0 up. City could have collapsed; instead they responded within seconds as Lomas's cross was volleyed home by Brightwell. The goal had a catalytic effect and Coppell's first half-time team talk seemed to work as the visitors dominated the second half, playing the kind of confident free-flowing football which had been sadly lacking earlier in the season. Kinkladze, in particular, revelled in the wide role once held by his new boss and the home side struggled to contain the brilliant Georgian. Rosler hit the post and saw two penalty claims waved away before Andy Impey handled a Kinkladze shot on the line to earn himself a red card and allow Kinkladze to level from the spot. A tiring City failed to take advantage of the extra man and complete the comeback, but a vocal travelling support left Loftus Road talking more about promotion than relegation having seen their side dominate a football match for the first time in months.

Predictably, that optimism evaporated in a lame 2-0 defeat at Reading in which Lomas was sent off for an apparent stamp on Phil Parkinson, but returned once more when Coppell marked his first home game in charge with a 2-1 win over Norwich City. Typically, Coppell was heralded with the minimum fanfare and the Canaries were duly despatched in similarly unfussy fashion, Nigel Clough easing some early nerves with a first-half opener before Dickov's neat chip over Bryan Gunn nine minutes into the second half made the game safe. Keith Scott set up a nervy finish with a late goal, but City deservedly held on for their first win under their new manager.

The returning confidence was in evidence again in Coppell's fourth match, a live Sky game at home to Wolves, but despite almost constant pressure and a stunning long-range effort from Jeff Whitley that thudded against a post, City had nothing to show for their domination. Instead, a late Wolves break saw Steve Bull show the kind of clinical finishing City had lacked and left Coppell with nothing to show from a game his side had dominated.

With Lomas facing a three-match ban for his dismissal at Reading, Coppell returned to Selhurst Park to bring in Simon Rodger on loan to face Southend United at Roots Hall and the new boy, nicknamed 'Jolly', slotted in comfortably as City raced into a 3-0 lead with a Rosler goal just before half-time and two second-half strikes from the sublime Kinkladze. Once again, City fans were forced to endure late nerves as the side destined to finish bottom of the table scored twice late on and pressed for an equaliser, but luck appeared to be shifting back City's way.

The weight of anticipation remained heavy on everyone's shoulders, but Coppell was beginning to make his presence felt. "The expectation of that football club and the supporters is massive, absolutely massive," remembered McGoldrick, almost by way of a public health warning that Coppell may not have read. "With City having been relegated and Manchester United across the road there was added pressure. On top of that, Steve was an ex-United player, though I never felt that was a problem and I certainly didn't think the job was too big for him. It felt like he was well capable of handling that football club and moving it on to better things."

Neal agreed, telling me: "Stevie hadn't done disastrously badly; it wasn't as if the results were affecting the situation. He was as confident as ever and he was putting confidence and knowledge into the players before every game. Never too much, but enough to say 'beware of this', or 'let's go out and express ourselves'."

If there were underlying health problems, they weren't exactly showing, so why was Coppell just one week away from walking out of the club, just as matters on the pitch appeared to be improving, albeit slowly?

Paul Hince, chief sports writer of the *Manchester Evening News*, admits that no-one saw it coming, though the spot-the-difference nature of the manager's two main press conferences was a dramatic window on the pressures of football management. Hince told me: "I knew Steve as a player because I had played for City and we had come across each other a few times. I knew he was extremely bright and he'd done such a terrific job at Crystal Palace that I genuinely thought after years of dross he'd be the one to take us back to the top flight.

"In his first press conference he was very articulate and very confident. I remember coming back and saying 'that's it now, we are finally moving in the right direction again'. But 30-odd days later he was doing another press conference to announce he had quit. That time he looked physically ill. Really ill. He had lost a great deal of weight in a short time, and I am not talking a pound or two, he looked almost skeletal."

The speed of the departure and the bizarre circumstances around the second press conference, with no questions allowed and security guards posted on every door to keep reporters inside until the departing manager had cleared the building, led to more speculation than fact. If Coppell was simply suffering from stress, what had caused it? If stress was merely the reason given to hide the truth, what were the real reasons behind the departure?

"We felt there must have been something more to it the minute we walked into the press conference with security people all around the place. They even stopped us going out afterwards to see if we could have a word with him outside," Hince told me.

"We were told there was no point asking a question because it wouldn't be answered and that, coupled with how ill he looked, was what led to the rumours that there was something seriously wrong with him. All sorts of rumours started to circulate, not least AIDS. Our news desk reporters were phoning all the AIDS hospitals and asking 'can you put me through to Mr Coppell' hoping that one of them would say 'certainly sir, he's in room 28'. It was all completely unfounded, but that was at a period when AIDS was becoming more and more of an issue and it was one of the things people looked at if they saw someone had lost a great deal of weight."

Though the headline writers swept the City floor looking for scandalous rumours, it was not beyond the realms of possibility that Coppell was suffering a serious illness which he wanted to deal with privately and away from the public glare. Some years later another Manchester favourite, Brian Kidd, quit his role as England's assistant manager with the minimum of fuss in order to undergo treatment for prostate cancer, yet the real reasons for his departure were not divulged until he had made a full recovery.

Hince revealed: "Kidd was another shy manager, like Coppell in many ways and very introverted. He disappeared off the scene for a while and it turned out that he'd had prostate cancer, but he didn't want to announce it because he felt it would be unfair to the people he underwent chemotherapy with. He thought it would be like boasting to their families and saying 'I made it'.

"We have never known what happened to Steve Coppell in the weeks following his departure from Maine Road. I'm not suggesting Coppell had cancer, but he did look ill and it might be that he has recovered from something but chosen never to speak about it for the same reasons as Kidd."

Several years after his departure from City, Coppell underwent a series of cardiac tests after a heart murmur was investigated, though he was given the all-clear and there has never been any suggestion that he suffered the problem during his short City tenure. Having been through cardiac tests and treatment myself for many years, I know the stresses it can cause but can only imagine the added strain of coupling those anxieties with such a high-profile role. Even so, it may be churlish to seek alternative causes given that my GP assured me that stress can indeed strip stones off a sufferer in a matter of weeks, though he did also point out that some patients gain weight due to 'comfort eating'.

Whatever the cause, whatever the symptoms, Coppell was, in so many ways, a victim of bad timing. Journalist Bob Harris, a close friend of Coppell's, explained: "Journalism at that time was changing. It was getting dirty and the red top war between the *Sun* and *Mirror* was in full flow. You look at Bobby Robson, the loved Bobby Robson, who was treated appallingly," he added, recalling a media campaign to remove the England manager that peaked with the headline 'In the name of Allah, go!' after a 1-1 draw in Saudi Arabia shortly after England had crashed out of the 1988 European Championships, losing all three group games. "It was happening everywhere and Steve was just unlucky he was caught in that trap.

"He actually used to laugh about it. One rumour claimed he was caught in the shower with a player and I rung him up and we just laughed. The truth always comes out in the end. Always, without a doubt. If there was anything sinister to reveal, we would know it by now, but there has not been a word on Steve. Never. If there was anything really sinister at the time I for one would have known about it. I wasn't a bad journalist!"

Harris was closer to Coppell on a personal level than most journalists ever get and Hince was close enough on a professional level to agree that the truth will always out. He said: "Professional football is like a village – if something sordid happens in the dressing room at Southampton they will know about it in Newcastle within a few hours – if there had been anything about Coppell's departure it would have come out. These things always come out in the end with a manager; if he has done something terrible, or even if it is something as simple as he couldn't get on with the chairman, or he fell out with the chief executive because he had too much influence.

"In all my time covering City, I have rarely known a manager who has left or been sacked without me finding out what went wrong, either at the time or further down the line. But in Steve Coppell's case: no idea! I was a City player and have covered them for donkey's years and knew most of what went on in the club, but I never got anywhere within sniffing distance of why he actually went – unless it really was just as simple as he realised he made a mistake and could not go on. It could have been that – we always look for more complicated reasons, even when they are not there.

"I remember as a player when I left City and signed for Charlton Athletic; within a week I knew I had made a dreadful mistake. I couldn't tell you why, I just felt that this was the wrong club for me. It's horses for courses and when you are involved in football you sometimes get that sort of feeling."

The fact, it seems, is less exciting than the fiction. Stress was the official reason for Coppell's exit and, to this day, seems the most likely explanation, but only in that it was merely the tip of the iceberg. The underlying causes of his dramatic decline in health were clearly many and varied. The job was undoubtedly more stressful than he anticipated, not least because he started to feel he was not going to get the financial assistance or support that he thought he needed. Yet, whatever was said in private, it also appears clear that any expectations of financial help were based on assumption, rather than any public promises from the chairman. It may not have been a coincidence that Coppell quit in the same week as City announced their latest fiscal results. The club announced a working deficit of £3 million for the past financial year, compared to a profit of £203,000 for the previous year, leaving them with debts of £26 million against an asset base of £33 million. Just as Coppell's reconnaissance period was concluding, the transfer kitty would have been empty.

It certainly seems clear that any figures put on the funds available to Coppell at that time were purely speculative. Before City announced their 12-month results, there had been widespread claims that Coppell would have £5 million at his disposal, but when that figure was put to the new manager in a Radio 5 Live football forum in Manchester during his first week in charge, Coppell's response was: "that's not what he [Franny] told me."

According to Hince: "The whole team needed to be rebuilt. I think Steve had probably been in to see Francis Lee and said 'I think we need that' and was told 'sorry, we haven't got the money for it'. Somehow, though, I can't see Francis employing a manager, making an offer of funds available to improve the team and then just laughing in his face and saying 'you're not having it'. Certainly Francis Lee never came out at the time and said, 'we've got Steve Coppell and now he's going to have a £15 million war chest', but the assumption was there from everybody. You bring a new manager in and you expect him to improve the team by bringing new players in.

"The story at that time was that he'd given Coppell six matches to assess the team; Steve must have gone and told him what he wanted and Francis looked at it and said 'you are not getting it'. The rumours were that he said to Francis that City were going to go down with what he had and said, 'you are not taking me with you'."

The first item on Coppell's shopping list when he arrived at Maine Road was apparently a new goalkeeper. Reports at that time suggest his number one target, Watford's Kevin Miller, was deemed too expensive at £2 million and so too was his second choice, Luton's giant Iain Feuer at £1 million. Instead, Coppell was encouraged to take a look at Australian keeper Mark Schwarzer, available from Kaiserslautern for a modest £250,000. Schwarzer spent a week training with City, playing a behind closed doors friendly with Wrexham, before eventually signing for Bradford City and his presence seemed to inspire the under-pressure Dibble who had a fine game at Swindon. But even a string of outstanding saves, including a penalty stop from Kevin Horlock, could not keep City in the game as two Wayne Allison goals secured an all-too-comfortable win for the Wiltshire side in what turned out to be Coppell's last game in charge.

Whatever the truth over the levels of funding made available to Coppell, if the chairman – a former player turned business millionaire with strong opinions – had tried to influence his manager's transfer targets or team selection, it would have been an intrusion that the single-minded Coppell would not tolerate. "You wouldn't do that to Steve Coppell, he would just be out the door," Hince added.

Coppell's close friend and players' union man Gordon Taylor agreed, telling me: "I was never quite sure what went wrong at Manchester City, though he had a chairman in Francis Lee who I knew as a larger than life character who would not get involved in owning anything without wanting to have his say. In fairness,

Franny was a top player and a top businessman. The reality is that Steve would always be prepared to take the consequences over things as long as they were his decisions, but he would certainly not be willing to accept the consequences over decisions that were not his."

Taylor highlighted another factor that would have weighed heavily on Coppell's increasingly strained state of mind, telling me: "Steve was very much the family man. A lot of football things used to happen on a Sunday but Steve wouldn't attend. He was always adamant that Sunday was the time for his family, especially his son."

Coppell's mood over the goalkeeper situation would therefore not have been helped by the hectic schedule of away games which had meant the new manager had little time to settle. Complications in his personal life might have been easier to deal with had Coppell been able to spend more time at home and less on the road. Instead, the strain his marriage had suffered during his early days as a manager was this time tested to breaking point as his life became one long road trip. Coppell had written in his autobiography of his early steps into the management game with Crystal Palace: 'It was tougher on Jane, as I was off to live in a flat in London while she looked after our house, her job and her sick father. If we had a weekend match in the north I would stop off in Cheshire, otherwise she would catch the train to London on a Friday night.

'On a typical weekend the uncomplaining Jane would arrive at Euston on Friday night, we would grab a quick drink and snack in a wine bar, getting back to Surrey in time for me to make my telephone calls and for Jane to do the laundry. On Saturday I would be off to football while Jane would go to the shops to buy my weekly groceries, clean the flat and look for a house. Providing the game was not too far away I would be back in time for her to cook dinner. On Sunday morning I would call in at Selhurst Park to see if there were any injuries from the day before and then, if I was not due to watch a player in Ireland or on a local park, we would look at more houses before I drove her to Euston in time to catch the 6pm back north. Added to all that, I am a bad loser and more often than not returned home in a foul mood after suffering the latest setback. Those were the black moments when I would wonder what the hell I was doing in the job.'

A decade on, the strain of management had taken its toll and while Jane remained in the Surrey home with 10-year-old Mark, Coppell headed back to Manchester to take on the City job. The manager's reasons for originally wanting a job closer to home were becoming painfully clear.

Harris, who helped Coppell pen those original words in *Touch and Go*, explained to me: "During that time at City he was going through a divorce and he was terribly upset at not seeing his son every day. It was very difficult and awkward. There is a strain on marriages in football, but Steve made a point of going to watch the players he wanted to buy and would come back in the early hours of the morning. It's hellish.

"Going to City was the greatest mistake of his professional career, but while there were clearly problems you can forget all the lurid stories. That was all nonsense. As far as I know, there was no awkwardness at working with Franny Lee, but I don't know at what level the problems were because he didn't divulge to me. We are all still guessing at the answers and we don't know the whole truth, but stress still seems the most logical explanation."

Perhaps the most significant witness in the investigation into what caused that stress is Dave Bassett, who seemed set to accept the City challenge before stunning everyone by staying at Palace. Working with Coppell at Palace, Bassett was perfectly placed to offer his director of football a reference for the job, but Coppell never asked for his opinion.

"I would go for runs with Steve on occasions at the training ground and it was surprising that he went there without asking me anything about it. He knew I had turned the job down so I was taken aback that he didn't ask me why, though that is not to say whether or not he would have taken it," Bassett told me.

"If he had asked, I would have told him that, in my opinion, Francis Lee was the wrong type of chairman for Steve Coppell, who in my opinion is a manager who has got to be allowed to get on with it. I was aware that Franny Lee would be too powerful and too demanding for Coppell's personality which would result in wearing him out." Or, to put it more simply, Bassett added: "I reckon Franny Lee would have driven him mad."

Bassett explained the research on which he based his opinions: "I had two interviews at City and I was close to taking the job. I met Franny Lee and the problem for me was that he was a successful and powerful man that wanted his say. I felt he would have been very hands on and demanding, whereas at Palace Ron just let me get on with it most of the time.

"The chairman of a football club commands a certain amount of respect but I just felt that at City I would have been spending too much time and energy on the chairman. Franny had his own business and was a hands-on chairman. That's just the way he is, he wants to be involved and that is fair enough, but for me to be successful as a manager all my energy has to be in the right places – the players, the staff, the recruitment and the media. I was of the opinion that Francis Lee would have been on the phone every day.

"I also felt that City had too many 'moles' – people reporting back to the chairman. Ron had one or two at Palace but there were never any problems; they would tell the chairman what was going on, but that was that – end of story.

"After my second interview I said, 'let me go away and think about it' and then I got a phone call from someone in the media saying City had organised a press conference to announce me as manager. I just thought *fuck you, I'm not going*".

Instead, Coppell took the opportunity that Bassett had turned down, but soon the combined pressures outlined by those closest to him at that time took their toll.

McGoldrick could see the strain playing out, adding: "He was going through a period in his personal life that meant it wasn't the right time for him and he never really got a settled base because in the first five weeks of his arrival we had three away games. He would be in Manchester for two days then out on the road, then he'd stay down south for a while and we would see him again on a Friday. He was going through a bad stage in his life and maybe it was just too much for him."

Symons believes it is only with the benefit of hindsight that Coppell's players became aware of the pressure he was facing. "It came as a real shock that he went, but looking back he looked like a man with the weight of the world on his shoulders," Symons told me, adding: "He lost a lot of weight, went really gaunt and he didn't look good. As players, you just get on and play football and you don't really notice too many other things around you, but as soon as it all happened I sort of looked at Steve and realised he didn't look so great. He was normally such a healthy looking feller.

"You do feel the pressure at City as a player, without a shadow of a doubt. It is a huge club and there were a lot of things not right behind the scenes at that time, so it may be that he realised how big a job and how big a club it was and thought he wasn't able to get everything the way he needed it to do the job right."

Coppell, though he may have been doubting the wisdom of his decision to take the job, was intelligent enough to know when something was not right – and he was never afraid to confront an issue with total honesty. His Palace walk-out had not been due to stress or hurt pride, it had been a brutal statement of the need for change at the club which had given him his first chance in management. So when it became apparent to Coppell that his new nomadic lifestyle would not be compensated by his own interpretation of the tools required for the City job, the manager told Lee straight. It simply wasn't the role he had envisaged. Expectation was the killer word; City's expectations were hard for Coppell to live up to, while his own expectations of the support he was to receive looked unlikely to be met.

Coppell wanted out. There and then. But Lee and his board were wary of treating the British football public to yet another City circus. They told Coppell he was free to leave, but only if he publicly shouldered the humiliation of his departure. Desperate to get out as soon as he could Coppell agreed and, in my view, he has regretted his agreement ever since.

Hince added: "This was a time when the club was being mocked all over the country – there were managers who wouldn't touch that job with a barge pole.

Francis would have thought, *finally I have got a decent manager*, but then ended up with egg all over his face, so he would not have been well pleased."

Yet, despite that displeasure, Lee then did something that few would have predicted. Hince told me: "Years later, Francis showed me a letter. Even though Steve resigned, Francis offered him a payment of £30,000, which he was not obliged to do. That was a lot of money and I saw the letter that Coppell wrote back to him thanking him but saying 'no, because I haven't earned it', but underlining that he appreciated the gesture."

Lee's act of goodwill hints at a level of concern that had not been obvious as Coppell faced the music on 8 November 1996, the watching football world gawping in disbelief while his players and staff tried to come to terms with what was happening.

Chris Evans interrupted his *TFI Friday* show on Channel 4 to announce the decision as Coppell struggled to force out the words: "I'm not ashamed to admit that I have suffered for some time from huge pressure I have imposed upon myself and, since my appointment, this has completely overwhelmed me to such an extent that I cannot function in the job the way I would like to.

"As this situation is affecting my well-being, I have asked Francis Lee to relieve me of my obligation to manage the club on medical advice. I am therefore resigning for personal reasons. I'm extremely embarrassed by the situation and I would like to apologise first and foremost to Francis Lee and his board, who have done everything in their power to help me."

That press conference was borderline cruelty – if Coppell was suffering huge stress then parading him in front of the cameras could not possibly have helped – and City's players found it painful viewing when they sat through the TV news later that day.

"It was just numbing for us; a real feeling of shock and disappointment," McGoldrick remembered. "I was disappointed, devastated in fact, but when I saw that press conference and saw how emotional things were for him at that time I thought, *hang on a minute, he's more important than the football club*. His health was paramount and although we were bitterly disappointed, we knew that as long as Steve was going to be okay then that was the most important thing.

"Maybe it was a little bit insensitive of the club to hold that press conference – maybe Steve didn't have to be there and they could have done it as a board on their own. But in a way perhaps they had to do that because they had been through so much turmoil in the previous year with changes of managers and being relegated. There was upheaval going on at the club at the time with boardroom struggles and Fran coming in."

While fans drew their own conclusions and the newly-established internet chat rooms continued to go berserk with scurrilous and libellous rumours as to the real reasons behind the split, Coppell's friends and former players felt able to read between the lines and get a little closer to the truth.

John Salako watched the drama unfold and recalled: "He went to Manchester City as an ex-Manchester United player. City at the time were in turmoil and were badly run; there were huge expectations, but they were rudderless with no systematic approach in the way they were running the business. I think he looked at the situation and thought, *this is not for me. I can't work like this with these people.*

"Steve wants to be in control and make his own transfers and he will make his mind up pretty quick. He's very intelligent and astute and does not have the need to be successful and on the front page of newspapers or in front of the cameras with the lights on him. I was looking at pictures of us walking out at Wembley against Manchester United in 1990 and even then he's in the background. He's suited to those clubs who let him do that."

Another hero of that Wembley season, semi-final matchwinner Alan Pardew, also drew his own conclusions from seeing Coppell's press conference. He said: "I was at Barnet at the time and, although I never knew what happened, I just remember seeing him on the TV and thinking, *that is so Steve.*

"If he is not happy, if he doesn't feel right and doesn't think it's working, he will be man enough to walk away. It was quite understandable to me; he was a legend at Manchester United and was going back to Manchester City – probably not his best career move – but when you leave a club like that, people think that something sinister must have gone on, and that was never the case.

"I had a similar situation myself at West Ham about which I will always hold to my counsel. That is our right as individuals. The rumours I heard about me at West Ham were unbelievable and Steve had that at City too."

Coppell's former United team-mate Lou Macari had been linked with the Maine Road job, but insisted the stability the pair enjoyed as players with United was far removed from the insecurities of the role at Manchester City, a club crying out for a calm managerial hand at the helm. He told me: "The press lads wrote various things, but the real reason was simply that if he wasn't happy he wouldn't hang around. He certainly would not have encountered the same atmosphere as when he joined United as a player; it was never uncomfortable once you were at Old Trafford – we had all types of lads and we all shared the spotlight."

Coppell has never felt comfortable in the spotlight, though his desire for a quick getaway from City meant it was impossible to escape the media glare as rumour and ridicule engulfed the football world. Coppell could have quickly nipped those newspaper and internet rumours in the bud, but chose to ignore the speculation and retain his dignity, even if it meant the rumour-mongers would have a field day feeding on the scraps he had left behind.

"It was a private moment in my life and I don't want to talk about it. But it wasn't what it seemed," he told me during his Reading reign, as close to spilling the beans as he is ever likely to come.

He did not even tell those closest to him the full extent of the problems he had faced, as Bassett explained. "We didn't talk about it. Steve is a very private man and it was not for me to tell him what I thought. We never discussed it, though he knew that I knew and I knew that he knew. Even so, I had been surprised that he never said 'what about it? Why did you turn it down?'

"When Steve came back he'd lost a lot of weight. For a week or two there were all sorts of silly rumours; all a load of bollocks, but what happened left an indelible mark."

"I felt it was a very brave decision for him to make," Symons told me. "Whatever his reasons were, for someone after six weeks to say 'no, it's not right, I'm not going to do myself justice or the club justice', it's a brave thing to do and not an easy decision to come to.

There were some outrageous, quite terrible rumours going around about why he left. We knew ourselves as players that some of the things being talked about were an absolute load of rubbish but people love a bit of gossip and a good story and because his departure was so out of the ordinary the rumours came thick and fast.

"From a selfish point of view, you think, *oh God, here we go again,* but because of the mess the club was in at that time it almost wasn't that big a deal to start looking for a new manager. It had become quite a regular event at City at that time. City fans are fantastic supporters, but they almost enjoy the notoriety of the team being in disarray – their attitude was 'look at us we are still supporting our club even though it's a bit of a shambles'."

While those City fans who had expressed reservations of a former United player coming in at Maine Road adopted a 'told you so' attitude, others preferred a black-humour approach. If Coppell was stressed after 33 days, how the hell did he think they felt after years of supporting their club? The majority registered genuine sympathy and concern for their short-stay manager; ill health and ill advice were causing equal concern and Lee, rightly or wrongly, remained the main outlet for their frustrations.

"I think the fans were disappointed," Hince told me. "Even though he was a Manchester United footballer the City fans were really excited because they had a manager of his calibre. There was never any backlash from the crowd, even when City had lost matches under Steve they never sang 'you don't know what you're doing', which they used to sing on a regular basis to Alan Ball!

"He was highly respected by the City fans. They had no problems with him being a former Red and I still haven't changed my mind; I don't think they could have got a better manager. His knowledge of the game and his respect from the fans meant he was ideal, but something went horribly wrong."

The fans' respect hinted at an even greater potential loss to the city of Manchester, according to Hince's *Manchester Evening News* colleague David Meek, the newspaper's respected Manchester United correspondent. He told me: "The City fans would have welcomed him on to the Manchester scene and in many ways he might have bridged the hostility between the two clubs. Hostile was never his nature and being abrasive was never in his personality."

Lee bore the brunt of the fans' backlash, but responded by saying: "When you hear the things that were said it hurts, but I have made a large investment in this club and I will not be walking away. If I walk away from it now, I would be admitting defeat and missing out on what could be a much better period and brighter future for the club."

Coppell's sudden and dramatic departure also left Phil Neal in a dreadful position. Persuaded by his friend and former England team-mate to leave Cardiff and become Coppell's right-hand man, Neal suddenly found himself at the centre of another farce even more bizarre than the TV documentary on England manager Graham Taylor which had indirectly ridiculed Neal. The infamous documentary failed to show Neal in his true colours; that of a quiet and single-minded football man whose views are never less than straight-forward and honest. Forged from the same England mould that produced Coppell, Neal's straight-bat approach was exactly what City needed in a time of turmoil as he took on the dreaded role of caretaker manager.

"He never really explained it to me," adds Neal, with the air of a man mourning a loved one he never got the chance to say goodbye to. "I don't know what the reasons were – he was quite a secretive type of person and he coped with that on his own really because I don't think he ever explained the real reason why he left. I had left Cardiff managerless and, although I did have a couple of months after Steve left to try and impress the Manchester City directors that I should get the manager's job permanently, it was never going to happen."

Graham Taylor's own reflections having been sacked as England manager two years earlier, a vacancy Coppell had been tipped to fill, proved somewhat prophetic. He said: "It's like taking any job. Until you've done it the first time, you think about what it's like and then you suddenly find out what it really is like."

While Neal was the unintended victim of the fall-out, Coppell returned to the comforting bosom of Selhurst Park where he became chief scout, a position which allowed him to remain in the game, but still get over the shock of what had happened. "I was surprised at how much it took out of him. I think he found the club too enormous, but he weathered it," said Palace chairman Noades.

Coppell recovered quicker than City, who despite finishing in mid-table under new boss Frank Clark that season, were relegated again the following year. It took the appointment of another Quarry Bank School old boy, Joe Royle, to revive City's fortunes and steer them back to stability. Symons witnessed the full procession of managers and told me: "It really was a very messy time and it's such a shame because I have really fond memories of the club. It is a fantastic club, it really is, but they were going through a really bad time and unfortunately a lot of the players or managers at the club at that time had to suffer with it. It wasn't easy at all and because it was such a big club with such great tradition the pressure became even greater.

"These were good people who were coming in; Steve, Frank Clarke and Joe Royle were all really good experienced managers and they all found it very difficult at the club at the time. That is testament to what had gone on in the past and some of the things going on behind the scenes then. It's amazing to see the club now compared to how it was when I was there. I have got a lot of time for Steve and he obviously went on and did an excellent job at other places. So I'm convinced that with the right time he would have done that job at City."

As McGoldrick contemplated his own fledgling coaching career and the routes he might follow from Northampton, just as he did as a player two decades ago, he had some sympathy for his former mentor. "You talk about players picking wrong moves or it turning into a wrong move and it seemed to be that for Steve at the time," he surmised. "It was probably the right place at the wrong time for Steve – we will never know. Steve has always been and always will be a very private person; he focuses on his job and always has done. I'm sure Steve and all managers and players look back at things that happened in their career and realise that you quickly get over them. He was taking Crystal Palace up six months later, so he quickly got over it through his strength of character. That shows the person he is."

Hince, the former City player turned City journalist, talked in headlines as he added: "It remains a football mystery. If there was anything sinister then in all honesty it is the best kept secret of all time. I think many things had a bearing: he wasn't going to get the money he expected to build a team; his domestic problems and the fact he simply realised he had made a mistake. City just weren't the club for him, but nobody, apart from Steve himself, knows the real reasons why he didn't stay at City."

Finding out the truth about what really went on in a single month at Manchester City is about as easy as getting your hands on Colonel Sanders' secret recipe, or putting a name to Jack the Ripper, but my own opinion is that, just as Steve Coppell's teams become a sum greater than their parts, so too did the stress levels that led to his Maine Road departure. The break-up of his marriage and the distance between Coppell and the son he doted on were crucial factors in his struggle to find any semblance of a work-life balance. The realisation that he would not be able to sign the players he wanted, or spend the money he felt was needed, regardless of whether or not it had been promised in the first place, would only have added to the strain. In isolation, any of those factors might have been bearable, but add them to the pressures of life on the road and the huge expectations of City's fans and it is little wonder that Coppell's world caved in. If timing is everything in comedy, it must also be a vital ingredient in tragedy.

Lee, a City legend on the pitch, did not deserve the situation either and found it harder to recover from the experience as he remained the butt of terrace jokes long after Coppell had recovered his health and his pride. In true Ronnie Corbett style, I shall end this chapter with the best of them:

Franny Lee was in a supermarket when he spotted an old lady struggling under several bags of shopping. Franny leant down and asked her: "Can you manage dear?" The old woman replied: "Get lost! You got City into this mess, don't ask me to sort it out!"

The young Coppell takes on QPR's Ian Gillard at Loftus Road.

Tommy Docherty, the man who gave Coppell his chance in the big time at Manchester United.

Celebrating Manchester United's fortunate winning goal in the 2-1 1977 FA Cup final victory over Liverpool with Stuart Pearson.

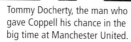

Celebrating with the trophy, Stuart Pearson and Sammy McIlroy. During the evening's celebrations Coppell would drop and dent the FA Cup.

Listening to new United manager Dave Sexton in training.

Coppell appeared in a record-breaking 206 consecutive matches for United between January 1977 and November 1981.

Coppell won his first England cap against Italy in November 1977.

Coppell scores past Scotland's George Wood in England's 3-1 victory at Wembley.

Scourge of the Scots: Coppell hammers in a shot at Hampden Park in 1980. He scored in each of his three appearances against the Auld Enemy.

Taking on Archie Gemmill at Hampden.

Showing all his flair in roasting the Romanian left-back in April 1981.

Carried from Wembley after Hungarian full-back Jozsef Toth shattered Coppell's knee in a tackle during the vital World Cup qualifier in November 1981.

Shaping to shoot against France in England's opening game of the 1982 World Cup.

Flying down the wing against the French.

Preparing to face West Germany in a crucial second phase game. It was to be the last game of the tournament for England's "little fly" as a reaction to a steroid injection left him sick and unable to face Spain.

Taking on Ronnie Whelan and (right) tackling Mark Lawrenson as United lose the 1983 League Cup final 2-1 to Liverpool.

In June 1984, Coppell became the Football League's youngest manager, taking over at Crystal Palace one month short of his 29th birthday.

Palace's devastating duo: Mark Bright (left) and Ian Wright. Introduced to the first team by Coppell, the strikeforce led Palace to promotion via play-off victories over Swindon Town and Blackburn in 1989.

Alan Pardew scores the winning goal in the incredible 4-3 victory over Liverpool in the 1990 FA Cup semi-final at Villa Park.

Leading out Palace for the 1990 FA Cup final alongside under-pressure Manchester United manager Alex Ferguson. "Inadvertently, we were the catalyst for an empire," Coppell said.

Ian Wright's introduction from the bench changed the face of the FA Cup final. Coppell unleashed the striker, who was coming back from injury, with 20 minutes remaining in normal time, and he scored twice as the game ended 3-3. Here he nets Palace's third goal of the game to put them 3-2 ahead.

Coppell joined Manchester City after the club had been relegated from the Premier League and begun the First Division season poorly under Alan Ball. His first game in charge saw a tumultuous 2-2 draw at QPR, in which Steve Lomas was sent off. Here fans celebrate Georgi Kinkladze's penalty ... and in the next photo Coppell looks on impassively.

It wasn't long before Coppell was moving on again, although under something of a mysterious cloud after few questions were answered in his farewell press conference with chairman Francis Lee.

Appointed Palace manager again following Dave Bassett's departure on 28 February 1997. Coppell had four separate spells in charge at Selhurst Park, as well as stints as Director of Football.

Getting the best out of Swedish international striker Tomas Brolin.

Celebrating winning promotion via the play-offs again, this time with Ron Noades after David Hopkin's last minute extra-time goal defeated Sheffield United.

Sharing the joy of promotion with son Mark.

Introducing Attilio Lombardo as Palace's new manager in March 1998.

With Palace perilously close to going under and in administration, Coppell enlists the help of comedian Kevin Day to publicise the club's plight in February 2000.

Red Nose Day: promoting Comic Relief in February 2001.

Coppell was appointed manager of Brentford by his old chairman at Palace, Ron Noades, who had taken over the west London club in May 2001.

Lloyd Owusu netted 22 goals in the 2001/02 season, which saw Brentford come so close to winning promotion to the First Division.

Martin Rowlands scores the opening goal in the vital final day of the season clash against Reading, but Jamie Cureton's goal 13 minutes from time gave Reading the second automatic promotion spot and consigned Brentford to the play-offs.

Goalscorers Lloyd Owusu (left) and Darren Powell celebrate Brentford's 2-1 win over Huddersfield in the play-off semi-finals and a place in the Millenium Stadium final.

Coppell applauds the Brentford fans after seeing the Bees reach Cardiff.

Coppell could only watch as his team were outfought 2-0 by Stoke City in the 2002 play-off final.

One of Coppell's earliest games in charge of Brighton was against former club Palace. The Eagles won 5-0, but Coppell began to turn around Albion's horrendous early season form and brought them back into contention to remain in the First Division against all the odds.

Brighton fans idolised both Coppell and his star striker Bobby Zamora (right).

On-loan midfielder Steve Sidwell was a key member of that Brighton side.

Zamora nets a penalty at Grimsby on the final day of the 2002/03 season. The must-win game ended 2-2…

… and Brighton were relegated back to the Second Division after only a single season in the First.

Brighton fans show their appreciation of the team and manager's efforts, despite the agony of relegation at Blundell Park.

Coppell's Royals reign got off to a victorious start as Reading won his first game in charge, 2-1 against Gillingham.

American international goalkeeper Marcus Hahnemann was a crucial part of Coppell's rebuilding plans at the Madejski Stadium.

Wigan's Jason Roberts scores the second goal in a 3-1 win over Coppell's Reading as the Latics secure a place in the Premiership and leave the Royals agonisingly short of the play-offs.

Coppell shows off his Manager of the Month trophy as Reading storm to the top of the Championship table early in the 2005/06 season. They would set a record for a 46-game season with 106 points.

Coppell and chairman John Madejski celebrate promotion to the Premiership for the first time in Reading's history following the 1-1 draw at Leicester in March 2006.

Coppell and his coaching staff say 'hello' to the Premiership.

Lifting the Championship trophy following the 2-1 victory over QPR on the final day of the 2005/06 season.

Coppell was awarded the League Manager Association's manager of the year award in 2006.

Signing autographs for Reading fans at the pre-season friendly against Bromley in July 2006.

Welcome to the Premiership. Reading found themselves 2-0 down at home to Middlesbrough on the Royals' top-flight debut, but fought back to secure a memorable 3-2 victory.

Coppell locks horns with Rafa Benitez as Liverpool win a League Cup thriller 4-3 at Anfield.

Coppell is calm amidst a sea of controversy during the battle between Reading and Neil Warnock's feisty Sheffield United in January 2007.

LMA manager of the year for the second year in a row: here interviewed by Sky Sports' Claire Tomlinson.

The 2007/08 season began with Coppell masterminding Reading's goalless draw at Old Trafford.

Reading's season began to fall apart after a 7-4 defeat at Portsmouth and despite Coppell's efforts the Royals won only 5 out of 26 matches to fall into serious relegation danger.

A last minute 1-0 win at Middlesbrough thanks to James Harper's goal (left) and a 2-0 victory over Manchester City at the Madejski, aided by Shane Long's opener (right), seemed to have set Reading on the right road…

…but six games without a goal in the spring of 2008 saw Reading sink into danger. Despite a final day 4-0 victory at doomed Derby, the Royals were relegated.

Having failed to prompt Reading back into the top flight at the first time of asking Coppell resigned, announcing his decision on 14 May 2009. He declared that he wanted a break, but insisted his footballing story was by no means over.

INJURY TIME BOMB

Tick tock, tick tock . . . every watch inside Wembley Stadium begins its countdown to Spain the moment Georges Konrath's whistle sounds for the start of the crucial final qualifier with Hungary. England need only a draw to secure their place, but are keen to qualify in style. Already confirmed as group winners, the only style Hungary have in mind is that of London's West End. They have not come to play with flair, they have come to buy flares . . . 90 minutes to go . . . tick tock, tick tock . . . England edge in front after 14 minutes, Paul Mariner's goal is scrappy, but celebrated as if it were a 30-yard screamer . . . 76 minutes to go . . . tick tock, tick tock . . . just keep possession and everyone heads to Spain; out of the corner of his eye Steve Coppell sees his marker, burly defender Jozsef Toth, hurtling towards him. All it needs is a quick push of the ball past him and a skip down the line and Coppell is away in space, while Toth will be forced to dust himself down and chase back . . . but Toth does not stop and, suddenly, Coppell is flying . . . 30 minutes to go . . . tick tock, tick tock . . . silence, a moment's silence, and then the crashing roar of pain with a backing track of crowd noise; shouting, abusing, encouraging. Coppell on his hands and knees, fire inside his left knee, the burning sensation of pain masked only slightly by the anaesthetic of adrenalin. Slowly, he crawls across the touchline, the nausea rising as the confusion contracts . . . tick tock, tick tock . . . Tony Morley is running on for his England debut as Coppell is crawling off, one man's pain another's gain . . . slowly there is clarity, but still pain. England's flying winger is now England's injured winger and as he limps to the England bench thoughts of White Hart Lane on Saturday, of Spain next summer, bring the pain to another level, a feeling of nausea in the pit of his stomach. But it will be fine. Steve Coppell injuries are rare – he has not missed a Manchester United game in four years – and this is nothing serious . . . is it? Tick, tock . . .

FEW OBSERVERS ARE better qualified to commentate on the emergence of Steve Coppell the player than *Manchester Evening News*'s former United correspondent David Meek. As United were celebrating their centenary year in 1978, Meek was chalking up his 20th year of covering the club, though the circumstances of his elevation to the role mean it is rarely an anniversary he celebrates. The Munich air disaster on 6 February 1958 tore the heart out of Manchester United – eight of the club's finest players among the 23 who lost their lives – but it also had a profound effect on British journalism. Eight of the dead were from Manchester's equivalent of Fleet Street – Alf Clarke (*Manchester Evening Chronicle*), HD Davies (*Manchester Guardian*), George Follows (*Daily Herald*), Archie Ledbrooke (*Daily Mirror*), Henry Rose (*Daily Express*), Frank Swift (*News of the World*) and Eric Thompson (*Daily Mail*) all died; and so too did Tom Jackson, who had covered United for the *Manchester Evening News* for a quarter of a century.

Meek, originally a political leader writer for the paper, was charged with filling the void left by Jackson's passing, but only on a temporary basis. Thirty-seven years later he finally gave up his temporary role, United's 1995 FA Cup final defeat at the hands of Everton the concluding duty in a career during which he filed more than 2,000 match reports.

Meek is a journalistic institution, so there was a feeling of genuine excitement as I prepared to talk all things United with someone who knows them better than most. David was excited too when we met, quizzing me on my Berkshire location; nothing to do with Coppell's six years in charge of Reading, but because of the Reading hockey team that boast a reputation in their game to rival United's standing in football. He loves his hockey, does David, and I could not help feeling something of a heathen as I admitted to only once having seen the title-winning club that goes about its business a mere two miles from my home.

Despite retiring from full-time journalism 14 years ago, David still covers the occasional hockey game here and there (as well as ghost writing Sir Alex Ferguson's column in the United matchday programme), so I promised to offer the Berkshire hand of friendship when his side, Brooklands, visit Reading in November. In return, he settled down to tell me all I need to know about Steve

Coppell, but surprised me when he started: "To be honest, as a local reporter I found him quite hard work." David was quick to elaborate: "I had looked at his background and thought, *we are going to get a high-IQ university-trained lad who will be very refreshing to interview – I will get some good pieces from him*, but it didn't work out that way. I don't think he was basically shy, but he put out that kind of demeanour in order to deflect publicity. He didn't want to be pressed in case his team-mates thought he was saying, 'I'm the big I am'. I got to know him slowly, but I always got the impression that he didn't want publicity or to be singled out; he wanted to keep a low profile in order not to offend or upset his new team-mates."

As United entered their centenary year in 1978, under new management in Dave Sexton and under pressure to mark the occasion with some silverware to follow Tommy Docherty's FA Cup triumph, Meek was enjoying the renaissance of a club he had seen taste European glory ten years earlier. He told me: "I really enjoyed it then. Steve joined at the right time in the sense they had hit the bottom, but Tommy Docherty made a few changes and I don't know if it was planning or by accident but the Doc came up with an all-guns-blazing attacking team and it was an exciting period in United's history. They had Stuart Pearson at centre-forward and two really fast wingers in a period where England had had the wingless wonders, so it was very refreshing and very enjoyable reporting United at that particular time in their history. Coppell was a key figure in that.

"When Tommy Docherty bought him from Tranmere, I remember writing with great irony that Steve came with a recommendation from former Liverpool manager Bill Shankly. Shankly had fallen out with Anfield a little bit and I quoted him as saying: 'I've had quite a bit to do with Tranmere and Coppell impressed me. He is quick, has good movement and a lot of courage. He can play on the right side, or in the middle or with a roving commission. Given the right kind of club, he has all that it takes to become a very good player – a real proposition. He's a great player in the making, like Kevin Keegan in so many ways. If I was still at Liverpool, he would be in my team'. So he effectively recommended Steve Coppell to United."

No testimonial would have filled Coppell with more pride than the endorsement of Shankly, whose teams Coppell had idolised from the Kop pen as a young boy, but the arrival of Sexton, a former Chelsea manager like his predecessor Docherty, meant a change of roles for the maturing young player. Where the raw teenager had made maverick progress up and down the wing, Sexton encouraged a more thoughtful role on the right side of United's midfield. Coppell was on every Sexton team sheet in the new manager's first season and, having played in the final 23 league games of the previous season, remaining ever-present was a remarkable achievement given Coppell's constant work-rate. Sexton brought out a more complete player as Coppell combined his natural gift of wing play with sheer graft and determination. Football supporters were quick to recognise the contribution too and in Sexton's first season at Old Trafford Coppell was voted 'most popular player in the game' by *Sunday Express* readers.

Meek explained: "Steve was ready for that change of styles. He was always an intelligent player and I think he realised there was a bit more to it than just going haring down the wing, so we saw him in a more creative role with more defensive work and trying to complement the team in other ways. Sexton was a tactician and encouraged that.

"I think the fans enjoyed Coppell's attacking instincts because it's always been the tradition since Matt Busby for United to play attacking and entertaining football and Steve fitted into that box fine. But they also admired him because he was a selfless player and would work for the team; as he developed he became more of a team player and they liked that. They liked his courage and his work ethic, so he was popular and the fans who did have contact with him found him a modest, likeable, friendly guy, which he was."

United's form in that first season under Sexton was patchy to say the least. After winning the opening two League matches of the new manager's reign the early signs were good, especially as Sexton had promised to brand his time at Old Trafford with a hallmark of attractive football. But, having been among the top three early on, United adopted a constant position in the middle third of the First Division, hardly the position their fans had come to expect.

Sexton shouldered the blame squarely in the media, but Coppell was quick to defend the new manager, who had been linked with the role some years earlier following the departure of Wilf McGuinness. "Given that we had the same players we had before he joined, it can only be that it was the players themselves who failed to fulfil their potential," Coppell said. "Dave Sexton was very introspective and at the same time kind and generous. He hit exactly the right note when he arrived by making the point that he was taking over a talented, successful side and saw no point in changing the status quo. He was as good as his word, standing back to let Tommy Cavanagh take those pre-season sessions and carry on with the sort of fitness training we had done in previous seasons."

Sexton, contrary to media reports suggesting Docherty's departure had left them bitter and unresponsive, had an immediate rapport with the players he inherited. Sexton was a different animal from his predecessor, technical and deep thinking and willing to listen to the opinions of his players; where Docherty had been more forthright and was hostile to any player who disagreed with his methods. But, in a results business, Sexton was under instant pressure to repeat the silverware success of the Doc. That pressure was even greater as United entered their centenary year, but with another modest league effort and having suffered an early League Cup exit at the hands of a Luther Blissett-inspired Watford, it was once again clear that the FA Cup offered the club its greatest chance of success.

"The FA Cup final almost felt commonplace," Coppell said. "We thought: 'Yeah, that's what we're about. You win six games and you win the Cup.' It was almost something that we concentrated on. We felt capable of beating any team on our day, so we always felt that winning six matches in a row was within our compass."

In 1979, however, it had taken eight games just to reach Wembley after United required replays in the fourth round against Fulham, the quarter-final with Tottenham and in the semi-final, where they had again faced Liverpool. Keen to rekindle the spirit of '77, Sexton and Cavanagh attempted to repeat as much of the preparations as possible, including a return visit to the Selsdon Park Hotel in Surrey. In fact, the superstitious Sexton even dug out the suit he had worn in leading Chelsea to their FA Cup triumph over Leeds nine years earlier and made sure he had a haircut and visited his mother in Brighton, just as he had done before outwitting Don Revie.

Much to the players' dismay, Cavanagh continued the superstitions by insisting his lucky Max Bygraves tape got a repeat airing on the team coach, though Sing-along-a-Max was the last thing on defender Brian Greenhoff's mind. Coppell's room-mate was known for his struggles with nerves and, the night before the Cup final, the anxiety over whether or not he would be included in Sexton's starting line-up overwhelmed him. Kept awake by his room-mate and his own anxiety over whether he should call for help, Coppell convinced himself to stay quiet, sure that anything else would signal the end of his pal's chances of playing. Yet Greenhoff ultimately took the decision out of Coppell's hands, calling physio Laurie Brown in a desperate bid to calm his nerves and get some sleep. "His chances of playing went with that call, though I still believe that Brian could and should have played," Coppell said later.

In fact, Greenhoff never played for United again, departing that summer in a £350,000 move to Leeds United. Whether or not the absence of Martin Buchan's trusted central defensive partner was significant in the opening half of that final will never be known, but Arsenal tore into United from the off. The brilliant Liam Brady laid on a chance for Brian Talbot to win a race with team-mate Alan Sunderland and poke the Gunners in front, then Brady worked his magic again, suppling the cross for Frank Stapleton to head the second, unmarked at the far post.

Arsenal were in total control and, despite an improved showing from Sexton's men after the break, Terry Neill's side looked as though they had comfortably held their rivals at arm's length. With 20 minutes left, Neill attempted to protect the two-goal lead by replacing winger David Price with defender Steve

Walford, but United grew stronger as Arsenal seemed to be guilty of some complacency. "In our heads we were already halfway up the steps to the Royal Box," Arsenal defender Willie Young later conceded.

It was Coppell who kick-started United's fightback, though there were only four minutes remaining when his free-kick found Jordan on the left and he cut the ball back for defender McQueen to sweep home from seven yards. It appeared little more than a consolation, but two minutes later Coppell sent Sammy McIlroy scuttling clear and the Northern Irish midfielder danced around David O'Leary and then the hapless substitute Walford before squeezing an effort past the outrushing Pat Jennings to send the ball bouncing in, almost in slow motion. It was a brilliant individual goal and seemed to have totally turned the game on its head. Arsenal looked shocked and beaten and Coppell later admitted: "I was so convinced that we were going to win that I could even see the headlines in the Sunday papers. The score would be 4-2. It was inevitable, we were tall and strong, full of running and they were shattered at having come so close, only to lose it. All we had to do was keep it for 100 seconds."

But United managed barely half that before the outstanding Brady took the game by the scruff of its neck once more and wrenched the cup back out of United's grasp. The Irishman, his socks rolled down to expose his aching calves, burst between McIlroy and Mickey Thomas and curled a left foot pass out to Graham Rix, who flighted a cross beyond rookie keeper Gary Bailey to the far post, where Alan Sunderland evaded Arthur Albiston and stretched out a leg to turn the ball home for the most dramatic of Wembley winners.

"It was like winning the pools only to find you hadn't posted your coupon," groaned McIlroy later, while Coppell added: "I have never switched from feeling elated to deflated so quickly."

Bailey, who had been promoted to first-team keeper by Sexton only in November that season, bore the brunt of the criticism over the next few days, but the dignified manager refused to blame individuals, instead reasoning that his players had shown a collective lack of concentration at the death.

"A lot of people blamed Gary Bailey for the goal, but you could start criticising long before the ball reached him," said Coppell, adding: "We should have killed it, fouled or anything at that stage. Dave Sexton described it as a cruel result, but it was as cruel for him as it was for us as it left him with nothing to show for his hard work and expenditure."

Coppell at least found quick consolation at that wrenching disappointment in the form of England duty, returning to Wembley just two weeks later and scoring in a 3-1 Home Championship win against Scotland. Coppell had become a regular in Ron Greenwood's side having made his debut in a World Cup qualifier against Italy at Wembley on 16 November 1977, effectively a dead rubber with England virtually guaranteed not to qualify for the World Cup finals in Argentina. But that game had at least given Coppell the chance to shine for his country having enjoyed a watching brief, but no action, in the final months of Revie's England reign.

Coppell's displays in his first full season with United had earned him a call-up to the Under-23 squad on his home patch at Old Trafford, where Gordon Hill and Brian Greenhoff joined him in the side as England won 3-1 in a game watched by Revie. Although Coppell felt he was only in the side because of injuries and the fact that the game was being played at Old Trafford, England's manager was clearly impressed and, following United's FA Cup-winning season in 1977, he named the young winger in his senior squad for the first time.

What made Coppell's draft even more exciting was that it was for England's tour of South America, with games scheduled in Brazil, Argentina and Uruguay. Crucially, Revie himself did not join up with the England party for the early stages. The story was that the England manager was on a scouting mission to run the rule over World Cup qualifying opponents Finland, though in time it emerged that Revie was in fact in the United Arab Emirates, negotiating a contract to take over as their national coach. Blissfully unaware of the international espionage taking place behind the scenes, Coppell revelled in the experience of his first England tour and his desire to maintain his fitness despite not figuring in the opening games of the tour meant he was a regular runner on the Copacabana beach, where his jogging partner became BBC television commentator John Motson. England secured a goalless draw with Brazil before Revie joined the party in time to preside over a 1-1 draw with Argentina in Buenos Aires and Coppell was thrilled when the England manager later told him that he would be given his first international cap by coming off the substitutes' bench in the final game of the tour in Uruguay. The young winger could barely contain his excitement as he sat on the bench during that match in Montevideo – probably the only man in the stadium with such levels of enthusiasm given the dour nature of the goalless stalemate – but as the minutes ticked by Coppell slowly realised Revie was not going to give him his chance. "I was disillusioned by the man," he said, adding: "If he had just told me I was going to be substitute I would have been happy because it was a step nearer, but to offer my first cap and then snatch it away was unkind."

The void that Coppell felt so intensely after that unproductive first tour was filled the following season when caretaker boss Ron Greenwood handed him his England chance against Italy. England's final chance of qualification for Argentina had all but gone when they failed to run up a cricket score against Luxembourg and so Greenwood took the opportunity to include wingers Coppell and Peter Barnes in the Italy squad, along with fellow newcomer Bob Latchford.

"I was extremely nervous before the game, but the night was one of the highlights of my entire career," Coppell said, adding: "I walked out of the tunnel at Wembley and felt hugely proud that I was representing my country. Before that game, my whole football life flashed before my eyes."

Greenwood's appointment on a permanent basis was good timing for Coppell, who became a regular in the England camp throughout the 1980 European Championship campaign, the qualifying tournament for the World Cup in Spain and the perennial Home Internationals, where scoring against Scotland became something of a habit. He netted his first England goal with the 83rd-minute winner at Hampden Park in his sixth appearance and repeated the trick the following season at Wembley to help ease the pain of that Cup final defeat against Arsenal. By then Coppell had won 14 caps and was a big part of Greenwood's ongoing plans, yet the day-to-day routine of international weeks had initially proved hard to adapt to for the naturally reserved midfielder.

'The problem with playing for England is familiarity and feeling comfortable and it took me about ten games to feel comfortable in the environment,' he said in Rogan Taylor's *Passion For The Game*. 'When you first go away with England you meet up on a Sunday and you're conscious of everything you do. Even when you sit down at a meal you want to use the right knife and fork and you want to eat properly and you don't want to do anything which draws attention to you. Football humour is cruel. Other players will make fun of you, pick you out, so you're very much shrinking into the pack all the time and it was only after I'd played a few games and I knew the people – the physio, the doctors, the manager and the coaches – that I felt comfortable and felt I could express myself properly.'

Greenwood's management style sat comfortably with Coppell, who was benefiting from the new manager's return to relying on wingers, a style long forgotten in English football. "Ron Greenwood's background was the academy of West Ham which was an adaptation of the Tottenham push-and-run. It was a passing game but he selected players who were successful in other environments," remembered Coppell.

"The dominant personalities of my era were the likes of Emlyn Hughes, Kevin Keegan and Trevor Brooking, with Ray Wilkins and Bryan Robson coming into the frame. These were hardened professionals, all of them, and I think they perhaps dictated the style just as much as the manager did. The manager selected the players, so he knew exactly what was going on, and I think he gave the players that freedom to impose themselves. Ron Greenwood always used to say, 'there isn't one captain in the team, there are 11 captains.'"

So much so that when Greenwood assembled his side at Hertfordshire's West Lodge Park hotel on a Sunday evening after the weekend's matches, he would send them off to the local pub with the order, "off you go and pick the team for Wednesday".

'Coppell and Barnes were essential to the pattern and I believed they were part of England's long-term future,' Greenwood wrote in his autobiography *Yours Sincerely*. 'They gave us width and flair, they were the edge to our blade, and I would have kept them in the team as long as I was in charge. Coppell fulfilled all my hopes: he was a little jewel, consistent, brave, a thinking raider, one of the names I always put down first. He was small, busy and elusive, a ferret of a player who worked the whole of the right touchline.'

Fielding a consistent side was also beneficial to Greenwood as his side cruised through their European Championships qualifying group, securing Coppell his first major championship appearance for the finals in Italy. 'We twice beat Denmark, Bulgaria and Northern Ireland and the only point we dropped was against the Republic of Ireland on the Lansdowne Road rugby ground in Dublin,' remembered Greenwood. 'Our form and shape varied a little but the side retained a solid, basic structure. Dave Watson played in all eight qualifying games, Ray Clemence and Kevin Keegan in seven and Phil Neal, Mick Mills, Ray Wilkins, Coppell and Trevor Brooking in six.

'The format was simple but adaptable. We were solid at the back, there was variety and enterprise in the middle and going forward we had width and pace. The side was experienced, too, and could adjust and improvise to meet the unexpected.'

Yet England's showing at the finals was strangely low-key as a side expected to challenge for the trophy were held 1-1 by Belgium in their opening game and then lost 1-0 to the hosts before a 2-1 win over Spain proved too little, too late for Greenwood's side. It was a disastrous tournament for England; the opening match was marred by crowd trouble and Italian police used tear gas in their attempts to restore peace, leaving England keeper Ray Clemence coughing and spluttering on the pitch as the clouds of tear gas drifted from the terraces.

Coppell was partly at fault for Marco Tardelli's winner in the game against the hosts in Turin, admitting: "I dived in to tackle the skilful Antognioni as he set up the move which led to the goal. All I had planned to do was stand up to the midfield player and shuffle him inside, but I was right in front of our bench and I was aware of Ron Greenwood shouting at me, telling me to tackle him. I should have followed my own instincts."

Securing their place at the 1982 World Cup in Spain proved more troublesome than expected too, as England struggled to qualify from a group they had been expected to breeze through. It had certainly seemed that way when Greenwood's youthful side thumped Norway 4-0 in the opener at Wembley, but a 2-1 defeat in Romania and an unconvincing 2-1 win over Switzerland at Wembley were followed by a laboured goalless draw with Romania before, worst of all, an England side that at last included Keegan were beaten 2-1 in Switzerland.

A 3-1 win in Budapest reignited England's charge, but a disastrous 2-1 reverse in Norway took qualification out of England's hands and signalled a level of trouble only slightly overstated by Norwegian commentator Bjørge Lillelien, whose theatrical summarisation at the final whistle has entered English football folklore. In a not entirely unrehearsed tirade Lillelien, a much-loved football and winter sports commentator in his home country, spoke partly in Norwegian and, to ensure English speaking fans worldwide understood the enormity of Norway's first victory over the English since the days of the Viking invasions, completed his commentary in rasping English:

"We're the best in the world! We've beaten England 2-1 at football! This is truly incredible! We've beaten England, England the fighters' birthplace: Lord Nelson, Lord Beaverbrook, Sir Winston Churchill, Sir Anthony Eden, Clement Attlee, Henry Cooper, Lady Diana – we've beaten you all. Maggie Thatcher, can you hear me? Maggie Thatcher, I have a message for you in the middle of your campaign. We have kicked England out of the football World Cup. Maggie Thatcher, as you say in your language in the boxing bars around Madison Square Garden: Your boys took a hell of a beating!"

As Coppell said, football humour is cruel, and on the back of an embarrassing defeat to a hapless footballing nation that had only once qualified for a major tournament – the 1938 World Cup – Greenwood was ready to answer calls from the media and the terraces and offer his resignation, only to be talked out of it by his players on the way home from Oslo. "He tried to resign on the way home on the flight back to Luton, but the senior players wouldn't let him," Neal told me. "We said, 'hey boss, come on, there is still one game to go, let's finish it out'. We were on the back foot in every sense, but, from a hopeless situation where I thought I was going to be denied a World Cup appearance, suddenly it all turned around."

Greenwood listened to his players, Coppell included, and vowed to see the qualification group through, and when an equally unpredictable Switzerland win over Romania saw the group table take another twist, Greenwood's England needed only a draw at home to Hungary to make good their passage to Spain. The task was made easier by the fact that Hungary were already safely qualified and, as Coppell put it: "The Hungarians were content with a couple of days in London, shopping for jeans and *Playboy* magazines, just as long as we did not embarrass them by scoring too many goals."

Even without playmaker Tibor Nyalasi through injury, Hungary's lack of effort was embarrassing, but gratefully received by a desperate England who were ahead on 14 minutes with a scrambled effort from Mariner. Both sides were happy to play out time after that, but one Hungarian defender remained clearly intent on making some kind of impression on the game. Toth, a burly 29-year-old built like Norman Hunter and possessing the subtlety of a brick and the turning speed of the QE2, was no match for the nimble Coppell, who set off on a run midway through the second half that was to dramatically shape his future. As the defender dived in, seemingly in slow motion, Coppell looked to make one of his trademark moves, pushing the ball down the line and skipping past the defender before sending in a quick centre. Instead Toth blocked his route with a thundering challenge that sent Coppell's free left leg spinning up in the air and left the winger in a heap on the ground.

In that moment, Coppell felt as much confusion as pain, but admitted in *Touch and Go*: 'The only other coherent thought I had in the next moments was of my knee exploding as if someone had let off a firework inside it. It was almost as if I had lost consciousness until the roar of the crowd gradually pierced my mind. I reached down to touch my leg which felt as if it was on fire and, thankfully, found that it was all in one piece – or so I thought at the time.

'The tackle had taken place right near the touchline and I crawled off on my hands and knees. By the time our physiotherapist reached me the substitute, Tony Morley, was already stripping off in preparation to take my place and I was lifted to my feet and limped back to the dug-out. The team doctor, Vernon Edwards, looked it over, but I was able to walk back to the dressing room unaided. I had taken quite a clout and it hurt like hell though there was no indication of just how serious an injury it was even when it swelled up like a balloon. Dr Edwards strapped it up tightly and gave me the usual anti-inflammatory tablets to take.

'After the game I simply carried on as normal, attending a Courage Brewery sponsorship function at the Conference Centre at Wembley before turning down the offer of a room at the complex's hotel in preference to driving myself back home to Manchester up the motorway. It was not false bravado, but just that I had never had a mechanical injury before and so did not realise the problems that they can cause. I kept telling myself that everything was fine while the increasing pain kept telling me differently. I even put down my failure to sleep to the normal post-match high as I lay in bed re-running the game and the tackle in my mind.'

The swelling around Coppell's knee made it impossible for the England and Manchester United medical teams to assess the full extent of the damage. Edwards and England physio Fred Street examined the knee after the game against Hungary, but their initial tests appeared to suggest there was no cartilage damage. The knee did not click or lock and, though Coppell was in obvious pain, he still had the full range of movement. United physio Jim McGregor's diagnosis was similarly hampered by nature the following morning and there was an element of guesswork when Coppell was told he had probably strained the collateral ligaments at the side of his knee. Having not missed a game for his club in a remarkable four-and-a-half season spell – a record-breaking run of 206 consecutive appearances for United between January 1977 and November 1981 – Coppell finally had to watch from the sidelines.

Stubborn and impatient, Coppell was determined to return to action quickly, despite the advice of McGregor and the United medical team. Uncertain of the extent of the injury, McGregor wanted Coppell to rest until a full diagnosis could be confidently offered and what no-one knew at that stage was that Toth's crunching tackle had, despite all the routine tests suggesting otherwise, damaged the cartilage. Without him knowing, the femur and tibia in Coppell's left leg were rubbing together largely unprotected, causing irreparable damage and making a bad injury significantly worse.

Oblivious to the wear and tear his knee was suffering and having struggled for form early in the 1981/82 season, Coppell was keen to impress Ron Atkinson, the flamboyant former West Bromwich Albion manager charged with bringing the swashbuckling style of Docherty back to Old Trafford after Sexton's more conservative period had been ended earlier that year. Sexton had been unfortunate; having lost to Arsenal in that dramatic 1979 FA Cup final, his side then finished runners-up to Liverpool in the 1979/80 season after eight wins in the final ten games left them just two points short of the champions. But near misses counted for nothing in the high-pressure scenario of the Theatre of Dreams and when United managed just ten wins from 37 League games in the 1980/81 season Martin Edwards called time on Sexton's four-year reign.

"I suppose I have to come to the conclusion that, despite my deep respect for him and my initial excitement at his arrival, Dave Sexton was not the right manager for Manchester United," Coppell said. "He introduced a lot of training routines designed to practise various elements of the game; he was a great technician and he wanted the players to do certain things a certain way. He even had a huge library of videos that he would use to illustrate his point and which would show the great players heading, shooting, tackling, crossing and so on. His training routines would incorporate practising these basic skills and concentrate on trying to improve technique, but how can you teach Martin Buchan to tackle, Gordon McQueen to head the ball or Jimmy Greenhoff to score goals? We could see what he was trying to achieve and would try and improve for him, but you could see how much better his coaching worked with the younger players."

There was change in Coppell's personal life too, as Atkinson's arrival in the summer of 1981 coincided with Coppell's secret wedding to childhood sweetheart Jane before the new season started. Jane organised the wedding in her maiden name, finalising the details while Coppell lived on the road for the best part of two months; heading straight from England duty in Budapest to a United tour of the

Far East and then home to Liverpool for his nuptials via a Pink Floyd concert and a date with his tailor in London and, finally, a stop at his favourite shoe shop in Manchester. Things did not exactly go to plan on the day, however. Although Jane had successfully managed to keep the news of their wedding from the papers, she could hardly have legislated for a shoe shop which gave her husband two left-foot shoes – "the salesman could only have been a Manchester City fan with a very warped sense of humour," Coppell recalled – nor a wedding dress company that provided her with the wrong gown, several sizes too large.

Best man Eric, Coppell's grandfather, then forgot the rings, not the news Coppell wanted to hear as he walked into church complementing his ice-blue suit with one black shoe and one blue before the errant right-footer was safely delivered in the nick of time. Blue was clearly the colour that day, for when the happy couple arrived for the reception at a Hale hotel they discovered that the flowers had been recycled from the wedding of Manchester City captain Paul Power the previous day.

Things hardly improved on the honeymoon as the posh Bermuda hotel owned by Everton chairman John Moores refused to allow Coppell in without a jacket or tie. Having only packed casual wear, the embarrassed England international was forced to borrow some hand-me-downs from the well-attired son of a family the newlyweds had befriended. So, it was something of a relief when Coppell pulled a red shirt of United back on for the club's first season under new management.

Big changes were afoot; reserve team coach Jack Crompton and physio Laurie Brown departed, while Atkinson moved quickly to plug the gap left by Joe Jordan's departure to AC Milan by signing Arsenal's Stapleton. Remi Moses and Bryan Robson soon followed Atkinson from his former club West Bromwich Albion; Coppell's first lesson that every player has his price after Baggies boss Ronnie Allen had insisted Robson would leave "over my dead body".

Coppell could easily have been part of the changing scenery too. Nursing an ankle ligament injury picked up in pre-season, the winger tried to play through the pain and continue his remarkable run of appearances when he should have rested to ensure a full recovery. His form, as a result, was poor and Atkinson dropped him to the bench for the Manchester derby in which Robson made his United debut – wearing Coppell's number seven shirt. "I should have learned my lesson then," Coppell said, "but the physiotherapists, doctors and surgeons can only help once the player has decided something is wrong."

Having been linked with Arsenal, Coventry and West Ham, Coppell insisted he wanted to stay and fight for his place, even turning down the chance of a £1 million switch to Upton Park. His attitude impressed the new manager and, after a substitute appearance against City ensured the appearance record continued, Atkinson restored the determined Coppell to his starting line-up.

"When Ron first joined United I don't think he rated me," Coppell revealed in an interview with the Manchester United website. "He had come from West Brom, where Derek Statham was playing at full-back. I never really felt I'd played that well against Derek – he was difficult to play against and initially I think Ron would have been happy for me to move on. He said I could go if I wanted to, but I said I wanted to fight for my place and I think he respected that. We got to know each other better and I began to play some of my best stuff for him."

Atkinson also rewarded Coppell's exemplary skills and attitude by making him a mentor to one of United's emerging young talents. The winger's new room-mate was teenage striker Norman Whiteside, who alongside Mark Hughes had steered United to the final of the FA Youth Cup.

'I suspect it must have been planned that the model professional was given the youngster to set me the perfect example,' Whiteside recalled in his autobiography, *Determined*. 'I know he comes across as being fairly dour, but Stevie was a great guy: bright, unselfish and genuinely interested in players and their development. He also had a nice, dry wit and, though I've forgiven him for banging on in his autobiography about how I shared a face with Russ Abbot, I'm still not sure if his regular pre-match night-time prescription for me was a wind-up or part of his mission to show concern for my welfare.'

The late night snack in question was a glucose energy bar, and Coppell's insistence that his room-mate wash it down with a cup of coffee was hardly orthodox. Whiteside added: 'He was an excellent athlete and had seen me struggle on distance runs. "Go on, have it," he said, "it will give you strength," so before every away game for the next year I tucked into the ideal snack to help me get a restful night's sleep: an energy bar and a cup of coffee!'

No energy bar in the world, nor any quantity of sheer bloody-mindedness could have masked the pain with which Coppell returned to United from international duty on 19 November 1981, the euphoria of England's World Cup qualification shrouded by the dark cloud of pain for Coppell. Yet even the injury he suffered against Hungary caused him to miss only three games – defeats at Tottenham and Southampton and a home win over Brighton – before reclaiming his place. The World Cup was calling and, despite the advice of the United medical team, Coppell was determined not to miss a moment more of his career than was absolutely necessary. In hindsight it was unwise, yet, as United ended Atkinson's first season in charge with a ten-match unbeaten run in which Coppell scored four goals to secure third position, captain Buchan recalls being dazzled by the winger's staying power.

Buchan told me: "I remember being quite pleased seeing those playing cards you got back then, because early in my career my playing card read 42-42-41-41 in terms of appearances in the season. I was pleased to play that many league games but what Steve achieved in playing 206 consecutive games was phenomenal. He also did it at an incredibly high level of performance; not only did he play all the games, he played to a very high standard in all of those. If I'd been manager, he'd have been the first name on my team sheet."

Ron Greenwood agreed. Steve Coppell, despite the injury which was unknowingly gnawing away at his joint, was off to Spain and the World Cup with England.

A KNIGHT IN SHINING ARMOUR

The London skyline dazzles from above and the aerial view Steve Coppell is treated to as the flight from Bangkok circles over the capital is every inch a sight for sore eyes. Darkness still holds its grip on the twinkling skyline and most of London remains asleep as regimented lines of streetlights and the faintest glow of moonlight afford the city a romantic glow.

The London Eye is an imposing new landmark alongside the river and Coppell smiles as one of his own milestones comes into view, Brentford's Griffin Park tucked away amongst the flyovers and industrial estates and apparently only inches from the river from this observation point. Coppell just about has time to reflect on his highly enjoyable year in that corner of West London and cranes his neck to look further down river towards the south east corner which had formed such a big part of his career in four spells at Crystal Palace. Eventually Coppell submits to the increasing pressure on his eyelids and spends the rest of the approach to landing snoozing off the jetlag. When he wakes, the usual cattle-herding exercise of reuniting passengers with bags mercifully keeps him from checking his watch too often – it is a little after 7am in London, but his body feels as if it is in another time zone altogether.

This was an annual ritual, the final leg of Coppell's month-long sabbatical to recharge his batteries on a beach far from the madding fields of English football. Only this time there was no job to return recharged for, unless this morning's meeting went well.

Dick Knight is not fighting sleep deprivation; he is fresh, shaved and high on early-morning caffeine by the time Coppell walks into the London hotel for their breakfast meeting. The Brighton chairman has waited weeks for this opportunity and feels ready to secure the Seagulls' new manager over coffee and a croissant, basking in the feeling that his club is destined for a return to better times under Coppell's guidance. Knight thrusts out a hand and welcomes the interviewee before settling back into his comfy chair and beginning his sales pitch. Brighton are a club going places, he explains, their new ground will be ready in less than three years and, together, the pair can ensure the Seagulls will move in to their new home as a club on the up.

The chairman looks up from his notes and knows he will be able to tell just by looking into Coppell's eyes whether he is the one to lead the renaissance. But he does not feel the steely engagement of a man with a vision, or the piercing stare of determination that so many have told him about. In fact, Knight sees nothing in Coppell's eyes that morning, nothing at all. In the comfy surroundings of the hotel lounge, the jetlagged interviewee has fallen fast asleep.

SELHURST PARK WAS Steve Coppell's salvation, a sanctuary to shield him as he rehabilitated from his Manchester City nightmare. Returning to the club as chief scout, a bruised Coppell was able to ease himself back into football before Ron Noades nudged him back into the limelight as the man to take over the reins once more following Dave Bassett's departure to Nottingham Forest.

Six months later Palace and Coppell were back in the top-flight, David Hopkin's long-range effort in the last minute of the play-off final at Wembley sealing victory over Sheffield United and a seat at football's top table once more for the club and its returning manager. Asked what Palace's promotion meant to him, Coppell replied: "Nine months of hell." He was fully cured.

Again his top-flight return was short-lived as, despite the signing of Tomas Brolin and Attilio Lombardo, who many Eagles fans still regard as the best player ever to pull on a Palace shirt, Coppell's side were firmly rooted to the foot of the table throughout the 1997/98 campaign. Having been made to wait until April for a first home win it was already inevitable that the club would be relegated when Noades revealed he was selling his controlling interest to boyhood Palace fan Mark Goldberg.

The new chairman fulfilled a lifelong ambition by selling his IT recruitment business and ploughing £23.8 million into dragging Palace out of the First Division and turning them into a European force. An ambitious shuffle of the managerial pack saw Coppell become Director of Football, with former Palace player and manager Terry Venables installed as manager. Goldberg reportedly paid Venables a staggering £130,000 just to hold talks with the club and then awarded him a £750,000 pay packet with a car and a house thrown in.

But the new chairman's empire was built on weak foundations; his purchase of the club did not include the freehold of the ground and Goldberg was left with negligible assets that led many of his backers to withdraw their financial support. Faced with mounting debts, the club sold high wage-earners, including Lombardo, while Venables also departed. A distraught Goldberg, his fingers badly burned, was forced to place the club in the hands of the receivers in January 1999, with Coppell the obvious choice to come back downstairs and take over the managerial reins once more.

He was back where his managerial career path had started, seeking a Palace renaissance, but this time in the grip of administration, rather than seeing it as merely a dark cloud on the horizon. Under the circumstances mid-table finishes of 14th and 15th were remarkable achievements, particularly in the 1999/00 season when relegation seemed a certainty.

On the verge of bankruptcy, Palace desperately needed a change of direction – and so too did Coppell when mobile phone tycoon Simon Jordan bought the club, lifting them out of administration. Midway through an uninspiring pre-season campaign, Coppell quit the club after failing to hit it off with the new owner and Jordan's promise of a new dawn began when he replaced Coppell with his assistant, Alan Smith, who rather sheepishly took over again just as he had done seven years earlier.

At the time Jordan was pragmatic: "Steve did a fantastic job for a number of years, but we now have a new manager and a new opportunity. Sometimes things change; a management style comes in and things evolve. If you don't evolve, you die." Yet, later, he revealed there had been an obvious personality clash. "Steve Coppell and I just didn't get on. I'd watched us concede 15 goals in three pre-season friendlies, so I asked what the hell was going on. Steve had a funny turn and left," he said, adding: "I found him very difficult. I walked in to see him, having spent more than £10 million on the club, and he was very strange. Uncommunicative, unhelpful. He was so negative he interfered with the signal strength on my phone."

On the face of it that may seem a harsh assessment, yet many other chairmen and owners would probably agree with Jordan's first impressions. The key, apparently, is to show some patience, though Coppell hardly gave his new chairman the opportunity to be patient, as BBC commentator and friend Jonathan Pearce pointed out: "There would have been a lifelong position for him there, but

Steve realised he could not work with a personality like Simon Jordan and went. I think that shows strength of character."

After a year's sabbatical, during which he was linked with a return to Tranmere Rovers as manager ("it was a rumour started by my brother and his family, who are season ticket holders there," he explained), Coppell and his old pal Ray Wilkins were lined up to take on coaching roles under Gianluca Vialli at Watford in the summer of 2001. Instead, he teamed up with another former ally, Ron Noades, who turned to him once more after taking over as chairman of Second Division Brentford.

It was the perfect fit and the pair were quickly back in harmony as the Bees made their best ever start to a campaign. Coppell's former England boss Bobby Robson was the only manager to get the better of him in the opening ten games as his Newcastle side recovered from Lloyd Owusu's opener in a League Cup tie at St James' Park to win in extra-time courtesy of Craig Bellamy's hat-trick.

"Brentford were as good as Chelsea were against us, I'll tell you," said Robson, before Coppell betrayed his own ambition in a post-match appraisal of his players. "As long as they have that desire to play at the top level, they will improve as players," he said. The desire for a return to the top flight clearly still burned brightly in Coppell – and his players did improve as they set about chasing down leading pair Brighton and Reading, two clubs that would play such a big part in his future.

Brighton, despite suffering a 4-0 hiding at Griffin Park that sealed a Brentford double that season, held their nerve to win the title at a canter, but Reading, managed by Coppell's former Palace charge Alan Pardew, stumbled across the line. Pardew was under pressure to deliver promotion to the ambitious Royals having lost in the play-off final at Cardiff's Millennium Stadium in 2001, despite having led twice, but five successive and nervy draws meant they went into the final game needing one more stalemate to hold off the fast-finishing Bees, their hosts in a deliciously scripted final game of the season.

It looked as though Coppell's side had timed their run to perfection when Martin Rowlands lashed home Owusu's cross to give Brentford the lead, but Pardew had the last laugh as Reading snatched promotion thanks to substitute Jamie Cureton's coolly lobbed finish 13 minutes from time to confine Coppell's side to the play-offs.

Lou Macari's Huddersfield awaited in the semi-finals, offering the diminutive Scotsman a chance for revenge over his old Manchester United team-mate following Swindon's suffering at the hands of Wright and Bright in 1989. Instead, Macari told me: "Steve did it again. At Huddersfield on the Sunday we battered them, but it finished 0-0 and then we lost the second leg at Griffin Park 2-1 having led 1-0."

Once again, however, Coppell's Bees failed to clear the final hurdle. Having come up agonisingly short against Reading, when barely 15 minutes separated Coppell from promotion, Stoke became the first team in 12 Millennium Stadium finals to win a match from the seemingly cursed southern dressing room. Brentford froze, and found themselves two goals down by half-time as Deon Burton opened the scoring before Ben Burgess scored an unfortunate own goal on the stroke of half-time.

Brentford's fans were outnumbered by four-to-one in the stadium, the legacy of a poor display and an LDV Vans Trophy final defeat to Port Vale in the same venue a year earlier. "It was harder to get the 'less occasional' fans to travel to Cardiff again and Stoke are a better supported club, so whilst the players froze a little, we froze a bit in the stands too," my Brentford pal Jon Restall admitted over a beer in our local.

Brentford had beaten Stoke 1-0 at Griffin Park only a month earlier, but largely because of the disputed dismissal of Stoke's Icelandic midfielder Arnar Gunnlaugsson – and Gudjon Thordarson's side looked intent on revenge. Brentford simply didn't perform and senior players, including skipper Paul Evans, who had so often dragged Coppell's side through adversity, seemed to go missing.

I don't need many excuses for a trip to the Duke of Wellington, but getting to the bottom of what went wrong when all seemed so right at Brentford was a good one. Jon, for his part, does not need many excuses to moan about Brentford and explained: "Some people criticised Coppell for not giving the players the 'hairdryer' treatment during the break. The reality, as we have learned over the last seven years, is that we were blessed with a very talented manager who we would struggle to replace for many seasons. Martin Allen's tenure was fun at times, particularly in the FA Cup, but he was never the tactician that Coppell was. The truth is that we had a truly talented team who, at times, completely dominated sides and the likes of Ingimarsson, Sidwell, Powell, Mahon, Hunt and Owusu all went on to play at a higher level following our own demise."

The separation was immediate, Brentford condemned to another year in Division Two, while Coppell, shackled once more by a lack of club funds as Noades battled for its very survival, called time on his brief encounter with the Bees. Heading off for his summer of recuperation, Coppell remained blissfully unaware that Brentford's league double over the champions that season had caught the eye of Brighton chairman Dick Knight, who unexpectedly found himself without a manager after two successive promotions when Peter Taylor resigned at the end of the 2001/02 season.

Knight could talk all day about Steve Coppell. In fact, it is probably fair to say that he could talk all day about anything to do with football, if our thoroughly enjoyable dinner in Brighton is anything to go by. In between mouthfuls of spaghetti and gulps of red wine at the Topolino restaurant, as Brighton's beachfront prepared to welcome Prime Minister Gordon Brown for the supposed speech of his life, Dick and I discussed politics of a football kind as well as football psychology, football phone-ins and football stadia. But mainly we talked about Steve Coppell.

"It was at this very table that I sat down for dinner with Steve and offered him a ten-year contract," Dick told me. "He had been with me almost exactly a year, but by then I knew exactly what I was dealing with. Initially Steve is very hard to communicate with, but once you get past that innate reserve what comes back is loads of common sense, logic and intelligence. He has intelligence beyond football and is the most complex manager I have worked with. He's also therefore the most challenging, but also the most rewarding once you get the communication going.

"I wanted him to stay with us until Brighton were in their new ground and, hopefully, in the Premiership – and I wanted him to take us there and then help develop the next manager of Brighton. But when I offered him the ten-year contract he said, 'I can't take it, Dick, because I may just have another opportunity and I don't feel comfortable with being offered that length of time'.

"When I'd said we would be in the new stadium, his reaction was that he wanted to manage in the Premiership, but that he felt he would never get a job with a Premiership club. If he was going to get back in the top flight he was going to have to take a club there. That is part of what attracted him to take the job in the first place, but he knew we hadn't yet got that permission to go ahead with the ground development and that financially we couldn't compete. In the back of his mind he knew that if he carried on doing well with us it was possible he'd get a chance with a club nearer to that opportunity, which eventually he did.

"It was almost exactly a year after he first joined us at Brighton that John Madejski approached me about Steve taking over at Reading. We were top of the Second Division, but Reading were a step closer to being able to fulfill Steve's Premiership ambitions. It still took him two weeks to mull it over, but I knew deep down he was going to take it."

Fifteen months earlier Knight had not exactly boasted the same sixth sense. Thrilled at the prospect of luring the former Crystal Palace and Brentford manager to the south coast, Knight's excitement had been washed away by sheer frustration after Coppell had snoozed his way through his job interview. First impressions last – and Knight was not impressed. The fact that remarkably high-profile names, including Harry Redknapp and Gordon Strachan, had been mentioned to Knight about taking over at Brighton underlined the potential of a club that was being strangled by planning politics and paying the price of the business greed of the previous regime, though neither manager was ever interviewed by Brighton's ambitious, yet realistic, chairman. "We just couldn't match their financial ambition," he told me. "The fact is that we had one sixth of the playing budget of the rest of that league because we were playing at a ground where you simply couldn't get any more in. A 6,300 crowd was all we could accommodate at the Withdean, no matter how high we went. When we won the Second Division we were full every week and when we moved up into the First Division we were still only going to get 6,300 in a league where the average is 18,000. We also lost half our revenue because of matchday costs and I had to allocate playing budget in relation to our turnover. I didn't need salary caps, I already had one of my own."

The simple maths of Brighton's situation meant Knight was able to narrow down his search for Taylor's replacement to two names. Coppell, the wily former manager of Brighton's fierce rivals Palace, who had made a name for himself weaving silk purses from the ears of sows; or Martin Hinshelwood, who as Brighton's youth team coach had developed some exciting young talent that was beginning to emerge through the ranks and was handed the role on a caretaker basis after Taylor's departure.

That Brighton were seeking new management at all was unusual, given they had just been promoted back to the second tier of English football as clear Second Division champions. "We won the league in May and Peter Taylor immediately resigned – and the reason he did that, I'm sure, is because he thought he would get back to being a Premiership manager having secured promotion. He thought he had rebuilt his reputation and would get a Premiership job on the back of it, so we were left with a very good squad of players but without a manager," Knight told me.

"I was well aware of Steve because Brentford had beaten us in both games that season and had played especially well at Griffin Park, where they beat us 4-0. We only lost six games out of 46 and two were against Brentford. I was torn between Steve and one or two others, but I also had this niggling thing about promoting from inside. Martin was the director of youth and had been a first-team coach [ironically having been forced to pack up playing because of a knee injury] and I was considering giving him a chance but knew there was an opportunity to try to persuade Steve.

"Steve was away on one of his sabbaticals, but Athole Still, his agent, noted our interest and was certain Steve would be interested, so I left it with him." There followed a period of three weeks in which Still, also the agent of then-England manager Sven-Goran Eriksson, attempted to track down his client.

"I was doing my nut and getting more and more frustrated that he had not made contact," Knight told me. "All I knew was that Athole said Steve wanted to talk, but had to keep making excuses about leaving messages at his last known point in outer Mongolia, or somewhere. After three weeks I'd seen some experienced names and, though Steve remained top of my list, I was running out of patience.

"Then Athole rang to say Steve was due back at Heathrow on the Saturday morning and would love to meet. I said he wouldn't because he'd be jetlagged – coming that way it's difficult to cope with the jetlag, especially if you are not an experienced flier. But he insisted that Steve knew he had kept me waiting and wanted to meet at the earliest opportunity, so we arranged to meet at a hotel in the West End of London. When I say it was initially hard to communicate with him, it's fair to say that we didn't hit it off straight away, simply because he was falling asleep on me. He kept nodding off throughout the interview. There was this guy I'd looked forward to seeing for weeks and clearly I was so boring that he kept falling asleep! It was funny, but I felt he had not made much of an impression because of it. The bits I got out of him were interesting, but he was so keen to have the interview as soon as he got off the plane that it backfired on him. Instead of waiting a day, he rushed it and that didn't work in his favour. So I decided to appoint Martin Hinshelwood."

You snooze, you lose. Coppell's loss was Hinshelwood's gain, and to celebrate the new incumbent was then treated to the sort of shopping trip every manager dreams of, especially those at a club with limited finances. Knight's continued good relations with former Brighton boss Liam Brady, who still lived in the town despite taking on the Arsenal youth director's role, meant Brighton were first in the queue for taking a look at the Gunners' young emerging stars, with a view to taking them to the south coast on loan. So it was with wide-eyed excitement that Knight drove his new manager to watch a pre-season reserve team friendly between Arsenal and Charlton. Brady and Arsène Wenger were both there to see a young Gunners side tear apart an experienced Charlton team and Knight was excited by what he saw.

"Brighton have always been my team, but I love watching Arsenal as my second team and I had an understanding with Liam that I could take their players on loan," Knight explained. "I already knew I could get Steve Sidwell, so I took Martin to watch him and see which other players might be available, but none of them had names on their shirts, so we only had numbers to go by. Sidwell was number eight and easy to spot because of his shock of red hair, but they also had a big stocky black midfielder playing wide right. He was absolutely outstanding and during the game I agreed in principle with Wenger to take Sidwell and told him I liked the right midfielder too.

"Arsène said, 'yes, he's good, though his brother is better' and he told me his name was Kolo Toure. So I had these two fantastic young players I might get for the entire season and I was so excited when I got back in the car with Martin for the journey home. I told him we could have Steve Sidwell and Kolo Toure on loan, but Martin looked back at me and said, 'to be honest Dick, I've not seen anything here that is better than what we have got at Brighton'. It was his call. I felt strongly about the pair, but I would never force players on a manager if he didn't want them."

Shackled by the finances and so fiercely loyal to his players that he was keen to reward their promise with a first-team chance, Hinshelwood handed debuts to three of his youth team players for his tough managerial baptism at Burnley and was instantly rewarded with an impressive 3-1 win, which could have been more emphatic but for two disallowed goals. That fine opening day victory was underpinned by a goalless home draw with Coventry and things looked good for Hinshelwood and his young team. Four points from two games was a welcome start to any manager's career, but ten games later Hinshelwood's record stood at four points from 12 games.

"We lost ten on the bounce," Knight winced, as though his spaghetti had just burned his throat. "Because he put three new kids in for the first game and we won, he stuck with them. As the losses mounted and with Bobby Zamora out injured, all it did was to drag the senior players down, so I called Athole and asked whether Steve had got over his jetlag and would he like to continue the interview. This time, we just hit it off and that same day he became Brighton manager.

In a reversal of fortunes to the unfortunate Hinshelwood, Coppell suffered defeat in his opening two games before setting off on a run which nearly saved Brighton's First Division status – and which undoubtedly enhanced his own managerial reputation. His first match, a 4-2 defeat to Neil Warnock's Sheffield United at the Withdean, saw the Blades awarded two controversial late penalties by referee Phil Prosser having trailed 2-1 with ten minutes remaining. That was hard enough to take without the bitter aftertaste of accusations of racism, Prosser reporting Brighton's fans to the FA for allegedly racially abusing him and Sheffield United striker Peter Ndlovu and backing Warnock's claims that fans had thrown coins at him.

Warnock took the heat out of the situation, stating publicly that his players had not suffered racial taunts, but the Brighton fans were starting to turn on their own after Coppell's next game in charge saw him take his new team to his former club, Brighton's bitter rivals Crystal Palace. "Steve got a standing ovation from the Palace fans, but we then lost 5-0 and it's the only time our fans ever turned on me," Knight told me, the memories of the reaction that night more painful than his recollection of Andy Johnson's hat-trick. "Some of them were asking what the hell I'd done, accusing Steve's team of capitulating to the old rivals."

Yet Coppell quickly won the fans over as he turned to familiar faces in a bid to inject some steel into the fragile side he had inherited. Knight explained: "As soon as he arrived at Brighton, he wanted to go back to Brentford to sign a couple of players who had been with him there. Obviously Sidwell, as we had already been given permission to sign him, but also Ivar Ingimarsson and Stephen Hunt. We signed Ivar and he was wonderful, a lovely guy who has something more to give football in his later life. He played alongside Danny Cullip and was a commanding presence and a very cultured player who never lost his cool. Then Steve asked if we could afford £22,500 to sign 'a little winger at Brentford' and I remembered Hunt having a particularly good game against us in that 4-0 win for Brentford. I was surprised he wasn't in the team when Steve said, 'I can get him out of there', but we couldn't afford him, so I stopped it happening. I always regret it, not least because he is such a good crosser of the ball, but Hunt's progress since then underlines that Steve can spot them early."

Coppell also turned to Simon Rodger, who had served him so well at Palace – and so briefly at Manchester City – as well as bringing in experienced defender Dean Blackwell and Reading's Tony Rougier, who became a real cult hero at Brighton. "He was a hero because he scored significant goals," Knight told me, recalling a game at promotion-chasing Ipswich where Rougier's double hauled the struggling Seagulls back from 2-0 down to force a draw at Portman Road.

Knight added: "Fans love players that try, even if they are not best quality. Rougier was a very talented player, but was inconsistent, yet Steve got so much out of him that the consistency level went up 50 per cent. He loved Steve Coppell and Steve got the best out of him. That team was full of players like that. They were all experienced players and Steve had got rid of the struggling youngsters in the team and brought in experience which he forged with players who had helped us win the league easily the previous season; players like Cullip, Charlie Oatway, Richard Carpenter, the goalkeeper Michel Kuipers and, of course, Zamora.

There was one exception. Adam Virgo, an unused sub in Hinshelwood's first game, had survived Coppell's cull, but failed to gain a regular starting place, despite an impressive reputation. "Micky Adams really liked him, but Steve had no time for him. He let him go out on loan to Exeter," Knight told me. "Two years later, after Steve had left, we sold Virgo to Celtic for £1.5 million which just proves that Steve doesn't get it right all the time, though he did text me to say 'great deal Mr Chairman' when we got that much for a player we would never have expected to sell for more than £400,000.

"Steve was ruthless with players who were not up for the fight and the only way we could battle relegation was with experience. He was masterful at getting more out of players than even they might have thought they were capable of and, as a result, he gained their utmost respect. They never felt close to him and they didn't get close. They were in awe of him."

Knight cited Coppell's reputation as a player as key to his subsequent success as a manager, saying: "When he played, he would put the ball in a corner and go after it and you would think the odds were in favour of the defender, yet more often than not he would get there and get his crosses in. By a combination of no little skill and sheer determination he has always had the ability to carry through what he sets out to do and he possesses a single mindedness about him, almost to the exclusion of everyone else."

Playing in the image of their manager, Brighton fought like dogs to secure an unlikely survival. I interviewed Coppell for the BBC Sport website towards the end of the campaign, after a 4-1 hammering of a Wolves side that was later promoted through the play-offs suggested survival might just be within reach, and he told me: "We do have that spirit of a team who for the past two seasons have won promotion and now they are under pressure. That pressure has made them bond together and gel together a little bit tighter."

Then, defying his claim that he never looks at league tables, he added: "Some weeks, you look at your team and the points you have got and you think it is going to be too big a mountain to climb. But the performance and the result we had against Wolves made us realise that if we continue like that we can get out of it, no problem. I think if you asked any one of our squad at the moment whether we can get out of our situation then the answer would be yes. As long as we don't have the team splitting into cliques and little groups of threes and fours we have got a chance. Roll on the next match and we'll see what happens."

In the end they took their survival bid to the final day of the season, but eventually fell five points short of Stoke, the very team that had denied Coppell's Brentford in Cardiff 12 months earlier. "We were relegated with 45 points from 46 games, but when Steve took over we'd got four from 12. I'm confident we would never have been relegated had he not fallen asleep on me," Knight laughed.

Relegation and the rising costs of the public inquiry into the Falmer Stadium project forced Knight to accept a knock-down price of £1.5 million from Spurs for striker Bobby Zamora, a sale which summed up the scenario Brighton were faced with and one which meant the chairman knew he also faced a battle to hold on to his manager.

"I loved it there and I always knew that if I was going to leave it would have to be to a really big club," Zamora told me. "Copps made it clear he wouldn't stand in my way and that he wanted me to do well and challenge at the best clubs. It was brilliant to know there was no pressure, but that once I was ready to go he would back me all the way. It made me comfortable in making sure I chose the right move when it came.

"A few clubs came in and made offers, but I wasn't interested and I loved working with Steve. The team we had was good and everyone worked hard for each other, but when Copps came in his tactics steadied us and it was easy to adapt. He talks to you one-on-one, but he is quite quiet; he keeps himself to himself but you know where you stand and he is straightforward and tells it how it is. It is hard to describe and you just know what he is saying even without him saying the words. Some will say what they think, but he says what you need to hear and he says it in as few words as possible."

As well as wanting the best for his players, Coppell was fully behind the Falmer stadium project at Brighton and the development was one of the main drivers for his accepting the job in the first place. So it was no surprise when he went public with the club's predicament, saying: "What's killing us – and killing is the right word – is the public inquiry into the Falmer Stadium project, which is just a drain. It's costing millions. It's a big black hole. Bobby was going to go because we were desperate for the money to help with the inquiry. When you look at QCs, who earn more on an hourly basis than footballers, you can see what it is costing. We are in the midst of a struggle that will determine the prosperity of the club, but paying the price."

Knight was more aware than ever that Coppell, even above the irrepressible Zamora, was pivotal to the club's future. He said: "I'd had an enquiry of £3 million from Bill Kenwright at Everton earlier in the year, but I wanted to keep Bobby for the season and the main reason Bobby wanted to stay was because of Steve being his manager. Though we were a struggling Division One team and Bobby had been out injured for around two months, Steve taught him so much and that period of working with Steve was invaluable to him.

"When Steve joined it was not long after we'd gained local planning permission for the new ground, so I gave him a two-and-a-half-year contract and said by the time it expired we'd be in our new home. That would have been the 2004/05 season yet we are now looking at the first game being in 2011/12, seven years late. In reality, we've had three public inquiries; we were approved locally in June 2002 and got final approval in July 2007 – even then we faced another appeal that cost us another year.

"When Steve came to Brighton I made it clear we were fighting for a stadium and our battles were already part of football folklore. He totally bought into that and even after he left he showed his character by coming back to join us on political conference marches on Brighton seafront. But, because our ground was so important to the plan, I knew it would be difficult to stand in his way when Reading came calling. In Steve's case the grass really was greener because John Madejski was in a position to provide him with what he'd needed and it became clear to me that I had to let him go. The last thing he would do is show overt delight at getting the Reading job – in fact he was reticent and felt genuinely bad – but at the same time he probably felt he was in the last chance saloon in terms of ever getting back to the Premiership. He wasn't going to get a better chance and, although I wanted him to stay and we had a great team, it was all about the stadium.

"The negotiations on compensation were no problem whatsoever, though John had been a little embarrassed when he first contacted me – he said, 'you're a mate, but I want your manager'. I knew John well enough – he would entertain me in his luxurious boardroom and I would entertain him in my makeshift boardroom at the Withdean which had, earlier in the day, been used as a crèche – so negotiations were easy enough. I told him I was prepared not to stand in Steve's way, but said, 'if he wants to go then this is what I want in compensation – and I don't want any arguments'. I'm fair but hard when it comes to business, so I agreed a figure with John that was fair. From start to finish, the whole business lasted no more than ten days."

Reading's Director of Football Nick Hammond confirmed the timings, telling me: "He was the last one we interviewed because I'd asked Dick Knight for permission to speak to Steve, but they had three games in a week that were crucial to them and Dick said to me, 'you can speak to Steve, but here's the compensation that we want and you can't talk to him until these three games are out of the way'. I knew that the Reading fans were going to be thinking 'come on, sort this out' because of the situation the club was in after Alan Pardew's departure, yet I also knew that the guy who was probably favourite to get the job could not even speak to us for more than a week."

Hammond was under particular pressure given that he had just been elevated to the role of Director of Football and his first task was to steady the Reading ship after the acrimonious departure of their manager to West Ham. Yet, while Coppell was the obvious choice, Hammond had been hoping to pull a slightly less predictable rabbit out of the hat for his first trick at Reading.

"I guess, as a person who was just going into the role, my first thought was to have someone who was not the obvious person; someone who people would look at and say 'crikey, that's an interesting appointment'. But when I spoke to Steve he had that natural calmness and authority about him and we had just been through a turbulent few weeks with the Pardew departure, so I thought we'd found a guy who would bring the calmness and experience that the group needed.

"I recommended Steve and when he met the board and the chairman the next day they immediately liked his honesty. There was no PowerPoint presentation, there were no whistles and bells, it was just very straightforward sensible conversations. After those two meetings in 24 hours, he was the unanimous choice for the job. Looking back, I am really pleased with the process and how it all went, but at the time I was a 36-year-old former goalkeeper interviewing an ex-Manchester United and England international who had already become a successful manager in his own right. I knew full well he would have been looking at me and thinking, 'what's this all about?', but that was the starting point of our relationship. It probably took about six or seven months for it to get to the point that it was a good working relationship, because my role was so new."

Knight, for one, knew it would take time for Hammond's relationship with his new manager to grow. But this was business, nothing personal, and one thing that Knight knows inside out is business. As the last of the diners in Topolino's started to make their way out towards the beachfront, Knight blew the flame off a sambuca and offered me a wafer-thin after-dinner analogy.

"Football is a business but the product is totally unpredictable. If you are Cadbury's and make chocolate then your end product is totally controllable, but in football it is not. In my view it comes down to management and therefore the most important relationship is between the chairman or owner and the manager. Steve was only with me for a year, but we had a wonderful relationship."

I really could talk to Dick all night and the staff at Topolino's were clearly worried we might do just that as Dick began to regale me with another story from when he sat at a different table in this very restaurant. Our waitress, the daughter of owner Angelo, wandered over to clear our table and Dick turned to her in search of some form of reassurance as he told me: "It's not as if I am here every day, Stuart, I wouldn't want you to think that.

"I'm not, am I?" he said, turning to our young waitress. "Often enough," she said, then added with a smile: "your usual double espresso, Dick?"

A SPANISH SUMMER

Cue John Motson: "Away go England, left-to-right. Ray Wilkins, looking for Steve Coppell straight away; testing Bossis the left-back of France." (Coppell, wearing number five on the back of his red Admiral shirt of England, stoops to pick up a ball rolled to him by England captain Mick Mills and winds up for a long throw into the France penalty area, launching a well-aimed fizzer towards the head of Terry Butcher in a clearly deliberate move). Motson's narrative continues: "And, on the far side, already the French marking up man-for-man. Mariner's on the near post, Butcher has pushed well forward ... there's a header in there ... and a great chance for the first goal ... and it's there, BRYAN ROBSON! ... Bryan Robson, number 16, pounced there in the first minute. What a start for England! Amazing! Mariner and Butcher caused problems from the throw and Robson was on hand to score his fifth goal of the season."

Shirtless England fans wearing cropped denim shorts and flip-flops leap up and down on the San Names terrace behind the goal as Jean-Luc Ettori, the France goalkeeper, bends to pick the ball out of his net with only 27 seconds on the clock. Tickets with a face value of as little as 60 pence are showing an instant return on the investment for the travelling English supporters. On the pitch, there is a sense of disbelief too. Coppell tries to congratulate the scorer of the fastest goal in World Cup

history, but can't get near him and so just waves in his direction, as he turns to trot
back to the halfway line, Kenny Sansom gives him a quick hug and seems to aim a kiss
at Coppell's right cheek, in recognition of the winger's part in the goal. Coppell offers
a sideway glance and rolls his eyes in suggestion that he can't quite believe what has
happened (the goal, rather than Sansom trying to kiss him). Graham Rix follows up
with a congratulatory slap of the cheek and England's 1982 World Cup campaign is
off and running.

THE 1982 WORLD Cup draw, farcical though it was, could hardly have been kinder to Ron Greenwood's England. As one of five previous winners of the competition, England were seeded with Argentina, Brazil, Italy, West Germany and the hosts, Spain, although right up until the last moment protests from nations including Belgium and France threatened the English seeding. Having failed to qualify for the previous two tournaments, England's right to a seeding was naturally questioned, but as winners in 1966, Greenwood's side were the convenient seeds for a draw which would involve 24 teams for the first time.

The draw itself was a shambles; some of the miniature footballs containing the names of the 18 remaining teams should have been left out for the first stage of the draw and Scotland were initially placed in Argentina's group when they had, in fact, been paired with Brazil. One of the miniature footballs broke in half mid-draw and the giant wire bingo-style cage housing the team names continually jammed. For the millions watching back home on television, it made for an evening of comedy to rival the debut of John Sullivan's new sitcom, *Only Fools and Horses*, but for the Spanish organisers it was hugely embarrassing.

Greenwood, though, would have been happy with England's Group Four draw, which pitted them against lively underdogs in France and Czechoslovakia and rank outsiders Kuwait. Best of all, England were allocated Bilbao as their base camp, delighting not only Greenwood and the English Football Association but also the Basque nation, which had been cheering the England team throughout their qualifying campaign in anticipation of their arrival.

Greenwood had already travelled over for part of an English charm offensive, taking an England team to play in a testimonial for Jose Rojo, but Brit-Basque relations were already strong – founded in the 19th century when British sailors introduced the game of football to Spain – and Bilbao itself was as much a home-from-home as Greenwood could have hoped for. Cool, green and often inclement, Coppell might have noted it was at times more Southport than Spain. To go with the British climate, England packed a few luxuries from home – or to be more precise sent over an articulated lorry packed with 120 training kits, 8 playing kits, 30 footballs and huge quantities of breakfast cereal and brown sauce.

Even so, there remained a tense backdrop to the competition in the form of heightened Spanish security. England fans' reputation for hooliganism in Europe went before them and a Spanish police force already guarding against the potential for terrorism in their own country were not prepared to tolerate any misbehaviour. The confused scenario was underlined when the England team arrived, to be greeted by cheering locals and a lobby full of security guards armed with machine guns. When the England squad turned up at their training ground for the first day, there was a tank parked on the drive.

It made for a strange environment, but Coppell had an immediate calming influence in room-mate Phil Neal, who was as quiet, single-minded and studious as the Manchester United winger he had marked for Liverpool so often in recent club matches. When I caught up with Neal to recall those six weeks of Spanish summer, he was strolling around his local garden centre, killing time before heading off to see Liverpool play Aston Villa in the Premier League later that evening. The decorative pathways lined with ornamental shrubs ensured the memories of a lush Bilbao hotel garden easily returned, though thankfully Wyevale has not yet resorted to armed guards.

There was plenty of time to kill in the summer of '82, and Neal kept up the horticultural theme as he told me that Ron Greenwood's approach to that World Cup provided the belief that both room-mates would one day end up in management. "The arena that Ron created in '82 sowed the seeds in both of our minds, I think," Neal recalled.

"Stevie and I were team-mates, room-mates and had six fantastic weeks that probably convinced us both that we could go into the management side of it when we finished our playing days. The camaraderie and knowledge that Ron put into us is the stand-out memory. He took all the best coaches in the English game – Bobby Robson, Don Howe, Terry Venables, Dave Sexton – they were all there, so we didn't just listen to Ron's voice for those six weeks."

That training set-up, coupled with the warm welcome from the Basque nation, meant that England's camp was a relaxed and happy one, despite niggling injuries to their two senior players, Kevin Keegan and Trevor Brooking. "The Basques were really lovely and we felt at home very easily and very quickly. They gave us mementos before we had even kicked a ball – we had bottles of wine depicting the year of our birth – and there was also a real camaraderie created by Ron and his staff. They knew when to give you a break; after a long season in England, six weeks in Spain can seem longer and longer and you need that different environment. You need to let your hair down socially as well and the staff knew how to withdraw. Too much information leaves you drained, so it was all about trying to get a perfect balance.

"Steve and I discussed things and made little notes along the way, but we also enjoyed a beer with Ray Wilkins or a laugh and a giggle on the bus, taking the Mickey out of Joe Corrigan, who would thump you on the arm with a right good rap if you pushed it too far. The staff would put on a social occasion, like wine tasting or a trip to the cinema, and Stevie and I had a game of tennis and some golf with FA secretary Ted Croker, who had taken his rackets and golf clubs and everything else. We were all keen sportsmen and a challenge on the tennis court was just as good as having a warm-up with Don Howe at times."

It was, however, during Howe's final technical session on the morning of the opening group game on Wednesday 16 June that Greenwood had a last-minute revelation that would see Coppell unhinge France in the opening seconds of the opening game. 'I felt that Coppell was the man to have a go at Max Bossis, whom I'd seen turned inside out by Northern Ireland's Noel Brotherston in Paris,' recalled Greenwood in his autobiography, *Yours Sincerely*.

'Our preparation was complete, but there was one possible variation which occurred to me. One of our set-piece drills was Sansom's long throw from the left to Butcher at the near post with Rix providing an alternative and Robson moving up late. "Let's do it on the right as well," I said in the dressing-room. "Steve reckons he can make the distance but we don't seem to use him, so let's have Terry at the near post for him as well. Exactly the same."'

The new routine got its first airing in the very first minute as Coppell's long throw was flicked on by Butcher for Robson to hook home the then fastest goal in World Cup history, the perfect start to a fascinating match played in sweltering conditions. The typically-British weather which had greeted the team ten days earlier had given way that very morning to searing heat that generated on-pitch temperatures in excess of 100 degrees and England looked on the verge of collapse when they came in at half-time, pegged back by Gerard Soler's 25th-minute equaliser.

Back in the sanctuary of the San Names dressing room, several England players complained of feeling faint and so cold towels were applied and salt tablets handed out with the hot tea during Greenwood's tactical team talk. Whether it was the tea, the towels or the tactics, England raised their game and France buckled after Robson scored his second, a header from a Trevor Francis cross.

Coppell then combined with his United team-mate Wilkins to set up Paul Mariner for England's match-winning goal, Mariner's fifth in his last four internationals, but Coppell's international duties were not quite finished as he and Rix were the two players summoned for the routine post-match drug test. Dangerously dehydrated, it took the pair nearly two hours to produce a urine sample, while Mariner, hardly the fleshiest of footballers, was discovered to have lost 11 pounds in the punishing Bilbao heat.

England, though, were buoyant after an impressive victory and Coppell, despite feeling utterly drained, revealed: "I always remember the feeling after that game – it was almost as if that game was winning the World Cup."

"It was a phenomenal start and we were all up for it then," remembered Neal. "We came in through the back door in qualifying, but we were going to give one hell of a tug to win it and the belief that Ron and his staff gave was a boost to all of us."

The mood in the England camp was increasingly high; the Falklands war ended during the opening week of the tournament, lifting a dark cloud which had lingered over the nation throughout their preparations, while several players were receiving good news from back home. Robson, presented with a gold watch for his record-breaking opener against France, received the news that his wife Denise had given birth to their second daughter the day after his two-goal heroics, while Kevin Keegan was awarded the OBE in the Queen's birthday honours. As Keegan's room-mate, Brooking, already had a similar honour their room became known as the 'royal suite', though injuries meant neither player was ready for a royal appointment with the Czechs, despite West Ham doctor Brian Roper flying out to Spain to give Brooking an injection in his injured groin.

Their continued absence meant that Greenwood named an unchanged team for the game against a Czech side held to a 1-1 draw by Kuwait in Valladolid. Peter Shilton in goal behind a back four of captain Mick Mills, Butcher, Phil Thompson and Sansom; Coppell again on the right flanking his United colleagues Robson and Wilkins and with Rix on the left. The in-form Mariner and pacy Francis remained up front and it was Francis who put England in front after a mistake by goalkeeper Stanislav Seman. A Jozef Barmos own goal sealed a routine win and guaranteed a second-phase place despite an ordinary performance which was matched by a grey day in Bilbao.

Francis then scored again as England edged past Kuwait 1-0 to complete a clean sweep of Group Four victories and send them through to a second round group also featuring West Germany and the hosts Spain.

The opening game of the second phase sits vividly in Coppell's memory, even though the game itself was far from impressive. He recalled: "We had a 0-0 draw with Germany and I always remember playing in that game against Hans-Peter Briegel, who was a giant of a man. In the first five minutes I went up to him and tackled him, or tried to tackle him, and he sort of brushed me away and said, 'get away, little fly', which always sticks in my mind."

Germany then beat the Spaniards 2-1, which left England needing to beat Spain by two clear goals to reach the semi-finals and, when favourites Brazil were beaten by Italy the day before Greenwood's team faced the hosts, there was a feeling that World Cup glory was potentially just two goals away. "We thought we were so close to winning that competition," recalled Neal with a sigh.

Four games in less than a fortnight had taken their toll on Coppell's knee and the injury which had threatened his place at the tournament finally forced him to sit out the action. It was an agonising absence, emotionally more than physically, as Coppell looked on from the sidelines at Madrid's magnificent and newly refurbished Bernabeu Stadium. The £3 million refit turned the Bernabeu into a 91,000 all-seater stadium and the England team had a potential refit too as Keegan and Brooking were finally declared ready to play, though only from the substitutes' bench if and when Greenwood needed to play his trump cards. 'They wouldn't have lasted the full game, so how could I have handled my substitutes if someone else had got injured?' reasoned Greenwood in his autobiography.

Cologne's Tony Woodcock took Coppell's place in the side, but made way when Greenwood finally moved to give Keegan his World Cup debut. A minute later, Brooking replaced Rix and immediately injected a new skill level into the game, yet England had only 25 minutes to save their World Cup. The 33-year-old Brooking would not play again until the following March and Greenwood knew his introduction was a high-risk strategy. It was a gamble that so nearly paid off; Robson brilliantly created a chance for Keegan, but the Southampton striker somehow steered his header wide of an empty net, a miss he was never able to explain. Then Brooking carved out an opening for himself, but saw his poked effort blocked by Luis Arconada.

"We didn't get through and the feeling in the dressing room afterwards was just one of devastation," remembered Coppell. Neal, who had enjoyed only a few minutes of pitch-time during the tournament, knew his last World Cup chance had probably gone at 31, though Coppell still had Mexico in 1986 and possibly even a 1990 appearance ahead of him.

"I knew it was my last World Cup – I was a few years ahead of Steve, so he would have felt there was another one in him," recalled Neal. "You couldn't help but think to the future and you do learn lessons along the way. It was a learning experience and there were things from that trip which I think we both took into management."

Though neither of the room-mates knew it at that time, management for Coppell would come sooner than the next World Cup.

ASCENT OF THE ROYALS

The acoustics in the Madejski Stadium dressing rooms are resonant, capable of carrying the merest whisper or of turning a manager's shout into a deafening boom. But today the home team dressing room at Reading's custom-built £50 million home is silent, save for the occasional scrape of studs on floor, the bubble-wrap pop of cracking knuckles, or a cough. A nervous cough, probably.

The players sit in silence, most of them staring at the floor as they wait for their manager to make his way down from high in the stands, his vantage point for the first half. Like chastened schoolboys sent to their room after being told "just wait til your father gets home".

It is an atmosphere few of them are accustomed to. With only two defeats in their 40 league games, Reading are already assured of Premiership football next season and victory over a Derby side for whom the spectre of relegation still looms would seal the title if Sheffield United fail to win at Stoke. Steve Coppell's Royals, though, have simply failed to get going.

Half-time lectures have become rare at Reading, not simply because there has been more to celebrate than commiserate since Steve Coppell's arrival in October 2003, but because the manager is not prone to tantrums. "Shouting and screaming at you makes one person in this dressing room feel better, and that's me," he had said when he first arrived at the club, two years earlier.

Even when the door handle does finally turn and the manager enters the room, the stillness hangs for a few seconds more; a moment frozen in time. When the silence is at last broken, when Coppell begins his summing up of the first half of a game which could define the season, it is not the reaction any of them had been expecting. "I am disappointed in you," Coppell says in monotone annunciation, "so disappointed."

The brief delivery is replaced by the returning silence, giving the players a moment to understand the verdict. Every chastened schoolboy knows, deep down within his innermost fears, that he will be able to deal with the rebuke of a returning father, that it is the anticipation which heightens the anxiety. But paternal disappointment is an altogether harder emotion to handle.

Coppell elaborates only briefly before leaving his players to their own thoughts and heading for the dugout to take in the remainder of the action. Five Reading goals later the final whistle heralds a pitch invasion from the home fans, a swarm of buzzing excitement that sweeps the players down the tunnel and back in to the dressing room. Minutes later, a full hour after he had left that room, Coppell is turning the handle again and entering the champions' dressing room, where the acoustics are in full effect.

STEVE COPPELL'S SIX seasons at Reading were eventful to say the least. Having stepped into the breach to steady the ship after the acrimonious departure of his former pupil Alan Pardew to West Ham, Coppell's influence on the team was swift. With barely any budget remaining when he arrived in mid-October 2003, Coppell nevertheless managed to stamp his own hallmark on a team moulded by Pardew's hand. Reading's ninth-place finish in 2003/04 was modest, yet full of promise, and when the Royals raced to the top of the Championship by Christmas in Coppell's first full season the Midas touch he had shown at Palace was being introduced to rural Berkshire. Reading fell away woefully in the New Year though, failing even to make the play-offs and with a revenge-inspired victory over Pardew's Hammers the only glimpse of their early season form. But his team learned from that chastening experience the way his Palace players had used the pain of losing 9-0 at Anfield, and the two seasons which followed for the Royals were nothing short of remarkable.

Graeme Murty was firmly established in Pardew's side when Coppell arrived and became the inspirational leader of the new Reading. Murty was the former Reading captain by the time we caught up to talk about Coppell, yet his move to Southampton remained fresh enough to mean he talked about his former manager as though they were still in tandem. These were recent memories, not distant ones, and most of the stories were of lessons learned from a man Murty clearly believes is the master tutor.

There is something almost unnatural about seeing Murty in a kit that bears the badge of any team other than Reading, yet something instantly familiar about the way he walked off the training ground and over to meet me, laughing and joking with the younger Saints players who hung off his every word; most of which are punchlines.

"I'm always happy, you know that," he said after I commented on how well he looked as we settled into the home team dug-out alongside Southampton's immaculate Staplewood training pitch. Murty looked at home there, the instant ease with which he settled into the surroundings and the words he chose suggesting that a future in management beckons. Tucked into the corner of the dug-out, a recovery shake in one hand following a tough morning of early season training, Murty still looked every inch the player, yet could just as easily have been a trainee manager, getting used to the feel of the hot seat. He told me: "I have already talked to Steve about picking his mind if I decide to go into coaching and managing. As a footballer, you do reflect the people you have learned from and I think that comes through as a manager as well. I think I have been very fortunate to learn from some very good managers and coaches but in Steve Coppell I have learned from a great one. He is someone who conducts himself in a manner that I would be proud to emulate. If people were to compare my integrity and my honesty with his in later years, I don't think I could have a greater compliment paid to me."

Murty's relaxed demeanour in his new surroundings created a scenario not unlike that of Coppell's arrival at Reading, where Murty remembered the new manager seamlessly becoming part of the landscape at the club's Hogwood Park training ground. "There is no distinct sensation of him coming in and taking over; he just seemed to be there, watching," Murty told me. "It wasn't a nice atmosphere at Reading at that time and there was a lot of uncertainty around following Alan's decision to leave, but then we had someone coming in who knew what he wanted and knew the methods he was going to use to get those things. He left us in no uncertain terms as to how he was going to go about it. When a club has a change of manager players have to prove themselves to the new guy and at that stage it was hard because Steve Coppell doesn't give a lot away. He doesn't show a lot in his expressions or his voice, so every day you keep on striving to do that little bit more. Sometimes you do too much through trying to impress, so you have got to be strong, do what you know you are good at and be yourself.

"Pardew and Coppell are chalk and cheese. Alan Pardew managed in your face; a high-tempo, loud, confident cock-of-the-walk kind of bloke who demands something from you every second of the day; Steve Coppell is very much into the self-discipline side, where you are responsible for your performance. He thinks if you are not motivated then you shouldn't be playing football. You have to want it; you really have to be self conditioned, self motivating and self aware and I think that is something that playing under Steve helped me become. You have to know your roles, know what you are good at, what you are not good at and play to your strengths. I think Steve helped me identify them as well as anyone else.

"Even now my overriding sensation of him being at the club is the very watchful nature of the guy. He is not expressive, he doesn't shout and scream or bawl and throw things. But you know for a fact that everything you do, whether it is on the training pitch or in the canteen or in the weights room, he knows about it. It gets back to him and he factors it into his thinking. He doesn't feel the need to comment on anything but you know if you are being a bit of a dick he'll see it and there might be a little black mark that goes against your name. You have to endeavour to get rid of those black marks as often as you can."

The manager's understated entrance was very deliberate. Director of Football Nick Hammond, whose first task in the newly created role had been to find Pardew's replacement, told me: "I met Steve on his first morning and asked how he wanted to work it, whether he wanted the players in a room at the training ground or at the stadium. He said, 'no, we'll just train' and that's how he did it. He wandered out and watched them train, in the breaks in training he started to introduce himself to a few and he had five minutes of chat at the end.

"I saw it at the very start and it never really changed, he just allows things to evolve. He observes and sees the dynamic and then deals with it in that way. There was no big entrance, there was no big meeting, it was simply 'let's get to work'. Then he started to change things slightly and began to put his own mark on what was going on."

Coppell's first signing for Reading was a significant one, Ivar Ingimarsson leaving Wolves in a £100,000 deal just two weeks after Coppell's arrival. Amy Lawrence noted in the *Observer* that, just as dogs have a habit of resembling their owners, so football clubs are often a reflection of their own manager. That is particularly true of Coppell – loyal, hard-working and utterly focussed; he would probably keep a gundog – and largely a result of the players he surrounds himself with. Ingimarsson, having faithfully represented Coppell at Brentford and on loan at Brighton, is probably the finest example of that trait.

Hammond explained: "Steve likes familiarity, he likes to know in a player what he's going to get. He doesn't like to be surprised and with Ivar he knew exactly what he was getting. Ivar had played for him at Brentford and at Brighton and we knew him well. He was out of the team at Wolves and he was a good take at the time, a player who has proved to be an outstanding signing for Reading Football Club.

The significance of the signing was not lost on Murty, either. He said: "I think Ivar has played for him more than any other player and it speaks volumes that he is the ultimate professional. He makes sure he takes care of himself, he gives everything in training and you know what you are going to get. He is Mr Reliable and I think he is the archetypal Steve Coppell footballer."

It was, Murty insisted, important to Coppell to set his own tone on the training pitch, despite often adopting the role of general on the hill while others carried out their duties on the front line. "He's got his guys who run the coaching sessions the way he wants and he has got his senior pros who dictate the character of the training sessions, but he is the one who will pull you aside and have a quiet word if it is good, bad or indifferent. He is the one who will tell you what he wants to see and the things that you can influence – and there are no wasted words.

"He was very, very keen on the whole being more important than the individual and it didn't matter if you were Cristiano Ronaldo – if you didn't fit into his mentality and his ethos you weren't playing. When you get a group of very like-minded people and put them in with that mentality, with someone as well respected as Steve Coppell drumming that into you, good things can happen. It was in those first months at Reading that he laid the groundwork and the foundations for the things that would come to pass."

Coppell was also quick to demonstrate his knack for spotting a lower division talent, having paid £150,000 for Cambridge striker Dave Kitson at Christmas despite others being put off by the forward's injury troubles. Gillingham thought they had completed a deal to sign the striker, only for Reading to snap him up on Christmas Eve, prompting a holiday phone call to Hammond from Gills chairman Paul Scally that was not exactly dripping in festive cheer.

Less controversial were the signings of wingers Bobby Convey and Glen Little, while Coppell also returned to his former club Brentford to sign central defender Ibrahima Sonko and striker Lloyd Owusu on free transfers. For Little, the move finally represented the chance to play for his hero, 10 years after modelling Coppell's crossing techniques as a teenager at Palace and 20 years since having his prized Steve Coppell pictures signed.

Little said: "It was a no-brainer really as I was out of contract at Burnley, so I joined Reading. It was a relief to finally get the chance to play for him, as I was long gone and playing in Ireland by the time he returned to Palace. The next time I came into contact with him was when I scored what turned out to be the winner for Burnley at Brighton when he was manager there. He came in at half-time and gave me a bit of stick."

Like Murty, Little's impression of Coppell when he first arrived at Reading was one of Godfather – in the Don Corleone mould rather than that of Christian responsibility, though arguably both are relevant. "I remember someone telling me 'he sees nothing, but he sees everything' and that sums him up perfectly," Little told me. "We all knew he was sharp; it was all logged upstairs."

Coppell's Royals jigsaw was beginning to take shape, but by the time he took his team to Wigan on the final day of the 2004/05 season the dream of promotion was all but over. Paul Jewell's side needed victory to ensure a first ever season in the top flight, but Coppell knew that if Reading secured a better result than Pardew's fast-finishing Hammers then a play-off place would be theirs. It was Wigan's party, a 3-1 win sweeping the Latics to the Premiership while West Ham won at Watford to leave Reading trailing in seventh, but Coppell was quick to turn the *schadenfreude* to his own advantage.

As Jewell and Wigan chairman Dave Whelan sprayed champagne and their players enjoyed a lap of honour around the JJB Stadium, Coppell forced his side to stand, watch and applaud the home side's success. Later, in the sanctuary of the dressing room, he told his players to learn from the defeat and to use it as their motivation the following season.

"It took watching Wigan celebrating on the pitch to make us realise what we were missing out on," Murty told me. "We knew that we could have dragged them back into the play-offs with us if we had beaten them, but we just didn't have the belief when it came to it. Steve showed us that you have to have the disappointments and work with them and you have to take everything that you have learned, the good as well as the bad, and put them into practise the next season. There was no quantifiable reason why we tapered off that season, other than a good Christmas party perhaps! We didn't change anything, but we just fell away and I can't nail down what happened. We got to the end of the season feeling flat and unfulfilled but no-one castigates themselves more than Steve Coppell. When you work with him you work hard, but he wants to make sure you take care of yourself in terms of rest. When you have the summer off he insists you get your rest in and come back renewed. He said he wanted everyone fresh for the new season and no injuries in pre-season; one of his great sayings is that there are no medals in training."

While the players were getting their rest, Coppell was still working, travelling to Ireland to watch Kevin Doyle help Cork City to the League of Ireland title. By the time Reading's players reported for pre-season training there were two new faces at Hogwood, Reading chairman John Madejski parting with a modest £78,000 to secure Doyle and little more than pocket change to add teenager Shane Long to the deal as an Academy player.

"We went over to Ireland to watch Kevin and had six pints of Guinness before the game. What did I see in him? I can't really remember, it was all a bit blurred," Coppell joked after introducing the new boy. "He did like a pint of Guinness did Steve and he still does," smiled Hammond. "We had good connections in Ireland; the manager of Cork City at the time was Pat Dolan, who I was an apprentice with at Arsenal and is probably one of my closest friends in football, so we were aware of Kevin six months before we took him. Our chief scout Brian McDermott and I were fairly nailed on with him and Shane and sent Steve for a couple of trips out there. The first time Kev was okay, but the second game he played particularly well and Steve rang me and said he was happy, so I went to Cork and did the deal.

"Steve enjoyed the trips to Ireland; we had someone pick him up and look after him and he would pull his bobble hat down and coat collars up and go to the local pub, have a pint of Guinness then watch the game. I don't think he was anonymous, most times he got spotted, but he's not a great one for going to games. He didn't do an enormous amount of scouting because his focus was always the team. He was ferocious in terms of analysis of the opposition and would watch several full-length games of the teams we were playing the week before we'd play them. He would cut and dice video and his dissection of a game was outstanding."

Coppell invested significantly more money – a club record £1 million – in Leroy Lita from Bristol City that summer of 2005 and also brought in the out-of-contract Stephen Hunt from his former club Brentford, having failed to convince Brighton chairman Dick Knight to pay a fee the previous season.

With Convey now fully fit, Coppell had the balance he required, but his rebuilding work almost collapsed from beneath him when Reading lost their first game of the 2005/06 season, at home to Plymouth. On the back of the previous season's disappointment another defeat at Coppell's former club Brighton three days later could easily have spelled the end of his reign under ambitious chairman Madejski. Instead it sparked the start of something remarkable and a 2-0 win at Brighton was arguably as significant to Coppell as Manchester United's FA Cup final replay win over his Palace team had been to Alex Ferguson in 1990.

Murty readily recalled a pivotal week as he told me: "We should not have lost against Plymouth, we conceded two rubbish goals and were pushing for the win and sometimes you are guilty of thinking you will score and then switching off the defensive side. The players felt it was our fault, so we said, 'right, let's take this one on the chin and the manager can take a back seat. We will put this right'. Regardless of letting Steve Coppell down, which you feel quite sharply, we had let ourselves down so we knew we had to go and put it right."

And they did, with Little playing a central role. He told me: "To say Steve could have been sacked two games into the season is probably a bit strong, but funny things happen in football and who knows what would have happened if we'd ended the week at the bottom of the table? Instead we were practically top and never looked back. I scored the first goal in a 2-0 win at Brighton then we won 3-0 at Preston before we came home and beat Millwall 5-0 and really kicked on. We had the title wrapped up by the end of February. That's football, there are fine lines in the Championship."

The trip to Brighton also provided another fine example of Coppell being reverentially received by fans of his former clubs. The Brighton fans who had previously doubted the wisdom of appointing a manager so obviously worshipped by their bitter rivals Crystal Palace was clearly forgotten as Coppell received a standing ovation as he took his seat at the Withdean. "Steve always used to sit alongside me in the back row of the stand at Brighton, which is about five inches off the ground, and just before we played Reading our secretary told me Steve had phoned and asked if he could have his usual seat," Brighton chairman Dick Knight told me. "It was brilliant – there was a crowd of photographers down near the pitch pointing their cameras at us in the stand and Steve was receiving a fantastic welcome."

Victory at Brighton was pivotal for Reading and Coppell, but his one-game-at-a-time approach was a picture he had painted to his players in a series of meetings ahead of the new campaign, a method of one-to-one mentoring that had served him so well before and was almost certainly the legacy of the simple requests Tommy Docherty had asked of his teenage prodigy 30 years earlier. Little explained: "Before the start of that season the gaffer went round the team having individual chats with all the players and giving us tips on how to improve individually. Steve wanted to try different things and had a few ideas and there was a feeling that if things could just click we had a good chance of making the play-offs. In the Championship the top six is the aim and you know if it goes really well the bonus is that you go up.

"Never having got into the top flight in my career I was determined to make it work and one of the reasons I wanted to sign for the gaffer was the 4-4-2 that he liked to play. The first season we didn't really use the wingers right and Nicky Forster and Kits really were the only goalscorers, so Steve's hope for the new season was to get the ball wide and get the wingers scoring. I am a bit biased, but I always believed that if you could get the wingers playing well then the team would play well; they are the teams to watch. The spirit of the players was good and it was one of those seasons you are proud to be involved in, but of course we didn't know then what lay in store."

What did lie in store was a run of 33 league games without defeat following that opening game reverse against Plymouth. Coppell's team became unstoppable and it was no coincidence that he had completed his Reading refit in the image of the side that had worked wonders for him at Crystal Palace. For Bright and Wright, read Kitson and Lita or Doyle; Sonko and Ingimarsson dominated at the heart of defence in the mould of Eric Young and Andy Thorne; for underrated full-backs in John Pemberton and Richard Shaw, Reading had Murty and Shorey; Steve

Sidwell took the Geoff Thomas role; and there were wingers, always wingers in a Steve Coppell side.

But they also needed to be the right type, as Murty spotted so early on following Coppell's arrival. The correct mentality and work ethic are as important to a Coppell side as the job a player has been brought in to do. Get that mix right and the spirit will follow; the spirit of 90/91 or the spirit of 05 to 07, their origins are the same.

"Like Palace, that Reading team was more than the sum of its parts," Murty said, adding: "it was about good players, honest players put together effectively and with everyone knowing their jobs. If you talk about Steve Coppell teams throughout his career they have all been efficient. Every player knows his role and no-one is uncertain. The collective is the important part.

"More often than not going behind or even just being under pressure would see us respond and score; we responded better than anyone else in that season. Steve always said, 'your first reaction has to be a positive one' to anything that happens in the game. If you lost the ball, the next person's reaction had to be a positive one because that sparks the next guy; if we went a goal down, or if we were under pressure, we had to have a positive reaction. I have never seen a team that epitomised it as clearly as that team.

"When you walk over the line you play the way he wants you to play, but he doesn't make you robots. More than anything else we were efficient and while at times we didn't hit the heights we wanted to reach he kept banging on that if you are solid, strong and maintain your composure, then five minutes of your best will win the game. We did that 15 or 20 times in the season where we did well and kept going then, bang, we would have five minutes of really good stuff and we'd score two or three goals. Then we'd defend, but we didn't defend as a back five, we defended from Kitson all the way back. That was the thing for me, that everyone was willing to go the extra yard and no-one was willing to do just enough. One of Steve Coppell's mantras is 'just enough is not good enough' and he expects more of you. No matter what sort of player you think you are if you don't compete and you are not strong, if you are not physical and if you don't win your battle, you are going to let the team down and that is the worst crime you can commit.

"He has always said the team comes first; if you are out of the team you have got to get in the team, but you don't detract from the whole. Sometimes the people who aren't playing are more important than those that do because they can set the tone and make sure the ambience in the changing room is right. If you have got people who are negative and pulling energy away from the 11 then you are all going to lose and he doesn't suffer it."

There were turning points throughout that remarkable unbeaten run, but Little remembered a scrambled point at Hull as a particularly significant result. "I scored an equaliser with about 15 minutes to go and we were unbeaten in 14 games; if nothing else that unbeaten record kept us going. All of a sudden it was 19, then 25 and the unity and spirit grew stronger the longer we went on. There weren't too many huge escapes, Hull was probably one, but the biggest was Derby on New Year's Eve when Shane Long, who had never played before, came on and equalised in the 92nd minute. We had a will not to get beaten and when we finally did lose at Luton we were 17 or 18 points clear at the top. Promotion had pretty much taken care of itself."

Incredibly, Coppell's Reading were promoted before March was out, a 1-1 draw with Leicester at the Walkers Stadium securing the club's first ever season in the top flight, and it was only when that elevation was confirmed that the manager finally let his emotions show. Coppell had remained defiantly calm all season, persistently resisting the temptation and endless invitations to talk about promotion even when it became inevitable to the most cynical of sceptics. He said he never banned his players from using 'the P-word', claiming: "When you hear some of the shit they come out with, you might as well let them talk about promotion."

Even so, the relief was clear in the celebrations at the Walkers Stadium as Coppell broke away from the half-way line hugs to make a solo dash off the pitch and towards the Reading fans before tearing off his overcoat and throwing it to the baying mob. "We were waiting for someone to throw it back," remembered Murty, whose favourite moment amidst those celebrations came as Reading's players formed a line and ran towards the corner flag before diving together and sliding on their bellies towards their still buoyant supporters. It made for a theatrical finish, like the cast of a West End show taking their final bow but with a touch of footballers' bravado tagged on.

Then the coaching team took their turn; Wally Downes, Kevin Dillon and Coppell linking arms and trotting towards the fans as chairman Madejski applauded from the side. But as Dillon and Downes adopted their dive positions, Coppell let go and stayed on his feet, possibly mindful of the knee injury that ended his playing career also cutting short his day's celebrations, but also, I imagined at the time, nervous of returning home with no coat and grass stains on his knees.

"He let go," remembered Murty. "It was as though he was laughing at a joke that no-one else got and he is brilliant at that. If he hits you with a one-liner and you don't get it there's a little giggle. It's not a laugh, it's a giggle to himself because he knows he has got you. He is very dry and doesn't express himself to you openly but if you know what to look for he's a very humorous person.

"Leicester were brilliant that day. They sent champagne into the dressing room and wished us all the best and Steve was buzzing for the lads. He told us it was a fantastic achievement to be promoted so early and it was reward for everything we had done, but typically he then said: 'Right, you've got a big game coming up against Derby at home, so make sure you enjoy this and take as much as you can from it because these moments don't come along very often, but when it is time to go back to work you go back to work.'"

And that was the end of Coppell's promotion celebration as he returned to face the media, claiming: "I can't put into words what it feels like to win promotion, but I'd like to put it into a can and open it later." Then he was gone, preparing for the next game of Reading's juggernaut of a season. With six games still remaining, Reading probably could have lost the lot and still been assured of the title, but Coppell continued to adopt his one-game-at-a-time approach and was livid when his side failed to hit the high notes in the first half of what was a potential title-clinching game against Derby. No doubt mindful of the hype and hullabaloo which had taken Manchester United's eye off the FA Cup final ball in 1976, Coppell was adamant his players did not get caught up in the inevitable promotion party that was taking place off the pitch on April Fools Day at the Madejski. But, as Reading's fans 'ole'd' every successful pass and encouraged defenders to shoot from their own half, it was clear that the promoted side were coasting.

"When you have been awful for the first half you can get leathered by a manager, but that is not his style," Murty told me. "Normally it's a case of sit down, take a deep breath, get a drink, pause. Then he will tell you what you have done wrong. There are no histrionics, no shouting, no screaming, he just says 'this is what you did wrong, this is how you put it right'. He is very pragmatic, but when we came in at half-time having been rubbish against Derby it was the first time I have seen him disappointed in us.

"I have seen him angry, but never disappointed, and he told us our performance was unacceptable and failed to match the standards we had set for ourselves, or for him. When managers scream and shout you can scream back at them, switch off, agree with them or whatever, it's really easy to deal with, but when someone looks at you and very calmly tells you they are disappointed in you it's really hard to react against.

"We were sat there like kids; it was a killer. There were some hardened footballers in that changing room and they were all sat there like chastened little boys. We knew we had let ourselves down and we couldn't wait to get back out. When we came back later, having scored five in the second half, he was all smiles, saying, 'boys, you have won the title and you deserve it, thank you for responding in the right way, now let's go and enjoy it'. The lads were spraying him with champagne and he had a laugh and really enjoyed the experience, but even then you knew that behind the expression and behind the enjoyment he was thinking about the next game. He is just one of those people who doesn't switch off from it."

The focus remained as Reading put another five past Cardiff the following week, beat Stoke and forced Yorkshire draws at Leeds and Sheffield Wednesday, before Murty's penalty clinched Reading a 2-1 victory over QPR and broke Sunderland's record of 105 points in a Championship season by a single point to set a record for a 46-game season which has yet to be bettered.

True to form, Coppell saved his celebrations for his annual period of quiet reflection on a beach in Thailand, a beer in his hand as he contemplated his achievements and started plotting for a return to football's top flight. There are no witnesses to confirm either way, but rumour has it that the manager had a smile on his face.

BEERS, WHINES AND SPIRIT

There's an Englishman and a Scotsman in a bar and the Scotsman turns to the Englishman and asks: "What time should we be heading back?" The Englishman replies: "I reckon we could manage one more." Fits of giggles follow, not because it's the punchline to a joke, but because Scotland midfielder John Wark and England winger Steve Coppell are acting like a pair of naughty schoolboys and they know trouble is brewing.

Two World Cup refugees on the eve of crucial operations, Wark and Coppell are easing their pre-operative nerves with a couple of pints and a post-mortem of their relative frustrations at Spain '82. Just what the doctor ordered; except that their doctor knows nothing of their whereabouts.

David Dandy is one of the most sought-after specialists in football. A knee surgeon to the stars, he has patched up many an ailing athlete and ensured that careers are extended, or at times rescued, when others have failed to halt the decline. Yet as he had run through the intricacies of arthroscopy – a form of keyhole surgery of the knee – with his latest patient, the words had become drowned in a sea of harsh lights and the clinical aroma of disinfectant. Steve Coppell needs some fresh air and Dandy's staff are quick to suggest a stroll with Wark so the pair can relax ahead of their morning operations.

The sky is light and the air sticky as the pair made their way back out into the Cambridge streets with the directives "don't be late" and "follow your nose", yet on this balmy late summer evening, one of those statements will easily outweigh the other.

JOHN WARK HAD been afforded a little more time to prepare for his knee operation in Cambridge after the 1982 World Cup. Not only had his routine – a straightforward clean-out of a cyst in his knee – with world-renowned surgeon Dandy been booked well in advance, he also had the unwanted luxury of an early flight home from Spain after Scotland's brave, yet futile, three-game finals.

Like Coppell, Wark had been a major doubt for the trip to Spain, but had managed to put off an operation until after the finals. It may have been with an air of wishful thinking that the appointment was for 13 July, two days after the World Cup final, but the tournament was nevertheless something of a personal triumph for Wark. The Ipswich striker scored twice in the opening win over New Zealand and then set up David Narey for the goal which rocked Brazil in the second group game, only for the South Americans to roar back and win 4-1. A 2-2 draw with Russia saw Wark's Scotland eliminated on goal difference and he was on his way home to Ipswich while Coppell's England were preparing for the second phase.

"As usual, we were home before England," laughed Wark as we remembered that near miss, his chuckle hardly masking the painful curiosity of what might have been "had we not woken Brazil up". Wark was an unlikely source on my journey to find the real Steve Coppell, but we were thrown together by our publisher, who had recently launched Wark's memoirs, *Wark On*, and was keen for me to meet one of "football's nice guys".

Wark is proud of his own book – not least the reversible covers; red and blue interchangeable for launches in Ipswich, Liverpool, or Scotland – and was keen to tell tales to help me in my own biographical searches. "I didn't know Steve before we met at that clinic, though we had played against each other a few times, but we soon got talking the night before our operations," he remembered. "We both had our briefings about what was going to happen in the morning and when they told us we were allowed out for an hour for some fresh air or a walk we suddenly became a couple of naughty schoolkids! They were saying 'you can go for a walk' and we were whispering to each other 'we could go for a beer'. It was probably me who dragged him down the pub, but I don't seem to remember him taking much persuading. We went into Cambridge and found a bar that was packed with students and a few people recognised us, so we had to keep out of the way; we tucked ourselves into a corner and kept our heads down while we had a few pints.

"We were talking about football and the time flew by. I knew of his team-mates who I played with for Scotland, like Gordon McQueen and Arthur Albiston, and he knew a few of the England boys who played with me at Ipswich – Paul Mariner, Mick Mills, Terry Butcher and Russell Osman. Because we got talking we had a couple more pints and when we got back in to the clinic they weren't very happy. We told them we had been for a walk, but I think they could smell that we'd had a couple of drinks.

"But that was the culture in those days, everyone liked a little drink. I played for Ipswich and Liverpool and there was a drinking culture in those days and I knew United were like us too. Even over a few beers you could see that Steve was clued up; some footballers are not the brightest but he knows what he is on about. Just from that first conversation I expected him to go on and be a good manager.

"I didn't see him after that – we said 'all the best' and we had our ops at different times – but whenever I have bumped into him since we always talk about that night. It's never about the operations, always 'do you remember the time we snuck out for a pint?' Honestly, it was like two schoolkids."

Having missed England's final game of the World Cup after his knee had failed to take the strain, Coppell had virtually begged Dandy to squeeze him into his schedule before heading off on a holiday which would have delayed Coppell's comeback from injury. It was a timely intervention and the added anaesthetic of a few pints obviously did the trick as, less than six weeks after Dandy's operation, Coppell was not only declared fit to face Birmingham on the opening day of the 1982/83 season, but also announced his return with a goal in the 3-0 Old Trafford win. It was the first day and the first goal of the rest of his career.

Dandy's procedure had cleaned out the knee and removed the floating cartilage that had been causing problems for Coppell ever since that Jozsef Toth tackle at Wembley more than 18 months earlier. It was a much needed spring-clean of the joint, but something was still not quite right and after six games in the opening few weeks of the new season the workload was taking its toll on Coppell's fragile knee.

Coppell's problem was that the damaged cartilage between his femur and tibia was not providing its natural protective barrier, causing the two bones to rub together and resulting in an irreversible deterioration of the joint. Dandy's advice was to cut down on training, but as Coppell had always been a hard worker the advice was easier to give than it was for Coppell to take. Instead, Ron Atkinson gave his ailing star a fortnight off to concentrate on building up his leg muscles and when Coppell returned to action for big games against his boyhood idols Liverpool and the local derby with City, he had adopted a new mentality. "I was aware that I was not 100 per cent fit and made a conscious decision to take greater care and avoid the sort of challenges I had been used to," he revealed. "I managed to fall into a routine and felt I was playing quite well. I was using my soccer intellect instead of my legs and making the most of my experience to save unnecessary running and strain. To my surprise and delight I discovered that my brain was quite capable of looking after me."

He was, however, also increasingly dependent on anti-inflammatory drugs before every game, medication that played havoc with his stomach lining, but allowed him to continue on a game-by-game basis and then to rest, rather than train, as he looked to play through the pain until the end of the season when a second operation would improve the damaged joint, or at least ease the pain it was causing.

While Coppell was relieved with his new-found intelligent game, endorsed by inclusion in Bobby Robson's England plans as the new national coach sought to qualify for the European Championships in France, there was no escaping the fact that he was compromising, adopting the sort of self-preservation approach that a 35-year-old might attempt to see him through just one more season at the end of a long career. Coppell was only 28 and already others were noticing that the damage was starting to take its toll, not least his young United room-mate. It was massively ironic that Northern Ireland international striker Norman Whiteside would go on to have his own bright career cut woefully short by a crippling knee injury and he admits that his former mentor's battle with a similar problem was a psychological barrier he never overcame.

'Though he battled on through the World Cup and a last season with United, it was difficult to watch his athleticism ebb away as he battled through matches with a patched up knee,' Whiteside said in his autobiography *Determined*. 'His influence on me persisted long after he retired and not just through the good habits he passed on. It was a sad coincidence that we both succumbed to chronic knee damage and what happened to him was always at the back of my mind, and those of the consultant and medical staff, whenever my knee seized up over the next few years. I always tried to be positive when the familiar stiffness and pain returned, but the added psychological burden of knowing that Steve had not recovered was ever present and gnawed away at everyone's confidence.'

Manchester Evening News football writer David Meek could not help but notice the decline either. Meek had got to know the real Steve Coppell over many years of United coverage and admitted: "He had a real problem there, but being the kind of guy he is he didn't make a fuss about it. He didn't offer it as an excuse, he just got on with it and played as well as he could, but I think for those of us watching from the outside he didn't really hit the same kind of level again. I just don't think Steve was running at 100 per cent because of his injuries, so it made it difficult for Ron Atkinson, but Ron basically liked Steve's style of play as he had always cultivated wingers himself. He brought Lawrie Cunningham to Old Trafford and he liked people who could fly, but unfortunately at that stage of Steve's career he was hitting injuries and I think that affected his form."

Coppell's wings had been clipped, yet there were still enough glimpses of form to suggest that the best was yet to come. Scoring the second goal in a 9-0 annihilation of Luxembourg at Wembley was one such high, but a woeful goalless draw with Greece at Wembley followed to leave the European Championships out of reach for Robson's England. Not that Coppell would have been in France anyway as the Greece debacle proved to be his 42nd and final England appearance. It was not his final Wembley bow though, as his sixth goal of the season in the second leg of their semi-final against Arsenal completed United's march to the Milk Cup final where they faced Liverpool in a repeat of the 1977 FA Cup final. Adding to Coppell's single piece of silverware looked a fair bet when the 17-year-old Whiteside put United in front in the final, but Alan Kennedy equalised for Liverpool 15 minutes from time before Ronnie Whelan hit an extra-time winner to leave Coppell a beaten Wembley finalist for the third time.

United also secured another semi-final collision with Arsenal in the FA Cup, but Wembley was a tantalisingly cruel incentive as Coppell's fitness for the rest of the campaign was thrown into doubt when his fragile knee gave way in a League match against Sunderland on 4 April 1983. A routine tackle with Iain Munroe 30 minutes from time was not what caused the damage, but when Coppell twisted on landing it proved to be the final twist in the tale of his playing career. "It was a perfectly fair challenge, but I landed awkwardly and knew immediately I was in serious trouble," Coppell admitted. "To make matters worse, Lou Macari had gone off with an injury after only ten minutes and I more or less had to stay on or we would have been down to ten men. I stood out on the wing doing little more than making up the numbers for the last half an hour before hobbling off to the dressing room on the final whistle. The semi-finals of the FA Cup were coming up in a few weeks and I felt choked in the certain knowledge that I would miss it. I could not even face going into the players' lounge for a drink after that Sunderland game and all I wanted was to escape to the peace of the team coach. I was beginning to fear the worst."

In an attempt to keep his mind focused on being fit for the FA Cup final Coppell began to keep a diary, which became a kind of therapy for the injured star. The frank insight into the anger, frustration and ultimately sheer desperation he was feeling as he looked to battle back to fitness was first published in *Touch and Go* and offered a rare show of public emotion from the normally insular Coppell. He described it as his "confessional" and his words explain far better than mine the agonies of the period bookmarked by his second and third knee operations:

Wednesday 13 April
Though not normally a superstitious person, I found myself hoping that the date was not significant as I went to the BUPA hospital in Manchester for exploratory arthroscopy. It was reassuring to see the club physiotherapist Jim McGregor before I was put to sleep. When I came round Jim was still there and told me that when the specialist, Jonathan Noble, had opened me up he had immediately confirmed my suspicion that there was a tear in the posterior section of the medial cartilage. Closer inspection had also revealed that there was a large piece of cartilage lodged there which he had removed.

Thursday 14 April
I woke up early and lay on my bed feeling uncomfortable, sorry for myself and totally useless until the arrival of Noble at 7.30am relieved the boredom. He took the time to tell me exactly what he had done and even went to the trouble of drawing a normal healthy joint and tracing its deterioration from the fateful tackle in November 1981 until this last operation. Considering my doubts before the operation, it all sounded like good news and I began to perk up enormously. However, Noble then went on to explain that the cartilage is there for a reason, namely to stop the bones rubbing together. These bones should be hard and shiny rather like a ball bearing, but since the tackle and the damage to the meniscus one section of the bone had been rubbing against the other causing a great deal of harm. Far from the bone being hard and shiny, it was dull and the surface resembled photographs of the moon's surface. Noble was completely honest and told me that he envisaged me playing at my present level for a further two seasons with intermittent problems and then, after that, it would all be downhill.

Friday 15 April
Noble said how pleased he was with my knee and set me the target of getting fit for the FA Cup final if United are successful against Arsenal tomorrow and, if not, to rest it until next season. He told me to start with very gentle quadricep exercises and even the prospect of those felt good. I took a souvenir of the operation – a little jar containing the pieces of removed cartilage.

Saturday 16 April
The day started well and the leg felt good. A university friend, Brian Barwick, who works for BBC Grandstand, had made arrangements for me to watch United's semi-final against Arsenal from the comfort of the BBC television studios. I thought it sensible as I can't bend my leg 90 degrees and sitting in the Villa Park stands would have been very cramped, not to mention the fear of getting my knee knocked.

A little voice inside my head kept telling me that it would be better if the lads were beaten and then I could have my three months' rest without feeling any pressure or missing the final. Once the game got under way that thought was drowned by the possibility of all my mates losing to a poorer team in such a vital game when Arsenal scored the opening goal through Tony Woodcock, but two fabulous goals from Bryan Robson and Norman Whiteside capped a tremendous fightback and the lads were through to Wembley. Then that little voice kept telling me that I now had a chance to give it a try, but I decided to be completely honest about it with both the club and myself and to admit if I was not fit enough to do the team and me justice.

Sunday 17 April
A pleasant, restful Sunday. Light exercises went well, the leg felt much improved and I was even walking better. A very encouraging sign for Wembley and my future!

Tuesday 19 April
My leg felt terrible. I tentatively removed the bandage from around the knee and noted that there was a lot more fluid than yesterday, so I put the leg up and rested. I was in bed by 8.30pm and needed a couple of tablets to ease the throbbing.

Wednesday 20 April
The operation was a week ago today and though there was less fluid on the leg than yesterday, it still felt sore. After feeling so good it seemed all wrong to have this relapse and, try as I might, I could not think what I had done to bring this about. Jim McGregor took one look and feared that the swelling, coupled with the redness, was a sign of infection. Within 45 minutes we were in Salford Royal Hospital for an appointment with Noble. To test the amount of inflammation Noble used his lips, sensitive to half a degree of heat, to conclude that the knee was not overly hot though both Jim and I, using our untutored palms, had thought otherwise. The heightened colour was nothing more than the antiseptic solution used to clean the area before the operation. He insisted it was only temporary and if the knee was not used everything would be fine, including my chances of playing in the Cup final. I was bandaged from knee to crotch.

Thursday 21 April
My leg was sore and uncomfortable and the only way to ease it was to lie around and do nothing but watch television, with the result that I am becoming an expert on snooker.

Friday 22 April

Instead of taking the bandage off, Noble told me that I would be best not to move the leg all weekend and he strapped me up in a leg-length back splint. I headed reflectively to Manchester city centre and the north-west premiere of the World Cup film *G'Ole*. It bought back some good memories and the close-ups of the players inspired me towards preparing myself for the renewed target of the Cup final.

Saturday 23 April

The monotony was broken because it was match day and United were playing Watford. I joined in the ritual pre-match meal at the Midland Hotel and watched Laurie Cunningham and Ashley Grimes score the goals in a 2-0 win, but I felt like an outsider and must already be sounding like an embittered ex-professional moaning about the lack of characters in the game.

Sunday 24 April

More improvement. For the first time in a week I could perform straight leg lifts with my toes pulled in. I stepped up the exercises confident in the knowledge that Noble would give the OK for the splint to come off, but he dashed my hopes by telling me to keep it on until Tuesday, adding that I would feel the benefit of the extra 24 hours in a couple of weeks.

Tuesday 26 April

An appointment with Mr Millwood, who had apparently cured Sir Stanley Matthews when he was on the brink of retiring and then helped him play until he was 50. He began the examination by telling me that the splint was useless and that I was to take it off.

I began to wonder just how he achieved an OBE when he reprimanded me for being 'useless' and a 'dope' because I was awkwardly trying to copy an exercise which involved sitting on the edge of a table and swinging my leg. However, at the end of it all he announced that all would be well in a few weeks, he would see me next Thursday and that would be £15 please. I got a special rate as it is normally £20 for a first visit. Only time will tell whether he has any healing knowledge or is a quack. If he is a con-man then he is certainly a good one.

From there it was straight on to Noble who was nowhere near as pleased with my progress. There is still some fluid around the joint and he instructed me to take things very easily and concentrate on rebuilding my wasted quad muscles. He seemed to be suggesting that I must not expect too much. Was he trying to tell me something?

Wednesday 27 April

I gave the day over almost entirely to exercise, beginning with that one of Mr Millwood's. Then it was on to the club for body work, plus quads before finishing up at the Lymm Health Club where I had a strenuous session that left me feeling in a better mental state, but through it all the knee felt uncertain and sore around the affected area.

Thursday 28 April

Millwood manipulated the joint for a full 40 minutes in what seemed like a trance. I sat there wondering whether he was a complete fraud and when I told him I could not see him on Saturday because I was going to Norwich with the team he said I shouldn't be playing because I wasn't fit! I must admit the knee felt freer and that effect lasted all night.

Saturday 30 April

Three weeks to the final against Brighton and I was in pain all day – the same pain I'd had before the operation – at the back of the knee. It dug in so badly that I did no exercises at all.

Monday 2 May

The lads are flying off to Spain tomorrow and I went with them to the Hilton at Gatwick and, for no particular reason, got absolutely plastered. The manager came down to complain about the noise at around 3.30am, but after he had gone back to bed our behaviour grew progressively worse. I vaguely remember trying to toss Ray Wilkins' shoes onto a huge model aeroplane that was suspended from the ceiling in the foyer before finally crawling into bed at around 6am.

Tuesday 3 May

Suffered all the usual regrets when, after an hour's deep sleep, I crawled out of bed to go back to Manchester on the empty team bus. I arrived safe enough to keep my appointment with Noble, who told me that the fluid around the knee may well be a permanent fixture from now on. Apart from that he noticed a marked improvement and gave the go-ahead to start running and to use weights in my recovery programme.

Friday 6 May

Today I started cycling, which I intend to keep up, and jogging. The running was not as successful as I would have wished and Jim said it was because I would not 'let go'. He is right but I will not let go because the leg is simply not strong enough at this stage.

Sunday 8 May

I finally had to accept that Steve Coppell would not figure in the Cup final when I was told that to have any chance of selection I would have to play for the reserves a week tomorrow. My aim is now to get as fit as possible, even to the extent of doing daily quad exercises through the summer to build up my leg muscles.

Monday 9 May

I told Jim that I had more or less made up my mind that I had no chance of making Wembley especially as the jogging went badly again. He encouraged me to give it one more day and to try running, as increased pace is often easier than jogging.

Tuesday 10 May

The expected trial run turned out to be a non-event as I could jog only a couple of laps and, without the reserve match or Wembley being mentioned, it was decided that I should concentrate on quads only now until mid-June. Noble seemed quite pleased as he felt that I would still have difficulties in the future and that I should be thinking in terms of what I should do when they arose. Should I retire or should I have the complete cartilage removed for the sake of another year's football at the risk of being more disabled later in life? His words struck home, but I felt determined to do everything in my power to delay the judgement day.

Saturday 21 May

As if it was not bad enough missing a Cup final the day was ruined when we were told that those not playing could not travel with the team to Wembley. We were to travel in taxis that would follow behind. Remi Moses was so upset that he even threatened going home. I went with Bas Barwick, so that I could watch the match from the BBC gantry. The 2-2 draw was almost an anti-climax, albeit a welcome one after Gordon Smith missed a glorious chance for the Second Division club in the last minutes. The banquet went ahead and a handful of players went out on the town. It was all a bit of a damp squib.

Thursday 26 May

Everything has gone really well over the last few days and it was reflected in the fabulous four-goal win over Brighton in the replay as Bryan Robson scored twice to add to an Arnold Mühren penalty and a goal from Norman Whiteside. I even managed to scramble into a lap of honour, but I did not feel part of it. I was left to reflect that the Cup finals have been mental torture. I was really pleased for the lads, particularly the youngsters like Mike Duxbury and Alan Davies, but the realisation hit me that I should have been part of it.

27 May – 28 August

The days have drifted into weeks and the weeks into months as I have tried to push the future to the back of my mind and concentrate on the present. At least there has been plenty to occupy me having flown straight from the magic of Rio for a Channel Four television documentary to the unusual venue of Swaziland where Manchester United and Tottenham Hotspur were playing a series of games. I gave up any idea of training and, instead, played golf four days on the trot. It put a terrific strain on the injured leg and I was forced to develop a new stance and swing.

I returned home and finally paid some attention to my wife, Jane, and we set off for the United States on holiday. It wasn't fair on Jane but, without the buzz of a lot of people around me, I felt depressed as the feeling grew that there is no way I will ever play again. The more I thought of this the more I wanted to play. I wanted to share Jane's enjoyment of the holiday but couldn't, knowing that I was getting ever closer to going back to something I didn't want to face up to.

9 July

My birthday has always been a day for reflection in my life, a time when I have looked back over my achievement of the year before and areas in which I could improve during the coming year. I looked back on a year of affliction and disappointment and all I could see to look forward to was playing a couple of games and then struggling, playing a couple more and then struggling again and so on. Where, I asked myself, would I be in a year's time – would I be in football at all? On that day I knew that my playing career was over, but like an alcoholic I kept telling myself 'just one more'.

Monday 29 August

The season started today without me, but I am still training hard and hoping for a miracle and that first game of the season. I woke up not really in the mood for any kind of strenuous activity but kept telling myself that champions train when everyone else stops and so pushed myself to an 8am run on the local golf course. The damp, unpleasant morning reflected my own mood and I found it difficult to get going. Was it the weather which was causing the stiffness or was my knee still getting worse? I finished the run at a dispirited crawl.

Tuesday 30 August

My suspicions of yesterday were confirmed when I woke up to find my leg swollen and sore. Jim was amazed and could not understand why it had happened. I suggested that it had either been through running on hard ground or that my weights routine was too intensive. It provoked a heart-to-heart with Jim and we both voiced our doubts whether the leg would ever be strong enough for the type of football I wanted to play. One of my problems is that I cannot distinguish between the pain you train through and the pain by which nature warns you that you are doing yourself permanent damage. We both agreed that if I did play on for two years the damage I could do might be irreparable and almost reached the decision that I should retire. Though I have been subconsciously prepared for this for a long time I returned home inconsolable.

Wednesday 31 August

When I arrived for my appointment with Noble he asked me if I would talk to a young girl whom he had operated on the day before. She had broken her leg nine months earlier, it had become infected and this was her eighth operation. She was a United fan and I tried to cheer her up with a card and some chocolates. When we left her bedside I wondered if Noble had had an ulterior motive in taking me to see someone much worse off than me, but maybe I am just becoming a little sensitive.

This was my third visit to him this summer and he said how pleased he was with my progress. He insisted that the general trend has been upward despite the minor setbacks. He also told me that if there was not dramatic progress by Christmas he would operate again with an orthopaedic surgeon by his side to help assess the damage. Christmas seemed an awful long way off but on a completely mercenary level it meant that I should qualify for a new car from the club. I would rather have a new knee.

Thursday 1 September

I visited a rheumatologist called Professor Jayston and he explained that Noble thought my reactions were far in excess of my mechanical disability and he was hoping to find out why. After reading my case history and examining my leg, he prescribed a drug that I had not tried before and sent me for a blood test. I was loath to start taking drugs but as they were supposed to protect the cartilage I decided to give them a try.

Monday 5 September

I worked out a completely new fitness session:

    110 lengths in the swimming pool plus 200 hops in the shallow end
    10 pence worth of very light squash hitting
    extensive yoga exercises
    2 x 15-minute periods of cycling
    250 steps-ups, side leg raises plus straight leg and leg extensions

Tuesday 6 September

Typical of my impatience I put aside the slow build-up and really worked hard with three sessions well in excess of my planned programme which was a hard one even if I was fully fit. There is something inside me that drives me to do more once I have started. It is a kind of desperation and I forgot that once I get involved the pain lessens and it is only afterwards that I pay the full price.

Wednesday 7 September

Jim was late after the Arsenal game last night, so I began the warm-up on my own. When he arrived he was impressed by my 'Zico' legs! The joint felt good, but somehow different to any feeling I had felt before. I had a two-hour session of t'ai chi in the afternoon, but I was not happy about standing for that length of time and promptly wrote to the teacher giving some excuse for finishing my lessons. I felt drained after the full session the day before but still managed 110 lengths in the pool. There was no swelling but it still didn't feel right.

Thursday 8 September

My leg felt and looked 'podgy', but when I tested it I found I still had full range of movement and there was no reason why I should not carry on with the work. I received a telephone call from Derek Potter of the *Daily Express*, who told me that he knew how difficult I was finding it to recover and that he was wrestling with his conscience as to whether or not to break the story that I was finished. I don't think he will use the story but I decided to try and avoid the press for the moment.

Friday 9 September

My faith was misplaced. I received a very early telephone call from Peter Fitton of the *Sun* to tell me that Derek Potter and Bob Russell of the *Daily Mirror* had both broken the story that I was to retire. They know more than I do for, though the knee is puffy, it is not very tender and I can still move it fully.

Saturday 10 September

I had some limited sessions before and after the game against Luton Town. Watching these games is still very strange to me. For 70 or 80 minutes I was not bothered at all, just fully engrossed with the events on the pitch, but for 10 or 20 minutes I found myself thinking this could not be me sitting in the stand instead of playing. How could something as seemingly minor as this knee injury stop me?

Monday 12 September

I went to see Jim, hoping to start running. That turned out to be the height of optimism as Jim was confused by the state of my leg. If it can't stand the strain I have put on it then I have problems. All sorts of thoughts filled my head. Had I had the best treatment? Being hypercritical I didn't think so, but then again I am not knowledgeable enough to judge. I have always consciously tried to avoid swearing but it was the only way I could relieve my pent-up frustrations and I ran through my entire repertoire a dozen times on the way home in the car.

Wednesday 14 September
To hell with it. What did I have to lose? I woke up wanting to train and that is what I did. Just working myself into a sweat made me feel better.

Thursday 15 September
I woke up to discover that the swelling around the joint had gone down and immediately decided to go for a 45-minute run – I lasted exactly five minutes and limped back home. I went to a Tranmere Rovers' dinner as guest speaker and made a very ordinary speech. If they had known what was on my mind I am sure they would have understood.

Thursday 20 September
My next-door-neighbour Bob Carolgees asked me to appear on a television programme called *Hold Tight with Spit the Dog* . . . about my returning to the team after such a long absence. I couldn't tell him I was on the verge of retiring.

Wednesday 21 September
At last Noble was back from his holiday and I arrived early for my appointment. The decision was for an immediate operation. There is no alternative and it came as no surprise, in fact I was relieved that something positive was being done after biding my time for so long.

Friday 30 September
At last the day of the operation has arrived. No one needed to tell me that this was make or break, I sensed it. I went through the familiar pre-op checks and routines before going down to the operating theatre at tea-time to play my usual game with the anaesthetist of seeing if I could stay awake for longer than my usual count of three, which I couldn't.

It must have been two or three hours later when I came round and the first thing I did was to feel gingerly down the bed for the size of bandage, normally a good pointer to the seriousness of the operation. This time it told me nothing – or maybe I didn't want to know. A nurse brought me a glass of water and was followed in by Noble. "Good or bad news?" I asked. He signalled that I should wait until the nurse had left the room, but I knew from his face what the answer was. The tears welled up with emotion and frustration of the past few months and the dam burst when he said gently: "I'm afraid I am going to have to advise you to retire."

My world fell in on top of me.

The football world was in shock at Coppell's news, even though they had seen it coming from a distance. While Coppell battled with bouts of depression and slowly came to the conclusion that he would have to work hard just to be able to achieve the simple things in life which he had previously taken for granted, the letters and phone calls from well-wishers poured in. It was by no means false sympathy and Martin Buchan, who had already left Old Trafford by the time Coppell announced his retirement, well remembered the feeling when he heard the news. "What happened was cruel and I was devastated for him when I heard he was retiring. He was probably at his prime and had ten years of experience behind him; they say that is the time when a player peaks. We would have been in the treatment room together towards the end of my time there, but I'd had a good innings. I didn't feel sorry for myself, but I did feel sorry for Steve."

Buchan added: "It was a cruel blow to be cut down at the peak of his powers, but how he handled it was amazing. He just got on with it. He tried hard enough to get back, but perhaps because of his academic background he just got on to the next stage of his life. The tragedy was that the injury that ended his career came playing for England. It's a chance you take every time you go on the field, but for someone who had served United with such distinction to be injured on international duty is tragic and ironic. Who knows how many appearances he would have racked up for United had he stayed fit?

"You could see he wasn't happy himself with his level of fitness, but we never discussed it at the time. You have to remember we didn't have the sophisticated scanning machines back then; it's why Denis Law packed up ten years previously having had problems with his knee. If Steve was playing today, perhaps the injury would have been nothing more than a minor blip because of the improved technology and treatments."

Then, to underline the loss, Buchan told me: "I joined in 1972 and played with the best of them; George Best, Denis Law, Bobby Charlton, basically the final fling of the 1968 European Cup team. Of the players in my era, from the mid-to-late 70s, Steve Coppell was the most valuable player in our side."

It is a theory supported by Tommy Docherty, the United manager who saw enough in the young Coppell to give him his big-time break, who reflected on the end of his career almost as though he was recalling a death in the family. "It was a tragedy for United and a bigger tragedy for Steve. He could comfortably have gone on to play until he was 34 or 35 because he was in great condition and looked after himself wonderfully well," Docherty told me. "He was the best professional I have ever signed in my life, without any shadow of a doubt. In all the time he played for me, he never caused me one minute of a problem. Never. Hand on heart, from the day I signed him he never played a bad game for me; even if he was indifferent he would work his socks off. I can never understand how players today can earn more in a week than Steve Coppell earned in his whole career. The same goes for the Kenny Dalglishes, Tommy Lawtons and Tom Finneys; their wages would be a duck egg today. It can't be right."

Macari, completing my triumvirate of United legends, was another who shook his head as if in mourning of a footballing loss as he relayed the cold practicalities of a serious injury in that era: "People talk about a career in football being short, it certainly was for him and at that time you couldn't afford for it to be cut short. Your mortgage depended on playing football and winning games helped pay the mortgage with the bonuses, so it was a massive blow financially as well as emotionally. In a short career you couldn't afford to be out and not playing and you certainly couldn't afford to get an injury that ended your career.

"It is different now; when you sign your first contract at 18 or 19 you are an instant millionaire. These days you would know you are going to be okay financially, but then it would have been a worry for Steve. There was nothing in the bank making the situation look better – he wouldn't have known where the money was going to come from to pay the bills and that is possibly why he went into management so soon."

Having started his diary, Coppell believed he could find some form of therapy in writing a book, but depression overwhelmed him whenever he attempted to put his true thoughts in writing. Instead, he turned to his friend Bob Harris, then the chief sports writer with Thomson Regional Papers, who had been a trusted companion on so many England trips and had recently co-written Graeme Souness's autobiography.

"The book was difficult," Harris told me. "Steve originally wanted to write a book himself, which he was clearly more than capable of doing, but he just found it so depressing to have had to give up at the age of 28. There was so much still for him to do in the game and it affected him hugely, so he came to me and asked me to write it for him and I ended up nearly as depressed as him. Reading all the letters that had been sent to him was heartbreaking and there was very little joy in writing that book, other than his very special times with Tranmere, Manchester United and England. It was a beautiful career.

"At that time he had no intention of going into coaching or management, but by then he was in love with football – and once you are in love with football it is hard to get out of. His depth of knowledge meant he was wanted by clubs and he was by then very involved in the PFA at a senior level so he had made a lot of contacts. He was in great demand."

That PFA experience, in many ways, meant Coppell was well-placed to deal with the logistical and personal impacts of retirement, but it was an added loss as retirement as a player meant giving up the players' union. As chairman of the association for the previous year, and having been on the committee for a year before that, Coppell knew that as many as 15 professionals every year had to give up the game because of knee injuries and he also knew that his good friend Gordon Taylor would, as PFA general secretary, handle the practicalities of discussing insurance and compensation with United chairman Martin Edwards.

Taking care of the business side of football and allowing players to concentrate on the personal issues is what the PFA was formed for. The emotional aspect was down to Coppell. "It was a really difficult time for him," said Taylor, who got closer to Coppell than most others throughout his career. "The end of a career is always a frustrating time for a player and they have to go through the decision-making process of what to do next. Having to give up the PFA chairmanship only added to the problem for Steve, but I did my best to guide and help him."

Coppell's union experiences gave him a firm sense of reality, not just because of all the cases of retirements he had seen before his own, but most poignantly when Bob Kerry, the PFA's first education secretary, died of a heart attack during a fun-run just days after Coppell had announced his retirement from football. "It acted like a cold shower and suddenly everything was in perspective," said Coppell. "Here I was, 28 and in comparative good health, Bob was 42 and married with four children. When he died, he had been raising money for charity. The news of his death made me feel very humble and selfish and from then on I looked at things in a different light."

With a new sense of focus, Coppell's outlook on life changed overnight. Football may have given up on him, but he was not about to give up on football.

TEA AND SYMPATHY

The tables and chairs in the canteen at Reading's Hogwood Park training ground have been pushed to one side to create a stage. As performance arenas go it is a modest one, but for young apprentice Gary Frewen it may as well be the Royal Albert Hall, such is the pressure of the role he is playing.

Frewen has been handed the lead part in the annual gang show at Reading's Christmas party. The highlight of the performance is always the apprentices' send-up of the senior staff and tonight, ladies and gentlemen, the part of Steve Coppell will be played by Gary Frewen. If the young Irishman is nervous he doesn't show it but during the skit, as the teenager turns to exit stage right, he crashes into a pile of chairs and tables and stumbles to the floor. For a moment there is silence, until the intervention of Frewen's sidekick reveals it is all part of a well-rehearsed routine. "'Ere gaffer, you wanna watch that," calls the stooge as Frewen picks himself up off the floor and responds in a wicked monotone Scouse accent that disguises his Irish twang: "Well, you know me . . . I never look at tables!"

It is a punchline executed with such precision that it brings the house down, yet has the cackling senior professionals nervously turning in their seats to see if the victim of the satire is joining in the laughter. Frewen need not have worried, for the man laughing loudest was Coppell. His staff were laughing with him, not at him; Reading were laughing all the way to the Premiership.

ONE OF THE final journeys on my search for the real Steve Coppell was also one of the shortest; a few miles up the road on a sunny September morning to take in the greenswards of Reading's Hogwood Park training complex. Hogwood is an oasis of calm in the manic world of modern football and there are moments when the only noise you can hear is the sound of birdsong. Not on this day though, because James Harper had arrived to pick up his belongings having signed for Sheffield United earlier in the week. Harper broke off from shouting to Alex Pearce, Reading's new young vice-captain, across the car park to have a quick chat with me before climbing into his car and heading up the M1. "I love it here, I can't stay away," he told me, before outlining the footballer's occupational hazard of having to clear out accumulated junk from a house every time they change clubs. "I'm giving your book to Oxfam," he told me, referring to *Reading Between The Lines*, the result of the season I spent with the club following their promotion to the Premier League.

Much as I love talking to Harper (it's a little like being given a free ticket to the Comedy Store), it was not the midfielder I had come to see. Instead, I headed for the comfy leather sofas in the players' lounge, where Director of Football Nicky Hammond was ready to treat me to a ritual similar to one he enjoyed with Coppell for the best part of six years. "Steve hated formal meetings, absolutely hated them, but we would sit down almost on a daily basis and talk with a cup of tea," he told me as we settled down with a steaming cup of PG Tips. "We would talk through where the squad was at, sometimes across a desk, sometimes on the sofa, but as long we both had a cup of tea and were talking it didn't matter where we were. If there was anything I ever wanted to get into him or challenge him on the best time was seven in the morning with a pot of tea, because that was when he was his most receptive. He was an early bird and that was always the best time; we are both old-school in the belief that a pot of tea puts the world to rights.

"Because the conversations were so regular we both understood how we saw the team and how he was looking to improve things. It took a while, but I got to know him very well; as well as anyone does I suppose. I would challenge Steve on things and he would listen and, at times, he would take that on board and do things differently. I would allow him to get on and manage and be there to support him, that's the key. I think he was wary of our relationship to start with. He would say 'Nick, whatever way you look at it you are the face of the board' and I guess all managers are wary of the board because they are the ones who are, at some point, liable to say 'thanks very much, but enough's enough'. I'm sure in the early days he wondered what it was all about, but the role that I took on was completely different from the Director of Football role that he had at Palace.

"People get really hung up on the title of Director of Football, but there are general managers and chief executives at clubs who have the type of role that I have and the key to any of them is the relationship with the manager. You have to build a relationship of trust and an understanding of what the roles and lines of communication are and it didn't take Steve long to recognise that I was actually there trying to help him.

"I know now, because of conversations we had after he left, that he valued the role over a period of time. My aim was always to take as much pressure as possible off him and allow him to work in the way he wanted to. The chairman and the manager had a very good relationship and would have a beer together every couple of weeks after a home game. For me, Steve was a low maintenance manager and Sir John Madejski a low maintenance chairman; the fit was perfect."

Coppell's reputation was built on virtues of honesty and integrity, the watchwords of careers as a player and manager that bear remarkable similarities when played out in parallel. Yet Reading's promotion to the top flight for the first time in their 135-year history gave Coppell the chance to exorcise some top-flight demons and to repair a big-time reputation somewhat tarnished by the brevity of his Manchester City experience and the mystery surrounding his departure. During that first Premiership campaign he told me: "When I came to Reading the drive was to get in the Premiership, collectively and personally. I have been in the top division before and have a renewed respect for it. If you make mistakes it can break your heart, but I want to do well personally and for the season to go well for my players; it's human nature."

For the season to be a success, Coppell laid down a simple blueprint: "Be good enough to compete against the best and give them a game; compete with the others for the points". He told me: "You have to get yourselves up for Rooney, Saha and Ronaldo one week and then the next week it's 'oh shit, there's Drogba, Lampard and Terry'. It's constant, and if we lose to the big guys we might pat ourselves on the back but there is not a lot of honour in defeat. Losing isn't much fun and the elite teams are beyond the rest; for the others you want to be competitive."

For most of the summer ahead of their top-flight debut, it was a case of keeping the players' powder dry. Having been promoted so early, there was a long period – more than four months – of anticipation from players who had never before played at that level.

"We couldn't wait and he had to put the reins on us in pre-season," remembered Graeme Murty, the captain of that promoted side. "The boys were all saying, 'It's going to be so hard, so fast and we need to be quicker and stronger' and Steve was saying, 'It's a game of football; it's just a process'. We went to Sweden on a pre-season tour and were battering teams 10-0 and a few of us were saying there was no point. He would say, 'are you fit?' and we'd say, 'yeah'. 'Are you scoring goals?' 'Yeah.' 'Well shut up then, that's what I want.'"

Coppell wanted to head into the Premiership season with a squad of fit and healthy players creating chances, but above all he wanted them to enjoy it. The manager certainly seemed to be enjoying life and training was a daily joy, according to Murty. "The biggest smile we saw from him was during one training session when we were playing a two-in-the-middle circle and he came and joined in. Suddenly, there he was, this little bald feller in the middle of the circle. That must have been the only time he ever joined in and I said to him, 'What are you doing, gaffer? Your knee is shot.' He looked at me and said: 'You know what Murts, I just want you to be able to tell your grandchildren you trained with me once'.

"All the players were lashing the ball at him, properly smashing him and trying to catch him out, but he dealt with everything and I was devastated. At the end of the session we were looking at him thinking, *how good must you have been?* You could see he really enjoyed doing it and he was a little bit narked that he couldn't do it more often. It must have been so frustrating for someone as talented as him to retire so early, but I think he has got just as much enjoyment out of pitting his wits as a manager. Winning is something he enjoys and even if a result doesn't go for him he gets as much enjoyment from setting a team out and seeing it do well. He is very much into that and, from game to game to game, he worked out different ways of doing it."

The first match to plot and plan for was Middlesbrough, a team managed by Gareth Southgate who had come through as a young player at Crystal Palace under Coppell. An established Premiership side, Boro raced into a 2-0 lead through Stewart Downing and Yakubu and Coppell's blueprint appeared to have gone up in smoke just 21 minutes into the campaign. Andy Gray revealed during Sky Sports' live game the following day that he said out loud "welcome to the Premiership" when he heard the score on his radio. "That was exactly my thought," Coppell revealed after hearing Gray's comments.

Murty admitted: "We gave Boro far too much respect and we were wary of what they were going to do to us. We learned that lesson really harshly and, after we came back through Dave Kitson and Steve Sidwell, the manager told us at half-time to start playing our football and not theirs. You get to the Premiership and you think you have to prove you are a good footballer, but Steve's attitude was 'stuff that, be effective. Do what you are good at and make no apologies for it'. Then we got amongst them and went on to win 3-2."

It was a tough lesson from the master to former pupil Southgate, one of four Premiership managers that season who had played under Coppell at Palace (Alan Pardew, Chris Coleman and Iain Dowie completing the set). Southgate revealed after his Premiership debut: "We are all learning and me more than anybody. I have learned from everyone I worked with day-by-day and Steve is very experienced and somebody I enjoyed playing for. You can see his team play in a manner that is very positive and that is what I am trying to create. You have to be logical about it."

While Southgate was learning lessons from his first game as a manager, Reading were buzzing, though it was hard to tell whether the manager was actually enjoying the experience. "You can't tell if he enjoys it because he worries about it too much," Murty told me. "That night I watched us on *Match of the Day* and when Middlesbrough went 2-0 up they showed a picture of Steve in the directors' box. He was sat there with his finger on his chin and no expression on his face and the commentator said: 'Steve Coppell doesn't look very happy'. They went to him again when we scored to get back into it and he had the exact same expression on his face. 'Not much reaction there from Steve Coppell'. I sat there thinking, he's internalising everything and dealing with everything. He was thinking, *what can I change and what can I do there?* The process is going on and on and on. You think that he is going to go home and someone will flick an 'off' switch in his head and he's going to shut down but he doesn't, he just keeps going."

Neil Warnock once claimed that Coppell probably vented his frustrations away from the public glare, punching walls in the privacy of his own home. Everyone gets angry some time, he claimed. Coppell insisted: "I do let loose, but I don't do that. It is such a routine preparing for games, as soon as one game is finished you can't do anything about it so you go on to the next one and try to prepare for that. That's all I do, I just look at the next game and say can we win it? Yes we can."

The Bob the Builder approach, perhaps? It's not an altogether ridiculous analogy, given the simplicity with which Coppell likes to communicate his thought processes. "His greatest gift is the concise, clear way that he puts things over," Murty claimed, adding: "The hardest thing as a footballer is when there are so many instructions that you don't know what you are doing. He will put things over in a short clear pertinent way that you can assimilate and use.

"He enjoyed the process of improving the player, but he enjoyed the process of improving the team by making sure the organisation was right first. No-one has to be a superstar in his team and every time Reading were featured on TV the pundits always said 'they have no superstars'. Of course I disagree with that utterly, it's just that no-one was bothered who got the credit and Steve Coppell least of all. That is a very rare thing in football, but that's him, he is a very humble guy. His attitude doesn't change in the Premiership, but he says the higher up you go the more it is going to be about one-on-one confrontation. Can you win your battle with the guy you are up against? Can your mate help you out? You know Manchester United will be a good team and that Arsenal keep the ball for fun, but don't get caught up in what they do. He would just say 'that's you, go out and match yourself up'.

"He is famous for saying he doesn't look at tables and I don't think he does. He will look at the video of the opposition and the analysis sheet of them and they will tell him the way they play. Then the players get a report which says 'they do this and this to make this happen, so our process is to do this and this to get a result'. It could be Manchester United, Stoke, Burnley or Rotherham, anyone gets exactly the same.

"Arsenal was a classic. We were wondering how he was going to deal with them and he just stood there with a simple diagram and said: 'two centre-halves, two midfield players, little box, 40 yards apart, 20 by 20, that's them, that's what they do. They move like that, if we want to hurt them we have got to hurt that little box'. We were thinking 'what about the rest of them?' He hadn't talked about Henry, van Persie or Reyes, all he had talked about was this little box because he wants us to hurt them. Suddenly, you think, *he thinks we can hurt them*. You could almost see the lads thinking, *yeah, let's go*. It didn't work, because they were awesome, but that's not the point!"

Coppell had a simple explanation, adding: "The moment you say 'no, we can't win it' is the moment you have to have a word with the chairman and talk about making way for someone else. I'm not one to sit there and ponder what might be and what ifs, I'm very much focused on preparing for the now."

There were other issues that season that were impossible to legislate for. Reading had pocketed ten points from their previous four games when they entertained Chelsea on 14 October and the feeling was that Coppell's side had truly come of age. So too had Stephen Hunt. After breaking a Championship record for substitute appearances in a season of cameo roles, the Irish midfielder had to settle for more of the same in the Premiership before a late injury to Bobby Convey handed him his first Premiership start, against the champions. Before the game had a chance to settle, a collision between Hunt and Chelsea keeper Petr Cech in the opening minute saw the Czech international stretchered off with a fractured skull. Incredibly, Chelsea lost another keeper deep into stoppage time when Cech's replacement, Carlo Cudicini, collided in mid-air with Ibrahima Sonko and was taken to the same Reading hospital as his team-mate.

Chelsea finished the game with John Terry in goal protecting a 1-0 win, courtesy of Frank Lampard's deflected free-kick, but the result was lost as irrelevant in the aftermath of the match. Chelsea manager Jose Mourinho accused Hunt of deliberately hurting Cech and claimed the medical services at the ground had been too slow to react, accusations the player, club and emergency services all denied. Hunt was also the subject of letters containing death threats posted to the Reading training ground and Coppell was suddenly faced with the task of defending his club, his player and, to a degree, his own reputation whilst also attempting to prepare for the next game.

It is a Premiership baptism Hunt is never likely to forget and he remembered the club's handling of the aftermath to that game, telling me: "I knew after the game it was a serious injury, but was advised not to speak to the press and from that moment the club took control of me and wrapped me in cotton wool. There were comments made the next morning from all different angles, but it was impossible for me to respond because anything I said would be twisted. I knew I had to stay quiet, but that was the most frustrating thing when some people were probably thinking, *oh yeah, he ain't coming out.*"

It took a cool piece of man-management from Coppell, who had learned the hard way to sit on his hands, bite his tongue and say nothing following his departure from Manchester City, when the temptation to verbally lash out must have been huge. Typically, he used humour to draw the sting from the situation despite continued media attempts to reignite the row, saying: "After the game Jose Mourinho just patted me on the head. He's obviously frightened of me and didn't want to mix it. Scousers rule!"

Coppell retained a huge respect for Mourinho, but defended Hunt and his team vigorously, adding: "I would hope my team compete, but we are not physical, that is not a characteristic we could be charged with. The indicators are that we don't get involved in that kind of stuff, we just want to play and football is about that. The media can be over the top, but there are so many column inches and TV and radio stations forever looking to rehash your stories and keep them going. I understand it, but the focus is intense, that is why players understand they have a role model capacity and they have to be seen to be doing the right things as often as possible."

In a bid to help young striker Leroy Lita deal with the added attention coming his way, Coppell advised a simple trick. "He told me to imagine there was always a camera on my shoulder, filming me wherever I went," Lita told me.

Hunt, playing under Coppell for the third time in his career, could not have had a better guiding light at that time and said: "Steve Coppell was the man who gave me my chance at Crystal Palace. He was the one who picked me from the youth team and put me in the first team before he signed me for Brentford, where he had gone the year before. He tried to sign me at Brighton 'n'all, after he'd left Brentford to manage them, so I owe him a lot. I had every trust in the manager and I knew he believed in me."

It was a sentiment Hunt reiterated when he left Reading to join Hull, shortly after Coppell's own departure, proclaiming: "It's fair to say that without Steve signing me I would not be where I am today. In fact, God knows where I would have been – my path would have been very, very different."

BBC *Match of the Day* commentator Jonathan Pearce was an interested observer at that time and was not surprised at Coppell's handling of the situation, having known the Reading manager since his days covering Crystal Palace for Capital Radio. "The whole Hunt thing with Chelsea became a rabid affair and the way Steve diplomatically dealt with that was fantastic. His was the voice of reason," Pearce told me. "He is like that with most things – even if there is a bad decision on the pitch he will make his point, but make it eloquently and reasonably. He thinks before he speaks, but he doesn't take long to think because he's such a sharp man, such an intelligent man."

Reading were quick to move on from the Chelsea incident in as dignified a divorce as possible, though the division's underdogs did continue to take inspiration from others writing them off. Not least when Coppell inspired a 3-1 win over Spurs by pinning to the wall a press cutting which quoted Martin Jol as saying there would be 'a problem' if his side were losing to Reading. "You grasp at things," said Coppell at the time. "When you are their manager or coach they hear the same shit from you week after week, so it helps to hear different shit from someone else."

That was the first of four straight wins for Reading and they repeated that sequence twice more as Coppell's side continued to punch above their weight to leave them needing victory at Blackburn on the final day of the season to secure a UEFA Cup place. It would have been some achievement for Coppell, whose Crystal Palace team had been denied a place in Europe by the ban on English clubs in the wake of the Heysel Stadium disaster. Yet, while chairman John Madejski and Reading's players and fans all licked their lips at the prospect of a European tour, Coppell remained wary of the opportunity.

"He never once mentioned Europe," Murty told me. "With Steve Coppell it was just about winning the next game. Whatever happened he was a fan of saying you finish where you deserve to finish. He's absolutely right; luck, bad judgement or whatever, you finish where you deserve to, so don't go borrowing trouble from way ahead in the future, just deal with the game you have got in front of you."

A thrilling 3-3 draw at Blackburn meant Reading eventually fell agonisingly short of a UEFA Cup prize, but secured an impressive eighth-place finish in their first season in the top flight, not to mention a second-successive League Managers' Association Manager of the Year award for Coppell.

Not surprisingly, Coppell viewed it as a team award, telling me that summer: "There are so many individual agendas in football and I'm not naïve enough to think there aren't any here, but we have gone forward without the refrain of individual egos directing the ship. A collective force has given us something to reflect on. That is my warm feeling inside this summer and that was one of the few years I would have liked to extend."

The Ready Brek glow Coppell wore into that summer break would have increased when the fixtures for Reading's second Premiership season were announced as the Royals kicked off at Manchester United. "He loved Old Trafford – and he enjoyed going to Selhurst Park as well – but he just loved the idea that he was pitting his wits against Sir Alex Ferguson," said Murty. "It was the perfect first game for us; after the euphoria of playing so well we were coming back to play the champions and knew from minute one we had to be at it and doing the right things and sacrificing ourselves to achieve."

The point Reading earned in a goalless draw was the rich reward for another fine example of tactical planning from Coppell, who changed his usual 4-4-2 system for a team based on three centre-backs and man-for-man marking. "It was the hardest 90 minutes I have ever had because I marked Ryan Giggs," recalled Murty, almost wheezing from the memory alone. "Steve tried the system out in training and it was really hard to deal with, but we finally got our heads around it and when it came to the game we carried it out to the letter. So much so that when Wayne Rooney broke his foot, Michael Duberry followed him over to the side of the pitch where he was laid out getting treatment. I looked over and Duberry was stood next to Rooney while he was getting assessed by the physio; Michael was bouncing up and down on his feet and I shouted, 'Doobs what are you doing?' He looked back at me and said, 'I've got him!' and I just started to giggle. At Old Trafford, with 75,000 watching, I got the giggles – it was brilliant.

"Steve had a little chuckle too after the game. I came in and sat down and was drenched in sweat, totally fatigued. I had nothing left and was sat there with a recovery drink in one hand thinking, *I'll get up in a minute and have an ice bath.* Steve walked past and patted me on the knee and said, 'there you go Murts, I've extended your career by five years playing you centre-half' and walked off giggling to himself. I nearly threw my drink at him, I thought if I was going to have to do that for much longer he'll *shorten* my career!"

That hard-earned point, however, was not the start of another glorious drive towards Europe as Reading won just two of their opening eight matches and were involved in the highest-scoring game in Premier League history, ending on the wrong end of a 7-4 scoreline at Portsmouth. Wins over Newcastle and Liverpool did suggest Coppell's side were going to comfortably maintain their top-flight status, despite having struggled to significantly add new signings to a squad which had run away with the Championship two seasons earlier. The manager explained: "How can you reward people who have delivered everything you've asked for the past two seasons by saying 'thanks for everything you've done, but I'm getting in Carlos Kickaballs, who's earning four times more than you and we don't know if he can do as good a job'? I made what I thought was a logical decision and gave a huge incentive to the players who have delivered over the last two seasons, but now the responsibility is can they deliver again?"

Second season syndrome? It certainly appeared so, despite Reading's studious efforts to guard against it. "How can you combat it?" questioned Coppell at that time. "If you spend £50 million then it's not a factor, but that's not the way we do things here. Last year, the whole world and anyone who knows anything about Premiership football would say we over achieved. It's going to be less of a performance this year overall, that's inevitable."

Murty had a simpler definition of second season syndrome, telling me: "We just let ourselves down and we didn't have the same focus and unity that we needed. I think where before we had been fairly selfless and unified we became a little bit self serving and individual in our outlook. Rather than it going to people's heads, we looked at it and thought 'we belong here now' and that was the worst thing we could have done as a group. The gaffer continued to be very big on the processes of getting success and I think we missed out on those processes and just assumed it would be alright."

Reading again scored four times but lost when a four-goal haul from Dimitar Berbatov saw Spurs record a remarkable 6-4 win, the first of a run of eight straight defeats which left the Royals nervously looking over their shoulders. From a position of relative comfort, Reading were dragged into a relegation scrap as a 2-0 home defeat to Fulham gave Roy Hodgson's side renewed hope of an unlikely survival push. By the time Fulham travelled to Portsmouth and Reading to relegated Derby on the final day of the season, Coppell hardly needed to look at a league table to know his side needed to better whatever Hodgson's achieved at Fratton Park. If they failed Hammond felt he knew the consequences. "Steve was going to walk. He and I had spoken about it and he had made it clear to me that if we went down he would be going. He said it needed a 'new broom to sweep it out', a 'fresh start', so going to Derby on that last day I had in mind that if it didn't work out for us then he would go. I had sensed that it might have been a problem after we lost at home to Villa in February (the final game in that sequence of eight straight Premiership defeats). He was fairly flat and he was down, but then we beat Middlesbrough away, which was a big win for us at the time and he really came out fighting. He was more hands-on than I'd known him before in terms of the day-to-day, right in the middle of the players which wasn't his style. He was always more a stand back and observe type of manager but now he was right in the thick of it."

Had Reading found the kind of form they showed in that final game at Derby a little earlier in the campaign, survival would never have been in doubt. But when Harper, Dave Kitson, Kevin Doyle and Lita all found the net to seal a 4-0 win for the Royals, only their third win of the calendar year, it still wasn't enough as Danny Murphy's header secured a 1-0 win for Fulham at Portsmouth and completed a great escape for Hodgson's side as they edged out Reading on goal difference.

"I remember that last day of the season at Derby because of the excitement of the game," Hammond told me. "We played well and 20 minutes into the game I knew that we were going to win. In a way, our game became irrelevant and all that mattered to me was the Portsmouth game. With about ten minutes to go my phone went and my man at Fratton Park said that Fulham had scored. Sometimes the fates conspire and the run that Fulham had gone on in that final period was just unbelievable. Our defeat to Fulham wasn't a nail in the coffin, but it was a massive loss. If you look at our record against the teams in the bottom eight, if one result had turned around then we would have been OK."

With relegation confirmed, Hammond's immediate concern as he watched down from the directors' box was Coppell's reaction. He knew his manager could walk away before the dust had settled and knew Coppell would be keen to draw the attention of failure away from his players. "I went straight down to the dressing room even before the final whistle went because I wanted to be there; I just wanted to know what he was going to do. Steve, being the type of guy that he is, may have just turned around to the players in the dressing room and said, 'thanks very much for your efforts guys, but that's me, I'm done'. I was worried about that because I just wanted him to take some time to take a step back. When you are right in the middle it's very difficult, but you can't affect it with Steve; you can't just go and grab him as he is coming down the tunnel to tell him not to do anything stupid, you've got to let it unfold. He didn't do anything hasty, but when he left to do his press interviews I asked our press boys to feed back to me what he said." The feedback was not positive. Immediately, Coppell's first concern was for his players as he said: "I've been here for five years and the core of the team has stayed the same; they've done a lot for this club and they are feeling it in the pit of their stomach. Our dressing room is a sad and lonely place." Hammond's fears that Coppell would walk away after failing to arrest the team's slide towards the drop zone hardly subsided when the manager added: "Inevitably at the end of every season there are always changes and there will be here, mainly due to finances. But this isn't an occasion for thinking about me, we'll have a look forward some time this week, I'm sure."

Hammond remembered: "I was sitting in the dressing room, waiting, and he came back in and shook all the staff's hands. He shook my hand and he said, 'training ground in the morning?' so I left that night thinking he was coming in the next day to say he was walking."

Whether it was down to a night of contemplation or the Hogwood Park tea, Hammond instead found himself confronted on Monday morning by a newly-defiant Coppell. "I was ready to say 'listen Steve, it's all very raw, give yourself 48 hours', because I knew if you needed a manager to get you out of the Championship then he was still top of the list. I had already been through this process in my head but right at the start of the meeting he said, 'Nick, I want to stay and I feel that I've let people down'.

"I had to take it to the board, but the chairman has great respect for Steve and, of course, here was a manager who had been promoted for the first time in the club's history with a record number of points then had finished eighth in the Premiership in our first year there and won LMA Manager of the Year for two years running." Coppell was also as easy-going a manager as a chairman could ever wish to have, so there was never any real doubt that Madejski would not rubber-stamp the decision to honour the second year of his contract.

"I have never seen a manager be relegated from the Premier League and be unsackable and it just shows the high regard in which he is held at Reading – and in the wider football population," Murty told me. "People know he is a man of deep intelligence and deep integrity and if he had thought he couldn't do any more for the club and he'd taken them as far as he possibly could, he would have walked away. I had a meeting with him at the end of the season and we had about an hour's chat about what had happened. He was brutally honest and said we didn't execute well enough to deserve to be in the Premiership. As much as you take his technical and tactical skills into it, I think the honesty shines through."

Coppell had also been moved by a rather unusual sit-in by Reading's fans, who gathered in his car-parking space at the stadium to chant his name and tie banners bearing messages of support to the railings. "I hope they realise I've only got a small car; they won't fit many in there," Coppell had joked, but the significance of the modest gathering was not lost on him as he said: "From day one I've had a great relationship with the supporters here and I was tremendously flattered by the demonstration. It was terrific, it was warm and it got through to me."

Above and beyond the persuasive adulation of the fans, Coppell felt duty bound to honour the final year of his contract, having broken with his recent tradition of only signing one-year deals. Others were not so easily persuaded to stay, Kitson joining Stoke in a £5.5 million deal and Little tempted by another chance of Premier League football with Portsmouth.

Having spent most of the previous season sidelined by injury, it was a tough decision for Little to make – and an even tougher phone call lay ahead of him. He explained: "No-one gets really close to Steve Coppell, but I probably spoke to him more than most, though that's probably because I chat to anyone about anything. Leaving to go to Portsmouth was probably the hardest thing I have ever had to do and all I kept thinking was, *how am I going to tell the gaffer I am not going to sign?* I wanted another shot at the Premiership, but when I had to make that dreaded call I was worried I wouldn't be able to get the words out and was half hoping he wouldn't answer. It was hard because it was Steve and I was disappointed to leave what was effectively my home."

For Little, as with so many of the players with whom he has been associated more than once during his managerial career, Coppell was a mentor. I remember one specific recommendation the manager offered to his hapless winger after Little had suffered with a string of hamstring injuries, the latest of which had been aggravated by climbing the stairs in his own home. "What advice would you give Glen on dealing with his injury?" Coppell was asked at a press conference. "I have told him to move to a bungalow," came the quick-witted reply.

"Looking back, it is really disappointing how it worked out," Little told me, adding: "We had the best time of the club's history over those two seasons – we were all underdogs, but it was a wonderful club. He was the best manager Reading have ever had and the best they may ever have; I played my best football under him and I had respect for him because he let me play my game."

True to Coppell's traditions, he and the remainder of his squad returned for pre-season refreshed and ready for a new challenge and, with the likes of Doyle and Hunt having stayed, a swift return looked on the cards. Murty told me: "We sat on a little hill at the training ground and he said on the very first day of pre-season 'I am here to get promoted to the Premier League and if you are not here to do that you may as well leave now'. Everyone bought in to it."

Hammond added: "He took relegation very personally. He said to me 'I want one shot at getting us back up because I feel I owe that to myself and I owe that to the people connected with the club'. He is one of the most intense football people I have ever met; people look at him and say that he's reserved and some even claim he doesn't care because he's so laid back, but I have never actually met anyone who cares more. It means so much to him, yet he keeps it all inside."

Despite a mixed start as they readjusted to life back in the Championship Reading enjoyed a free-scoring run as they rekindled the brand of free-flowing football that had swept them to promotion two years earlier, equalling their highest win under Coppell in a 6-0 thrashing of Sheffield Wednesday, beating leaders Wolves 3-0 at Molineux and putting four goals past Crystal Palace, Swansea, Bristol City and Watford.

A three-horse race developed between Reading, Wolves and Birmingham but ultimately Coppell's side came up short, winning only 5 of their final 17 games as they ran out of steam and lost their nerve in the big matches. A home win over Birmingham on the final day of the season would still have been enough, but Coppell's side froze again and were beaten 2-0 as Alex McLeish's Blues sealed promotion. Even the *repechage* of the play-offs failed to reignite Reading's drive as they were beaten in both legs of their semi-final with Burnley and, within an hour of defeat in the Madejski Stadium second leg, Coppell told Madejski he was quitting.

Over the final dregs of our Hogwood tea, Hammond confirmed my own and many others' theory when he said: "Steve was ready for a break and even if we had gone back up I think he would have walked, though of course he would have been a lot happier in taking his break. He missed his son's graduation in the United States because we were in the play-offs and he was desperately disappointed about that; if nothing else he needed to spend time over the summer with his son."

Coppell barely hid that fact as he announced his decision, saying: "I feel it's the best thing, for both the club and myself, for me to leave. I apologise to the supporters; managers are judged on results and we had more than enough opportunities and firepower to have been promoted. That's the manager's fault and it was time to go, time for a fresh manager to come in, re-appraise and give a new lick of paint to the place. It's time for a tinker and that was right for the club and for me."

The metaphorical new broom identified by Hammond was being introduced, yet Murty insisted that Coppell's statement to the press was not merely a knee-jerk reaction to the disappointment of failure, but a manager protecting his players in one final act of falling on his sword. Murty told me: "He took it onto himself wholly and he didn't point fingers. After he walked away I said to myself, 'it's very clever the way he's done this', he had taken all the focus away from his team not achieving what we set out to do. Everything that was written and said the next morning was about Steve Coppell leaving, not one thing was about his team falling short. I hadn't been involved much that season because of injury and it takes someone to look at it like that to realise what a selfless act it is, and what an intelligent act as well."

Two days after Coppell officially quit the club, Reading called a press conference, not so much to explain the decision but to give the manager a chance to say goodbye properly and for all those involved with Reading Football Club to bid him farewell. A manager walking away from a failure yet revered for the previous work he had done, it was like seeing the QE2 officially retired, only without the fireworks.

"He has presided over the most successful era for the club and I thought it would be nice for everybody and for Steve to say goodbye," said Reading chairman Madejski, as I nudged my way through the crowd at that farewell press conference. Eager to know if our theories were correct I asked Steve whether he would have walked even if Reading had returned to the top flight and was surprised when he replied: "I don't think so. It would have been a consideration, I must admit, because nowadays you need very, very deep pockets in the Premiership. We had two years, the first was great and in the second we struggled right from day one. It's a game of finance, the secret of success is money for the best players and no-one enjoys a season where finishing fourth bottom is a great success.

"Last season I had a decision to make and I wanted to erase relegation and purge that through promotion. After the Burnley result, in my mind it became a full stop. My sole intention was to go up and I felt we were capable of more. I felt very lucky to be manager of this club, I served a long apprenticeship in management before I came here and everything fitted nicely, but it was time to move on."

It was as I shook his hand and wished him all the best that I decided to write this book; the end, in that respect, was the beginning. His final delivery was a trademark one and a fitting exit for a manager who had brought a razor-sharp wit to cut through his deadpan approach whenever the need arose. A young lady from a local radio station propositioned: "Steve, it's an embarrassing one, but I have been told by our listeners to ask: will you stay at Reading if I give you a kiss?" Coppell took a moment to consider an appropriate response, the silence agonising as a packed room of journalists hung on his answer, wondering exactly how the manager would sign off.

Coppell looked at the young reporter, now blushing at the public humiliation of such a non-football question. "Perhaps," he said, "we could discuss this in private?"

ARE WE NEARLY THERE YET?

IT IS RUDE to be late for a party, so it was with some haste that I made my way down Stevenage Road towards Craven Cottage, eight minutes before kick-off on the night the club celebrated their 130th anniversary. I could not be certain whether it was actually 130 years ago to the day that the club was formed as Fulham St Andrews Sunday School FC or whether a Monday night game against Hull City was just a convenient match in which to attempt to boost the attendance. Either way it was a good night to celebrate, and my son, Sam, and I, together with our Fulham-supporting pals the Barkers – Nick, Charlie and Tom – were in high spirits as we settled into our seats with roughly 40 seconds to spare.

I was in upbeat mood too as my search for the real Steve Coppell drew to its conclusion. I was at the Cottage to meet Bobby Zamora, one of a string of players who would call Coppell his mentor, but as I watched the game unfold it struck me how many bookmarks of my journey were on show in the game.

Zamora, the former Brighton striker who Coppell tried to re-sign for Reading, was being marked by Ibrahima Sonko, another Coppell favourite at Brentford and Reading, while Tigers' winger Stephen Hunt could boast three spells under Coppell's management, at Crystal Palace, Brentford and Hull. Danny Murphy, who scored the Fulham goal at Portsmouth that relegated Coppell's Reading and changed the fortunes of a club and its manager, was driving Fulham's midfield while Roy Hodgson, the manager who instigated that 2008 great escape, stood alongside Coppell's former Crystal Palace coach Ray Lewington in the technical area. Mark Schwarzer, the goalkeeper whose trial week at Manchester City may have been the catalyst for Coppell's hasty Maine Road departure, hardly had a save to make as Fulham cruised to a 2-0 victory.

The collection of coincidences made me realise what a small community football really is and Zamora, who scored the opening goal and made the second for strike partner Diomansy Kamara, underlined that fact by telling me that Coppell has been an occasional visitor the Fulham training ground since his departure from Reading. "He comes to training every now and then and he gets on well with Roy Hodgson," Zamora told me after the game. Does his influence rub off on the striker, even now, I wondered? "A lot of coaches come and watch Roy's sessions as he is well respected and they want to pick up pointers. Copps watches the training sessions, but he wouldn't suggest anything to me when he's not my manager – he's not like that," Zamora insisted.

Yet it is clear the Fulham striker is happy to see Coppell on a fairly regular basis and Zamora confirmed that he was denied the opportunity to team up with his former manager again at Reading. How different Fulham's anniversary party might have been had West Ham not blocked the move; perhaps a single Zamora goal for Reading could have been the difference between Fulham surviving or facing the drop and extending Coppell's Royals reign?

"He tried to sign me when I was at West Ham and if there was ever a chance to play with Steve again then I would have taken it, but it was out of my hands – West Ham turned down the bid," Zamora said. "Seeing him around the training ground from time to time makes me wonder what will happen now but he's a top man and I'm sure he will bounce back with another big job and do well at it. He's done well wherever he has been and people forget what he has done and what he achieved in getting Reading to the Premiership – and playing good football when they were there. Then they were relegated and people were talking about failure; it's ridiculous really."

Reading supporters clearly haven't forgotten. Twenty-four hours after I met Zamora, and just three miles north of Craven Cottage, the Royals fans were chanting Coppell's name again in the same breath as telling his replacement, Brendan Rodgers, that he was "getting sacked in the morning" following a 4-1 defeat at Queens Park Rangers. That very same evening, Coppell's former Palace protégée Gareth Southgate was handed his cards at Middlesbrough, three years after making his managerial debut against Coppell's Reading and despite having guided Boro to within a point of the top of the Championship. His replacement at the Riverside is Gordon Strachan, who as a player was bought by Ron Atkinson to replace Coppell following his retirement at Manchester United.

More evidence that the football world really is a small one.

And that community amongst which I have mixed over the past few months is in little doubt that Coppell has unfinished business. "What next for Steve?" is a question I put to all of those friends and former team-mates I spoke to and, while they may not all have agreed on the answer, they all concurred that Coppell will be back in the game before long.

Tommy Docherty, former Manchester United manager

"I didn't honestly know that Steve would go on to be a manager; but if you'd asked if he would be the future president of FIFA I'd have said yes. We want people like him to run football – great professionals, who know the game inside out. He should have been an England manager in the past, but is still a potential England manager of the future. Steve is the ideal candidate, he is so bright and intelligent and could sit the FA down and tell them how football should be run. I still hope he will be England boss one day. Learning is not a bad thing, of course, but there comes a stage when you have to decide what to do. Do you want club level, international management or an FA role? He has to decide what it is he wants more than anything else, but someone like him might come up with new ideas on how to run football."

Geoff Thomas, former Crystal Palace captain

"He is just having a rest. He can sit back and get a lager out, rather than jump at the first job that comes along. I actually think he could now get one of his best jobs yet and why not England? There was always talk of him being England manager and he would say he was not ready, but now he is."

Jonathan Pearce, BBC football commentator

"It's a different world these days, but I think one of the most remarkable things about Steve is that he's successfully bridged different football eras – the tail end of the old set up and post Premier League riches. It's such a vastly different game handling players these days and he manages to do it.

"I guess that Steve would like a chance at one of the big clubs, perhaps even Manchester United. The passion for United is still there; he talks with reverence about Old Trafford and United is still clearly, for him, the greatest team in the world.

"I'd love him to get the England job one day but I don't think that he will now. He's a private man and it's not in his character, he'd shy away from that type of thing. Once bitten – and he was with what went on at Manchester City – twice shy."

Brian Barwick, former FA chief executive

"I have twice been through the process of selecting an England manager and Steve would always be connected with the England job because he was so well respected. But I never seriously discussed it with him because he was very committed to Reading and to having a level of privacy in his life. He made it clear to me that he didn't necessarily want the job and I think Steve always saw the clubs he was at as the right level for him to enjoy a life and be a dedicated professional. The whole circus that goes with the England thing would just not have been Steve Coppell, but coaching the British Olympic team might be interesting and I don't write that off.

"The next thing in his life will be in football because he is a football man. He is hugely respected, well liked, vastly experienced, highly intelligent and football through and through."

John Salako, Sky Sports reporter and former Crystal Palace and Reading player under Coppell

"It will be fascinating to see where he goes now and much depends on how much gas is in the tank and how much desire is still there. I saw him a couple of months before he left Reading and he looked drawn and tired, then I saw him on a golf day in the summer and he had a spring in his step and the wrinkles had gone!

"He should have been part of the England team set-up in the past and he should be in the FA set-up now alongside the likes of Trevor Brooking, he'd be fantastic at that. Until the system embraces ex-pros for the good of the game that won't happen, but now would be the time to knock on his door. Failing that, he could be my Director of Football. He could oversee me and show me the ropes."

Eddie McGoldrick, Northampton Town youth coach and former Crystal Palace and Manchester City player under Coppell

"I think there is still life in Steve Coppell; I would like to think so. When the football fraternity know he is ready to return there will be clubs looking to employ him. He might feel he has a couple more years at club level, but I think that now is the time for Steve to be working somewhere within the FA and helping England as a nation to compete for the major finals and trophies. As England manager, you are constantly in the limelight and Steve doesn't like that, but there might be a little niche for him within the FA, possibly even at grass roots or youth level, and that could be the perfect role for him."

Lou Macari, former Manchester United team-mate

"There have been changes in the game and I am not so sure Steve will have liked those. It used to be that you turned up at the training ground, pulled on your tracksuit, went out and did some coaching then picked the team. Now it is not just coaching a football team, there are agents and other influences and everything about the game is different – the players, the owners, everything – and I am not sure he will like those changes.

"The least important things in the football world now seem to be commitment and loyalty and the game is full of prima donnas. That was never Steve and if players are not pulling their weight he would not be happy. So, unless he wants a particular job or wants a job for the money, I would think a different role in football is more likely now."

Gordon Taylor, PFA general secretary
"I always felt he had all the makings of a top-class chief executive. He was always thinking about the overall parameters and structure of the game, not just about being a footballer or a coach. He could see the broader picture and was keen on youth development and education; big into ensuring that youngsters had an education.

"I always remember a great quote of Steve's relating to young players. He said, 'They are like turtles in the South Seas. Thousands are hatched on the beaches, but few of them make the water'. That analogy was true for young players then and it's probably even truer today. One of the things that will have given Steve most satisfaction in his career is his success bringing on youngsters – players like Ian Wright and Mark Bright – he will have enjoyed that.

"He had all the potential to be a diplomat and he thought seriously about becoming a full-time administrator when he retired as a player. He is now in the elite group of managers with over 1,000 games to his credit, so his managerial career has certainly been a huge success. He is a real football man with a deep love for football and will succeed wherever he goes next."

Dick Knight, former Brighton and Hove Albion chairman
"Perhaps there is a complete change of career for him? When he came to Brighton, Steve had the most state-of-the-art video editing equipment and would edit tapes of opposition matches to show players who they were up against. No-one could get hold of him between 2pm and 5pm when he became the new Steven Spielberg, so perhaps there is a calling in film-making!"

Graeme Murty, Southampton defender and former Reading captain under Coppell
"Some people have suggested he could be a caddy for his son, Mark, who is playing professional golf in America, and I think he would love plotting the way round and telling his kid how to manage his game. But he would have to get on

the weights first – the bag would be bigger than he is and he'd need a trolley to carry it round!

"He would need a makeover too, because Steve has got the worst golf gear I have ever seen. Bearing in mind he is about 5ft 4in, he wears long shorts and the worst long socks ever – it is just horrendous. You would think that sartorially he might have some grasp of what looks good, but when you see his gear you think he must be wearing it for a bet.

"In reality, you would imagine he would come back as a manager or director of football somewhere. I can see him coming back into the Premier League with a big club and doing well, but I also think international football would suit him down to the ground and I wouldn't be surprised if he has an international calling. Failing that, he could be my Director of Football and I have already talked to him about picking his mind if I decide to go coaching and managing."

Nick Hammond, Director of Football at Reading
"From the conversations I have had with him, the indication is that he's all golfed out and I think he's ready to get back to work. He has got a big club in him, there is no doubt about that, but the amount of control that Steve wants in the way that he manages would be very hard to find at the top level. I think he will be very careful in what he chooses and if a massive job comes up and Steve Coppell's name is in the frame I don't necessarily think he's going to go. He is capable of a big job, but I think he'll be happy working at a small club with a small budget. He wants to be on the training pitch with players, I think that is when he is at his happiest and his preference would probably be to work with players on a day to day basis."

Kit Symons, Fulham scout and former Manchester City player under Coppell
"If Steve wants to go back into management he still has an awful lot to offer, but I wasn't that surprised when he left Reading because you could see he'd had enough at that time. But when a fresh challenge comes up and he is ready, I think a director of football type role would suit him down to the ground.

"He's certainly appealing to chairmen and boards as someone to deal with – he is not one to go and shoot his mouth off in the press and say ridiculous things. He really thinks about what he says and is very calculating. I think that is the sort of person most chairmen would like to have as a Director of Football.

Phil Neal, former England team-mate
"I think there is unfinished business and I think Steve will be back with a bang. It would be good for anybody to employ him and I would like to think he is destined for a big club, his education in football alone requires that. He's shown he can do it without spending zillions and he is good at little motivational things. The game

is a sad loss without him and he is one of those who is always employable. If I was a director and thinking how can I push this club forward then he would be one of the first names I would think of."

Glen Little, Sheffield United winger and former player at Crystal Palace and Reading under Coppell

"He was always at his happiest on the training ground and I think that is where he will return to. A lot of people will want him and he will be in demand and back in as soon as he is ready. If someone anywhere in football had a bad word to say about him I'd be surprised; he doesn't have too many enemies, that's for sure. Who knows, I could be his assistant, with him up in the stands and me on the touchline doing the talking!"

Martin Buchan, PFA executive and former Manchester United captain and team-mate

"It would be a crying shame if he is not back in the saddle soon. He would be a loss to the game – he's one of the good guys and football needs good guys. He's a great manager and such a nice bloke, with a very dry sense of humour."

* * *

I am very grateful to all those who met me and shared their memories and opinions, all valuable evidence in my search for the real Steve Coppell. Despite all the clues and my endeavours, I still feel Steve Coppell remains a footballing enigma, though I am closer to understanding the real reasons for his departure from Manchester City and know that his priorities will always be personal happiness and the son he idolises. I have also discovered in him a leading football personality who remains the polar opposite of the superstar celebrities of today's game.

In his autobiography, *1966 And All That*, Geoff Hurst placed Coppell above and beyond David Beckham in terms of ability, saying: "Beckham is a fine example of a player who has combined a rich and glamorous lifestyle with a successful playing career and happy family life, but I don't think he's the best right-side midfield player in Manchester United's recent past. Steve Coppell was a better all-rounder and had a greater range of skills than Beckham."

Yet that kind of glamorous lifestyle is something Coppell has never craved. Private and introverted – some would even say shy – those who know him best point to a funny, loyal and caring man who simply does not require his share of time in the spotlight. Paul Scholes is a better United comparison than Beckham, Best or Ronaldo.

Such is his lack of ego and preference for privacy that Coppell himself was one person I was unable to draw on as much as I would have liked in recent months, yet he gave me enough to confirm that he will be back in the business of football sooner, rather than later.

Fittingly, I offer the final say to him, words that confirm that the real Steve Coppell will not sit still for long. He said: "You wish your life away. Comparing seasons is a pointless exercise and we have to look at what is ahead of us, to keep coming back for more. It's not how many times you are knocked down, it's how many times you get up and your frame of mind when you do that.

"It was the right time for a break – normally you can't draw breath – but the focus is to come back some time in the future. You can't dictate when or where, that's for sure, you never know what is going to happen but I would like to come back to work.

"I am a manager, it is my job."